Preventing Autism

Also by Dr. Jay Gordon

Listen to Your Baby: A New Approach to Parenting Your Newborn

The ADD and ADHD Cure: The Natural Way to Treat Hyperactivity and Refocus Your Child with Jennifer Chang

Good Nights: The Happy Parents' Guide to the Family Bed (and a Peaceful Night's Sleep!) with Maria Goodavage

Preventing Autism

What You Can Do to Protect Your Children before and after Birth

Jay Gordon, M.D., FAAP
with Diane Reverand

WILEY

Copyright © 2013 by Jay Gordon. All rights reserved

Cover Design: John Wiley & Sons, Inc.
Cover Photograph: Courtesy of Gina Conte
Text design and composition by Forty-five Degree Design LLC

Published by John Wiley & Sons, Inc., Hoboken, New Jersey
Published simultaneously in Canada

This book sometimes recommends particular products and websites for your reference. Dr. Gordon is not affiliated in any way with such products or entities with the exception of his own website. In all instances, bear in mind that there are many products or websites other than those recommended here that may work for you or provide useful information.

No part of this publication may be reproduced, stored in a retrieval system, or transmitted in any form or by any means, electronic, mechanical, photocopying, recording, scanning, or otherwise, except as permitted under Section 107 or 108 of the 1976 United States Copyright Act, without either the prior written permission of the Publisher, or authorization through payment of the appropriate per-copy fee to the Copyright Clearance Center, 222 Rosewood Drive, Danvers, MA 01923, (978) 750-8400, fax (978) 646-8600, or on the web at www.copyright.com. Requests to the Publisher for permission should be addressed to the Permissions Department, John Wiley & Sons, Inc., 111 River Street, Hoboken, NJ 07030, (201) 748–6011, fax (201) 748-6008, or online at http://www.wiley.com/go/permissions.

The information contained in this book is not intended to serve as a replacement for professional medical advice. Any use of the information in this book is at the reader's discretion. The author and the publisher specifically disclaim any and all liability arising directly or indirectly from the use or application of any information contained in this book. A health care professional should be consulted regarding your specific situation.

For general information about our other products and services, please contact our Customer Care Department within the United States at (800) 762-2974, outside the United States at (317) 572-3993 or fax (317) 572-4002.

Wiley also publishes its books in a variety of electronic formats and by print-on-demand. Some content that appears in standard print versions of this book may not be available in other formats. For more information about Wiley products, visit us at www.wiley.com.

ISBN 978-1-118-38672-9 (paperback); ISBN 978-1-118-53987-3 (ebk);
ISBN 978-1-118-53998-9 (ebk); ISBN 978-1-118-54010-7 (ebk)

Printed in the United States of America

10 9 8 7 6 5 4 3 2 1

I could dedicate everything I do to my wife, Meyera, because she is there to support everything I do. Almost everything I do.

This book is also dedicated to the children and families who have taught me about autism and the spectrum. I have learned more from them than I learned in medical school, residency, or anywhere else. I have watched parents work harder for months and years to improve their children's lives than I could ever imagine working. They inspired me to write this book.

Dr. Gordon has changed the names and circumstances of the case histories included in the book to respect the confidentiality of his patients.

Contents

Foreword

I wanted my foreword to be written by the real experts: the parents I know who have actually dealt with their fears about autism. They have taken practical steps to keep their kids' environments as free of toxins as possible.

I am always surprised that so many people consider these concepts controversial. A recent study from a major university appeared to dismiss the great value of organic food. The response from more than one parent in my practice has been, "Intuitively, it just makes more sense to feed my children food without pesticides than to expose them to food with pesticides." It is hard to argue with that reasonable choice.

Some moms and dads who are committed to protecting their children from the damaging effects of toxins have contributed their thoughts to open this book.

> I try to live a very green life, and Jay Gordon affirms what I believe. I always go to him for advice on creating a clean and green environment for Nahla, the love of my life. "Get rid of the plastic! Jay is coming," is a common refrain in preparation for one of his house calls. There always seems to be a plastic toy around that happened to slip in with all the wooden toys! Jay is the first to say that no one is perfect.

We eat organic, healthy food at our house. Going to the farmers' market is one of our favorite activities, and we have Green Food delivered. Nahla is proud of what and how we eat. I've heard her say to friends, "Your cookies have a lot of sugar—sugar is bad for your brain." I had to take her aside to tell her that being so outspoken might become annoying. But she is learning a lifestyle that is important to me.

For my "What a Little Love Can Do" Project at the Jenesse Center, I have been helping to remodel housing shelters for battered women and their children. We have been environmentally conscious with the renovations, particularly the paint, flooring, and energy efficiency. The first apartment I worked on is the children's apartment, named Nahla's World after my daughter. I want to give these children a healthy place to develop and another way of looking at the world, part of a bigger life. I want to teach them they are worthy far beyond their circumstances. Taking good care of themselves and staying healthy is a big part of that learning.

Parents need good books. There is no guide that comes with being a parent. Jay's book embodies so many things I believe about raising healthy kids in a toxic world. His advice has meant a lot to me. I'm glad that his important message will be available to parents everywhere who are not lucky enough to have him as their family's pediatrician.

—Halle Berry

- - - - -

Dr. Gordon's book sheds light on the serious problems facing our children today. Over the years Dr. Gordon has cared for our children and shares with us important information about health-related issues. *Preventing Autism* is a book that takes the knowledge of a very exceptional doctor and gives us an important tool in safeguarding our children. We are grateful to have Jay Gordon in the lives of our children, and after you read this book, we are sure you will be as well. Enjoy!

—Giselle Bundchen and Tom Brady

▬ ▬ ▬ ▬ ▬

Embarking on the journey of new motherhood can be such a daunting chapter in life along with, of course, the mind-blowing joy that can also be overwhelming. We are bombarded by so many opinions, approaches, and so much to learn. As everything is a mystery to most new parents, it can take on such epic proportions. Fortunately, my experience with my first—and only—baby was indelibly affected by my relationship with our pediatrician, Jay Gordon.

Jay taught me everything I needed to know that wasn't innate about the beginning of our daughter's life. His humanity coupled with his unbelievable expertise is a rare and treasured asset. The importance of breastfeeding and his holistic less-is-more approach became our code, in spite of the fact that it went against so many of my initial impulses, which were informed by fear and the great unknown. I am so happy that babies everywhere will be able to reap the benefits and wisdom of this amazing, soulful, and generous man, and not just the lucky few to be in his practice.

Jay Gordon is unafraid of telling his truth. He has long been an impassioned advocate for babies everywhere, who have no voice and are not being protected against the harms of toxins that have proliferated in our society and are immeasurably hurting our young.

—Jennifer Grey

▬ ▬ ▬ ▬ ▬

Our family was blessed with two babies in just seven months. August, our five-year-old son, was thrilled to welcome his baby sister, Amaya. We adopted her in March 2011. We could not believe our luck when our lawyer contacted us that fall about Andrew, who had been born in July. We always wanted a big family. It was nothing short of a miracle. We found ourselves with a two-month-old and a six-month-old, and we've been loving every minute of the chaos.

Jay Gordon, our pediatrician in California, is passionate about how breast milk gives children the best possible start in life. I had written off the possibility of breastfeeding our two adopted babies, but Jay found a milk bank for us on both coasts. It didn't take much to convince Peter and me that our babies would benefit immeasurably from being nourished by nature's pure and perfect baby food.

—Mariska Hargitay

A recent study cited that nearly half of all children in the United States suffer from a chronic health condition. So what could the most costly healthcare system in the world be missing to produce such dismal odds for raising a healthy child? Sadly, this shocking statistic comes as no surprise. I look around, and see them everywhere—sick kids. I hear it from my weary friends who spend countless hours shuffling their children from one therapy to the next; I see it on the playground, where children must periodically disrupt their play to take a breath from their inhalers; I've had to explain to my own children why bringing in a sheet of brownies infused with walnuts to school could potentially kill a child with nut allergies. The cost of treating these illnesses is astronomical. The emotional impact on these families is incalculable.

Navigating this minefield of over a hundred thousand chemicals is no easy task. Fortunately, the endless challenge of reducing our children's toxic exposures and supporting a healthy lifestyle of organic produce, clean water, and plenty of fresh air have not been accomplished alone. Dr. Jay Gordon has guided my family every step of the way. His insights and expertise on both gaining and maintaining optimal childhood health in an increasingly toxic world have been an invaluable gift. Thankfully, Dr. Gordon has now taken his many years of research and holistic health practices, and turned his clinical pearls and experience into an important and timely book.

Dr. Gordon's comprehensive and thought-provoking work can serve as a resource for both first-time and seasoned parents alike. He's done the heavy lifting—making sense out of often confusing and conflicting health information and scientific studies. Although we "live and breathe for our kids," the reality is that they have to do that on their own. But what we can do is to become their best advocates. Arming ourselves through the pursuit of knowledge is an essential step toward turning the tides of this crisis. The stakes are high, and not just for our children, but for future generations to come. Dr. Gordon's book provides the fundamental tools to empower us as concerned parents as we reclaim our children's health, happiness, and well-being.

—Julia Roberts

Preface

Parents are very worried about autism. Everywhere they turn, they are bombarded with frightening statistics about the rising rates. They are confused because they get different messages from the media. With every magazine article they read and every report on the news they see, they are faced with conflicting information and heated controversy. Whether they are getting ready to have children or already have children, the couples I see every day at my office in Santa Monica, California, where I practice pediatric medicine, are deeply concerned. They desperately want to do what they can to protect their babies from developing autism spectrum disorders (ASD). Autism is now the number one health concern for families, and there is no close second. In support of that, I can offer some anecdotal personal experience. I have seen various cancers in children perhaps ten times in the past thirty-plus years. In that same time, I have taken care of hundreds of children with autism.

I try to see every family in my practice before their baby is born. At those prenatal meetings, parents always ask about vaccines. I put their concerns in perspective. Vaccines are a part of a much bigger question. I explain that autism is a complex disorder caused by an interaction of many factors. Vaccines may be part of what they have to consider when it comes to having a healthy baby, but they have to pay attention to the many toxins we are exposed to in our lives today. They desperately want to know what they can do to avoid the toxins that could harm their babies.

After their babies are born, the subject of autism comes up at every visit. I make a special point of reassuring parents by observing and discussing their babies' developmental milestones at each check-up. I give expecting and new parents practical steps they can take to safeguard the development of their babies. I provide a game plan for parents to follow to avoid toxic substances in their food, in their homes, and in their personal care products and suggest replacing their shampoos, carpets, household cleaning products, and plastic toys with safer alternatives. In *Preventing Autism* I put together the known facts as they stand today and give my interpretation of the research and my recommendations for reducing your family's toxic load. So many studies on autism are under way, and new and profound discoveries are made every day.

As I worked with my editor on this manuscript, the *New York Times* published three evidence-based science stories—all based on peer-reviewed studies—that cover issues and research I had already written about for these pages. These articles go beyond speculating about the causes of autism and the practical aspects of treatment to focus on autism causation and prevention. Books take a while to fly off the computer's screen into the hands of coauthors, editors, and friendly but critical readers. Every single day we share scientific articles about research that is so strong and relevant that it goes viral from a medical journal to the front page of a newspaper like the *Times*, online magazines and blogs, and the broadcast media. The findings, facts, fears, and practical applications to our children's health found in these studies resonate too well to stay buried in a journal. I will continue to keep the information updated on my website, www.drjaygordon.com.

The three *Times* articles deal with risk factors for autism, including the genetic mutations found in the sperm of fathers more than forty years of age, maternal inflammation during pregnancy, and the multigenerational effects of exposure to bisphenol A (BPA). For many years, we assigned increased autism risk to "old eggs." Now we know that the father's age plays a greater role in the genetic mutations that increase the risk of autism than the age of the mother does. Another study found that inflammation in the mother can be responsible for disrupting fetal development. The proven connection between inflammation and autism opens the door for research on prevention. The third breakthrough study reported by the *New York Times* shows that low-dose exposure to BPA, an endocrine disruptor found in plastic, can change the way genes are expressed, turned on and off, for three generations. It has become increasingly clear that chemicals and other environmental offenses affect the way genes are expressed in this generation of children and for centuries to come. And the impact is never good. Serious medical researchers are now filling in virtually all the gaps in understanding the causes of autism.

The science I have relied on to write this book ranges from proven to speculative. At the rate of current research, all of it will probably be accepted fact by the time a copy of this book reaches your house or your e-book app. In these pages, you will find explanations and solutions that pull together the most up-to-date information for you. *Preventing Autism* is neither an academic nor a scientific treatise. I wanted to write a book based on groundbreaking research and my own clinical experience. I know how busy future and current parents are. For that reason, *Preventing Autism* is concise, with lots of lists and sidebars to allow you to find important information at a glance.

My pediatric practice has given me an intimate view of the lives of families affected by autism. Many parents of children with autism come to me because of an unusual step I took in the middle of my residency training. I realized I needed a greater knowledge of nutrition, vitamins, and alternative medicine in order to practice the way I wanted. I accepted a Senior Fellowship in pediatric nutrition at the Sloan-Kettering Institute in New York City. Nutrition is a key element of biomedical therapy for autism. Families usually come to me after their children are diagnosed with autism. I know the importance of early intervention and how much we can do to help children move off their diagnosis. What I have learned is that all parents have to be informed about the latest research on autism.

I believe parents and prospective parents can take steps—even before conception—to protect their children from developing ASD, and science is proving me right.

I have been speaking out about preventing autism as loudly as I can for a very long time. I began talking about autism prevention and treatment about twenty years ago. I am very happy that medical experts and scientific researchers have joined me in this advocacy. During my thirty-four years as a pediatrician, my primary goal has been to give parents guidance on having healthy pregnancies and the healthiest babies and children. I have done whatever I can to contain the autism epidemic within my practice. I have cared for thousands of families, and the incidence of autism spectrum disorders in my practice is well below the national average.

I wrote this book to help inform you and to turn your fear of autism into an action plan to support a safe pregnancy and to protect your newborn baby. In *Preventing Autism*, I walk you through pregnancy and your baby's first two years of life as if you and your baby were my patients.

I believe we can stop the autism epidemic in its tracks. We can reverse the huge increases we have seen in autism spectrum disorders along with learning disabilities, allergies, and asthma. I have taken a leap to come to this conclusion. Large amounts of evidence exist, but sufficient proof does not—at least, not yet. I am confident that the research will come to support all of these ideas and theories. In the meantime, isn't it better to do something positive instead of feeling hopeless and fatalistic? I want to help you cut through the hysteria surrounding autism. *Preventing Autism* gives you clear, up-to-date information and a practical plan of action to protect your children for the first two years of life and beyond. I believe your children's future depends on it.

Acknowledgments

Diane Reverand listened to my thoughts, theories, experiences, and anecdotes and read my gathered research and data. Then using skill, persistence, and more brilliant talent, she turned this aggregation into a coherent, useful, and enjoyable book. It might as well have been magic, but Diane quickly grew to have the same passion for slowing the explosion of autism that I have. She read, we talked and wrote, and she became a newly minted literary expert on chemical toxins and the way they have an impact on genetic tendencies to autism, diabetes, ADD/ADHD, and much more. We wrote this book. Without Diane, there would really be no book.

My wife, Meyera, makes the rest of my life coherent and fills it with love, intelligence, and meaning. She supports everything I do, except the dumb things, and even then she guides me toward getting back on track. We've been together for more than three decades. Tired yet?

Simone, our daughter, gets it. She channeled her anger at the polluters into activism and ran for state legislative office in Oregon at the age of twenty-three, talking about cleaning up our world for the next generation of children. I hope she represents the voice of that next generation.

David Vigliano, my agent, persisted when publishers were reluctant to take on such a controversial book. He had the vision to introduce me to the best collaborator an author could have. Anthony Mattera, his associate, has been attentive, supportive, and on top of all the details. They have both been real advocates for the project.

Guy Oseary first listened to my ideas for this book and encouraged me to pursue it. He introduced me to David Vigliano, for which I am very grateful.

Britt Krivicich, Laura Borsenik, Lorri Horn, and Ted Rabinowitz helped me with research and information gathering.

Tom Miller at John Wiley & Sons had the vision to publish the book. His editorial suggestions made it so much stronger and more practical. We lost a fine editor when Tom left Wiley, but our new editor, Constance Santisteban, stepped right in. We never felt orphaned for a moment. Hope Breeman's close and careful proofread smoothed out all the rough edges.

I could not practice medicine the way I do without a terrific staff to support me. Lex Mech, Beverly Kitz, Jennifer Davidson, Holly Factor, Lisa Boehle, Tammi Burn, Ileana Hernandez, Ana Miller, Marci Tarle, Amy Hollis, Sophia Dibs, and Ranessa Loving help me to give my patients the attention they deserve. They keep the office running smoothly and contribute to the caring atmosphere that is so important. Lorri Horn is responsible for knowing everything that goes on everywhere in the office 100 percent of the time so that I don't sit in my office too long searching for new details to support my minority point of view. Ileana Hernandez has had to knock on that same office door to get me moving for well over twenty years. Bryan Sanders helps me with all things technological and works to make my website visible.

My two partners, Linda Nussbaum and Jody Lappin, cover me and will continue to take great care of my kids and families.

Alessia Gottlieb, the best child psychiatrist in the world, let me know when I was straying too far from the topic at hand. She bears no responsibility for inaccuracies, but she sure did help increase my batting average.

Thank you to Kahn, the best trainer in the world, for getting up so early and keeping me in good shape—for my age. Cheryl Taylor has been my website partner and the voice of www.drjaygordon.com

for fifteen years. I can't count the number of breastfeeding mothers and babies she's helped. She's amazing.

Thanks to Seth Greenland for his help every Saturday morning on the way up the hill with our dogs. And, of course, I acknowledge those dogs for taking me out for long meditative walks.

Introduction

You Can Reduce the Risk of Autism

Something is wrong. Something is going very wrong with our children. No matter what you believe is the cause, doctors and statistics are reporting a tremendous increase in learning disabilities, allergies, asthma, and, especially, autism spectrum disorder (ASD). Although many people use *ASD* and *autism* interchangeably, I prefer to use *ASD* because the term *autism* is not as all-encompassing. The term *autism spectrum disorder* covers a broader range of social, emotional, educational, and language problems. In 2008, the Centers for Disease Control and Prevention announced that about one in six children in the United States had developmental disabilities that ranged from mild speech and language impairments to much more pervasive disorders like autism. The CDC continues to report increasing numbers of children with autism. Ten years ago, one child in 150 was diagnosed with autism. The alarming new statistics indicate that one in eighty-eight children and one in fifty-four boys in this country have developed ASD by the age of eight. Newer studies from the United States and other countries have found that the incidence rate is even higher. One out of forty children in one Asian study had an ASD diagnosis.

All the speculation about the reasons for the rising numbers is less important than realizing that they are rising. Yes, we are defining and diagnosing kids earlier and more accurately than in the past, but I cannot believe that many "experts" and journalists dismiss the recorded increases and try to convince parents and doctors that these broader, more discerning criteria and diagnoses are driving the numbers up. It is not the whole truth. I agree that we are looking harder at kids with social deficits, children who are unable to relate successfully to their peers. We are looking harder at toddlers with delayed language, whose lives crumble in preschool because they cannot communicate with their classmates, have trouble forming typical friendships, and just do not know how to play productively. Greater awareness and changes in diagnostic practice cannot possibly be the only factor responsible for the dramatic rise in the diagnoses. Whatever the label, the behavior is observable in more and more children. There is nothing negative about raised awareness. Mainstream medicine now accepts and encourages the early diagnosis and treatment of ASD. Early diagnosis is considered crucial to minimizing or even reversing the symptoms. We can help a child develop to live a full, independent life. Why would we hesitate to do all we can as soon as we can?

More than 2 million people in the United States have autism spectrum disorders. ASD profoundly affects millions more in their extended families and communities. Family life is disrupted, and ASD puts tremendous demands on the resources of our education system. The economic cost is huge. Medical expenses are six times higher for children with ASD than for "neurotypical" families. The language, occupational, and behavioral therapies needed by children with autism cost an additional $40,000 to $60,000 a year or more, perhaps well into six figures annually for some families. The Autism Society estimates that the lifetime cost of caring for a person with ASD ranges from $3.5 to $5 million and is rising.

Families are spending billions of dollars without an increase in insurance coverage. Many of the families of children with ASD are losing their financial security, their homes, and their economic futures. In the United States, we spend more than $90 billion annually on autism, including research, insurance and non-covered expenses, Medicaid waivers, educational spending, housing, transportation, and employment. The cost of caring for the growing number of children who are on the autism spectrum will intensify our current health care crisis.

The Centers for Disease Control and Prevention have suggested that the huge increase in the number of environmental toxins to which young children are exposed might explain why the autism numbers have exploded. The focus of research now is the complex interaction of genetic vulnerabilities and environmental triggers. We have discovered that children at risk of developing ASD may not be able to effectively metabolize harmful chemicals due to genetics. Their bodies have trouble getting rid of heavy metals and other toxins. In combination, these toxins damage the brain and the rest of the nervous system and cause developmental delays.

The latest research shows that genes and environment can interact in a fetus or newborn child to change the way cells function all over the body, resulting in chronic inflammation in the brain and the immune and digestive systems. A child's rapidly growing brain is very vulnerable to injury from inflammation; a change in the ability to process information can be responsible for the development of autism. This explanation represents a very important breakthrough, because inflammation is treatable. If a condition is treatable, then it is preventable.

A recent opinion piece in the *New York Times*, titled "An Immune Disorder at the Root of Autism," by Moises Velazquez-Manoff, summarizes the work of a number of scientists, most notably Paul Patterson of the California Institute of Technology. The article spiked popular interest in the connection between inflammation, an immune response, and autism. The fact is that the prevalence of inflammatory diseases has increased dramatically in the past sixty years. Chronic inflammation has been found in most people who are autistic. Their immune systems are out of balance. Studies have shown that this inflammation is passed from a pregnant woman to her baby. A pregnant woman who develops a severe infection during her pregnancy or has an autoimmune disorder has a higher risk of having a child who develops ASD. If inflammation is at the root of many cases of autism, then we have a target for treatment.

In the past, the evidence for environmental causes of autism has been primarily anecdotal, but extensive studies are under way. Unfortunately, increased research usually follows epidemics rather than preceding and preventing them. Research is reactive to health threats that have already taken a heavy toll on society.

In 2010, the National Institutes of Health, in partnership with a number of government agencies, began the study of a generation, the $6.5 billion, twenty-one-year-long National Children's Study. Finally, a study has been designed to examine the effects of the environment on growth, development, and health in children. The study will follow one hundred thousand children from all over the United States from before birth until they turn twenty-one. The goal of this research is to improve the well-being and health of children and to understand the role the environment and environmental toxins have on health and disease. The project's ultimate purpose is to provide a basis for prevention strategies and health and safety guidelines.

We cannot wait twenty-one years for the findings of the National Children's Study before we take steps to protect our children and our families from toxins and other chemicals. It is going to take government agencies and science an entire generation to draw conclusions, but we have to act now for the sake of our children. We already have decades of conclusive scientific and judicial proof that environmental chemicals and other toxins harm pregnant women and children. The National Children's Study will inevitably make the connection between hundreds or thousands of chemicals and ASD. In the meantime, a whole generation should not remain at risk. Parents have the right to know now why we are studying these toxins and what can be done to stop exposing our children to chemicals, fumes, and other factors that poison their brain cells. These toxins interfere with and disrupt their bodies' development. I am certain that if we reduce exposure to these harmful compounds, we can turn the startling autism statistics around. My aim in this book is to provide a practical program to do just that.

Preventing Autism is divided into three parts: The New View of Autism, Protect Your Baby before Birth, and Protect Your Newborn. Part one will give you an understanding of ASD and how our thinking about the disorders is evolving. Part two will give you practical advice to help you create the safest environment for your unborn child. The science of fetal origins studies how the conditions your baby encounters in the womb can shape metabolism, temperament, intelligence, and susceptibility to disease. Environmental influences during pregnancy can increase the risk of developing certain diseases. We already know that cancer, cardiovascular disease, allergies, asthma, obesity, mental illness, and arthritis have fetal origins. Now we can add autism to that list.

From the time you even think about being a mother or a father, you should prepare your body and environment for a healthy pregnancy, and that starts with healthy eggs and sperm. Many toxins cause birth defects and have been related to the increased risk of ASD. These toxins can act during the first eight weeks after conception. Though autism can be triggered later, the disorder can originate very early in fetal development. You might not even know you are pregnant during that crucial time. There are immeasurable benefits if you take steps before pregnancy to minimize your exposure to toxins. If you have missed the opportunity to prepare for your pregnancy, please do not go into panic mode. Instead, you can focus on making healthy changes during your pregnancy.

Everything you experience when you are pregnant is shared with the baby you carry—the air you breathe, what you eat and drink, the chemicals to which you are exposed, your emotions, and the stress you feel. Your baby's health depends on creating an optimal environment for growth. That means avoiding harmful chemicals whenever possible in your food, clothing, cosmetics, cleaning products, and home.

"Welcome to Holland"

Sometimes you can do everything right, and your child will have developmental or other problems anyway. There is a limit to what you can control. When I discuss stopping autism, I do not mean to suggest that having a child with disabilities does not bring tremendous joy to parents and to a family.

The love that parents have for their children does not diminish if a child has disabilities. The commitment and unconditional love parents feel for their children are the same, if not more intense. I have seen the excitement of parents of children with ASD when their child smiles or his symptoms improve in any small way. These parents do not take their children's growth for granted.

I often tell the parents in my practice to read a piece by Emily Perl Kingsley that I find inspiring. She is the mother of a child with Down syndrome. She wrote an essay, "Welcome to Holland," that has become a classic. In it, she describes what it is like to raise a child with a disability. I think her imagery captures the experience beautifully.

Kingsley compares waiting for your baby to be born to planning a trip to Italy. You buy guidebooks and read information online to plan your itinerary. You learn some

Italian phrases that will come in handy. After months of preparation for a trip you have dreamed of for a long time, you make your way through the security check and finally board the plane for Rome. When the plane lands after hours in the air, the flight attendant announces over the loudspeaker, "Welcome to Holland."

You sit buckled in your seat and look around. Holland? What is he talking about? You're going to Italy. You have wanted to go to Italy your whole life.

There was a change in the flight plan. You are in Holland, where you have to stay.

After the shock wears off, you realize that Holland is terrific, too. It's just a different place. You need to get more guidebooks and check Holland out on your tablet. You have to learn a new language. Holland is less flashy than Italy, slower-paced. It doesn't have the Colosseum, Michelangelo's *David*, or gondolas. But there are windmills, tulips, Van Goghs, and Rembrandts.

For the rest of your life, you will say, "I was supposed to go to Italy. That's what I had planned." The loss of that dream will never go away. But you won't spend your life regretting that you did not make it to Italy. Instead, you will appreciate and enjoy the very special things you will find in Holland.

Studies have found many parental, prenatal, and childbirth conditions that are associated with ASD. Chapter 7 examines the known risk factors for autism. If you know the risk factors, you can eliminate those under your control when you are preparing to get pregnant, during your pregnancy, and after your baby is born. My intention is not to worry you. Being informed will enable you to work with your obstetrician to plan risk-reduction strategies. You cannot do anything about genetics, but you can stop smoking and drinking alcohol or become more careful about the medications you take. We look at how your family history will help you to evaluate whether your baby might be at risk.

Chapter 8, "Get Started the Minute You Think about Having a Baby," deals with preparing yourself and your partner for a healthy pregnancy. A woman's body is the baby's home before birth. Traditionally, pregnant women have taken steps to eliminate potentially harmful substances from their lives. In this chapter, you will learn what they are and that men have to make similar changes because the condition of the father's sperm has proven to be very important when it comes to ASD risk.

Chapter 9, "What to Do When You Are Expecting," gives you ten rules for healthy prenatal development. Since your baby eats and drinks everything you do, this is the time to drop your bad eating habits and to eat clean food, free of harmful additives and pesticides. You will find lists for foods you can eat to protect your baby's genes and to reduce damaging inflammation in your body. Chapter 9 also contains delicious, easy-to-prepare recipes that are packed with important nutrients that will promote your baby's healthy development.

"Home Detox," chapter 10, takes you through your house room by room to show you where there is toxic danger. I provide a practical list of safe cleaning products. You do not have to search for toxin-free alternatives; they are just a click or a phone call away. Recipes for homemade dirtbusters are included.

Chapter 11, "A Wardrobe Not to Die For," and chapter 12, "Beauty Does Not Have to Hurt," will open your eyes to all the endocrine disruptors and toxic chemicals found in clothes, cosmetics, and toiletries that can be transferred from you to your baby. Chapter 12 has extensive resources for safe grooming products and cosmetics, from shampoo to mascara, deodorant to sunblock. There is also a list of "Beauty Don'ts"—treatments you should skip when you are pregnant or breastfeeding.

Chapter 13 will help you to plan a healthy nest for your newborn, starting with finding the right mattress. From the paint on the walls to baby care products, you will learn all you need to know to create a clean environment for your baby.

Part Three focuses on the care and feeding of your baby. This final part of *Preventing Autism* covers how you can protect your newborn from harmful chemicals that can affect her developing brain during the first twenty-four months of life, a very active time when connections among neurons are being made. In chapter 14, "Feeding Your Newborn," I discuss the very important benefits of breastfeeding as well as the safest bottles. The chapter covers the transition to solid foods, including recipes for homemade organic baby food purees and toddler meals. There is also a list of the best ready-made organic baby foods.

Chapter 15, "Your Baby Is Changing Every Day," covers the developmental milestones of the first two years of life. The chapter includes a month-by-month guide to the early warning signals for developmental delays. Early intervention is so important in helping children with ASD. There is a limit to what a doctor can observe at an office visit. No one knows your child the way you do. You are in the best position to monitor your baby as he grows. I have included a Milestone Tracker in the Appendix that you can copy to keep a convenient written record. Having a thorough account of your baby's first two years will help your pediatrician evaluate her at various stages.

I have saved my comments on vaccines for chapter 16, because this issue is so loaded. The theme of this book is so significant that I do not want to distract attention away from it. This is not a book about vaccines. Throughout chapter 16 I focus on the big picture: how we can protect our children from the toxic chemicals that are everywhere in our lives.

I am not asking you to become a fanatic. Well, maybe I am a little bit. I cannot expect you to do everything I suggest in this book, because you and your baby cannot live in a bubble. I think protecting your children is worth a reasonable, practical, doable amount of extra effort. I am putting all this information in one place to make it easier while I make it harder. I want to help you understand the connection between the toxins you encounter every day and your baby's neurological health and development. I want to give you the knowledge to recognize the risks and to make informed choices. You and your baby will be better off with every simple step you take to live in a cleaner, healthier way.

Once you are aware of what toxic overload is doing to an entire generation of children, you will be motivated to take control of your family's exposure to toxins. You can demand more stringent safety standards for the tens of thousands of chemicals that are poisoning you and your children. We cannot continue on the path we are on. If each of us starts in our own homes, we can shield our children and put the brakes on the runaway autism crisis.

PART ONE

The New View of Autism

1

The Autism Epidemic

Something is happening to our children, and we have to stop it. I want to give you a sense of how widespread autism has become by taking a closer look at the numbers. More than 2 million people in the United States, and tens of millions worldwide, have an ASD (autism spectrum disorder) diagnosis. Throughout this book and elsewhere, you will see the terms *autism*, *autism spectrum disorder*, and *ASD* used somewhat interchangeably.

According to Autism Speaks, an organization founded by Bob Wright, the president of General Electric, because his grandchild developed autism, more children in the United States have ASD than the total number affected by cancer, diabetes, Down syndrome, AIDS, cerebral palsy, cystic fibrosis, and muscular dystrophy combined. In recent years, the numbers have increased 10 to 17 percent annually. Each and every case affects a family, then an extended family, and perhaps a small group of the family's close friends. It is not an overstatement to say that tens of millions of Americans are adversely affected by autism spectrum disorders.

Autism occurs in all ethnic and socioeconomic groups, but for unknown reasons clusters have been found in certain regions and in upper-middle-class families. Utah appears to be the epicenter of the autism epidemic. In Utah, one boy in thirty-two is autistic, the highest rate in the country. Environmental suspects are under investigation: the Great Salt Lake has the highest concentration of mercury of any body of water in the United States; the Kennecott Copper Mines produce dust and emissions; Utah has the highest rate of antidepressant use in the nation. Extraordinary elements in the environment of Utah are likely to have played a role in the state's astonishing autism rate.

California researchers have found ten clusters of autism in areas near Los Angeles and San Francisco. The clusters were located in primarily affluent areas:

- The Torrance, Beverly Hills, Van Nuys, and Calabasas areas of Los Angeles County
- The Laguna Beach/Mission Viejo area of Orange Country
- The La Jolla/Del Mar area of San Diego County
- San Francisco
- The Sunnyvale/Santa Clara area
- The Redwood City area
- Fresno
- Two other possible clusters are the Norwalk/Cerritos area of Los Angeles County and the Modesto area

Children in those areas are twice as likely to have autism as children in other areas. The clusters were found mostly among children with highly educated parents. Though access to medical services plays a part, environmental exposure could be more common in those areas. Some children of affluent families just have too much "stuff." I also believe these "affluence clusters" might be a result of increased travel and exposure to everything from airplane cabin chemicals—flame retardants and more—to more viral illnesses.

The Rising Numbers

The figures the Centers for Disease Control and Prevention release are researched by the Autism and Developmental Disabilities Monitoring Network. Every two years, they take a count of how many eight-year-olds have ASD in about twelve communities around the country. As you can see by the numbers below, the ASD epidemic is intensifying.

2002: 1 in 150 children had autism
2004: 1 in 125 children had autism
2006: 1 in 110 children had autism
2008: 1 in 88 children had autism

This is not a pretty picture. Autism has nearly doubled. Other statistics have shown that there has been a 78 percent increase in autism in the past ten years.

Thomas Insel, the Director of the National Institute of Mental Health, said in a statement on the rising ASD statistics that something in our environment is almost certainly driving the increase. Other scientists are joining Dr. Insel every month as the data continue to be published. This view is a departure from what has been considered the cause of autism in the past. Initially, the disorder was considered purely psychological; then, with advances in science, genetics seemed to be at the root of autism. Genetics can make a child susceptible to developing ASD, but those genetic vulnerabilities seem to be activated by external forces. The accelerating ASD epidemic of the past thirty years parallels industry's increased use of untested chemicals in manufacturing and in our food supply. This is not a coincidence.

The evidence for environmental causes of ASD had been mostly anecdotal, but recent studies have made the connection.

New paths of research are being explored that are very promising. They will lead us to a deeper understanding of ASD and therapeutic solutions.

As I mention in the Introduction, extensive studies like the National Children's Study are under way to explore environmental effects on the health and development of our children. If we remove environmental risks, the harmful effects on the body can be reduced or reversed. For example, if you stop smoking, you reduce your risk of developing lung cancer or heart disease. We have to identify and clarify the environmental triggers of ASD. If we reduce exposure to these toxins, we can prevent the disorder. Until we identify those triggers, we can generalize from what we already know. We might not be able to change the genetics yet, but we can look much more closely at chemicals and viruses and the inflammation they cause, and other possible triggers in susceptible kids. We can look more closely at family histories and individualize the care we give to families at risk. For instance, our advice to a family that has a child with ASD, three cousins who are on the spectrum, or close relatives with problems in social interaction has to be different from advice to families with no autism risk factors. If we work hard to utilize the knowledge we have of ASD to prevent it, we can save many more children from the developmental disorder.

2

The Changing View of Autism

Any doctor who did a pediatric residency twenty or more years ago has a story similar to this one: During a pediatrics ward rotation, when I was a resident at Children's Hospital of Los Angeles, our attending called the medical residents into one child's room. He told us that this was an unusual case, that we might never see another child with this severe disorder for the rest of our careers. We filed into the small hospital room, and there in bed was a four-year-old boy with autism. He was staring out the window, not even noticing the five doctors cramming into his space. He was destined to live his life in an institution. In 1978 there was no hope for this autistic child.

Autism was considered a static, unchanging, controversial, mysterious, and unchangeable condition then. We know now that is not true. Prevention and treatment can change everything. Autism is no longer a hopeless diagnosis. We can intervene with different therapies to reduce and reverse the symptoms of children with ASD. I want worried parents to understand that autism is no longer considered as monolithic as it once was. This optimistic assessment is radically different from when I started to practice medicine a little more than thirty years ago. Imagine the breakthroughs we will have in the next thirty years. As we learn even more about ASD, we will find a way to prevent it.

A Brighter Outlook

Here is a story with a happy ending. I wish all of my experiences with autism were this simple and worked out this well. Some parents do everything in their power to help their children but see no significant results. There always seems to be improvement, although sometimes nowhere near enough. I have seen how happy parents are when their child makes a simple breakthrough. A slight improvement is a source of joy.

Recently, I met with five-year-old Brian and his parents in the informal anteroom to my office. His parents had come to me three years earlier because they were concerned about Brian's delayed speech development. His pediatrician had reassured his parents that Brian's speech delay was normal. But they remained troubled. Their instincts told them something was wrong. Brian did not seem interested in what was going on around him. He was acutely sensitive to loud noises and resisted even the slightest change in his routine. Brian seemed different from other children his age, and his parents had come to me looking for answers.

After I listened to what they had to say and observed Brian, it did not take me long to recognize the problem.

They knew their child. They were right—Brian was different. He had autism. Rather than considering his condition beyond remedy, I was able to recommend a course of action, including language therapy, behavioral therapy, a new diet, and the reduction of toxins and harmful chemicals to which he was exposed.

Brian's parents never gave up. They talked to experts and read everything they could get their hands on. After two years, Brian was not only talking, but he was going to kindergarten and eagerly anticipating the arrival of a baby sister.

A diagnosis of autism no longer means a life sentence. The prognosis for enjoying life in the mainstream world has improved drastically from what it was just a generation ago.

All informed doctors and therapists now view autism as a treatable condition. Research is focused on finding new ways to predict ASD in infants, to identify it early, and to start interventions as soon as possible to reduce the severity of developmental problems. Recognizing the early signs of ASD can help children receive interventions that can change their future development. In the past, far too many children were diagnosed with autism between ages four and five. At that age, a child's brain is difficult to change, because it is more developed. The CDC and the Academy of American Pediatrics have recommended screening for autism at eighteen and twenty-four months with their formal checklist. If ASD is caught early, when the brain is developing at a rapid pace, the brain can be changed and molded.

I would like autism awareness to begin even earlier than eighteen months. I believe that healthy interventions can begin even before your child is conceived, while you are pregnant, and during your baby's first two years of life. *Preventing Autism* gives you guidelines for reducing exposure to the environmental toxins that can increase your baby's chance of developing ASD.

3

No Two Children with Autism Are Alike

Autism spectrum disorders encompass a range of complex developmental disabilities that almost always appear during the first three years of life and affect a child's ability to communicate and interact with others. The definition of autism has been expanded to a spectrum disorder because it affects each child differently and in varying degrees. No two children with autism are alike. This is one of the reasons we think ASD has many causes. The range of diagnoses along the ASD spectrum includes:

- Classic ASD or autism is the most severe end of the spectrum.
- Asperger's Syndrome is a milder, high-functioning form in which children have well-developed language skills but difficulty with social interactions.

- Pervasive developmental disorders (PDD) refer to children who have some ASD symptoms but not enough for a full diagnosis.
- Childhood disintegrative disorder occurs when children develop normally then regress and show ASD behavior between ages three and ten.
- Rett disorder or syndrome is a rare genetic disorder that mostly affects girls. What is promising is that scientists have found the single gene responsible for the reversal of development that produces symptoms of this disorder.

There has been some discussion about narrowing the spectrum for an autism diagnosis by focusing on classic autism. This would certainly reduce the numbers, but a staggering number of children will still have developmental disorders. The problems will exist, however they are diagnosed. Referring to the problem by another name does not change anything—except insurance coverage. The resulting cuts and exclusions in insurance benefits and special care could prove disastrous for families everywhere. Even worse, limiting the diagnosis could prevent some children with mild ASD from getting the help they need when it would be most effective. We have educational and financial obligations to these children and their families. Changing diagnostic criteria must not allow abrogation of this responsibility.

What Does ASD Look Like?

Until recently, autism has been defined only by behaviors. In the broadest sense, autism is a disorder of social communication that affects a child's ability to navigate, fit in, get an education, make friends, and live a normal, happy life in the social worlds of childhood, teenage, and adult years. There is a great variation in symptoms, but the main characteristic of ASD is isolation. In early infancy, a baby with ASD may be less responsive to people or resist cuddling or being touched. Children with autism often do not respond to their names. Some are overly sensitive to light, sounds, touch, smell, and taste, while others have blunted responses. They do not startle at loud noises or may be oblivious to pain.

People with ASD are very often unable to have normal social interactions. It can start with not making eye contact. They have tremendous difficulty reading social cues or interpreting what others are thinking. Their inability to read other people makes them appear to lack empathy. Retreating into their own world, children with ASD prefer to play alone. They can become fascinated by parts of an object, the spinning wheels of a toy car, for instance.

Language and communication are affected by ASD. Autistic children tend to speak late, often well beyond age two. Some children with ASD experience regressive autism. They gradually or suddenly lose their ability to say words and sentences. When they do speak, autistic children often use a sing-song or robotlike voice that expresses no emotion. They cannot start a conversation or keep one going. Often their conversations are obsessive, talking about topics like trains or dinosaurs. Some may repeat words or phrases verbatim but do not know how to use them correctly. Twenty-five percent of children with ASD do not speak at all.

Children with autism behave in a way that sets them apart. They often perform repetitive movements such as rocking, spinning, or hand-flapping. These movements are referred to as *stimming*, shorthand for self-stimulation. Some of these movements, like head-banging or biting, can be self-abusive. As alarming as these actions can be, experts believe they might act as a form of stress relief. Along with being aggressive to themselves, autistic kids can be physically aggressive to others, although without malice. I have had children with autism throw furniture around in my waiting room. They might move constantly or they might be extremely passive. The range of autistic behavior is sweeping. The key is that the behaviors are not normal.

People with ASD have a strong need for sameness. They tend to develop routines and rituals and become disturbed at the slightest change in those routines. When their routines are disrupted, they can react with intense tantrums. For example, my office is at 901 Montana. The front entrance is on 10th Street. One young boy refused to enter the office from the 9th Street entrance. He would only use the entrance on Montana that matched my mailing address.

Many autistic people have very narrow interests. Autistic kids can get stuck on a single topic or task. Once they get going about a subject they care about, they are not concerned about whether anyone else is interested. They take this narrow focus to an extreme. They become fixated on minutia and details. That is why some teenagers with ASD refer to themselves as geeks. They love creating their own worlds. They become preoccupied with Dungeons and Dragons, Star Wars, Star Trek, or Harry Potter.

About 40 percent of children with ASD have above average intelligence. Some of these children display extraordinary abilities in music, math, art, or academics. They are the savants we read about and see on television or in films. Their gifts are based on a cognitive style that researchers have found is shared by all people who are autistic. The *Wall Street Journal* reported that scientists from University College in London have found evidence that autism is not just a list of deficits but rather is another way of making sense of the world, a cognitive difference with benefits. Their study found that higher-functioning autism gives some people a perceptual edge, allowing those with ASD to process more information in a short amount of time.

Tennis Champ

Dan, age fourteen, has an interesting story. I remember his parents' prenatal visit very well. His mother announced her difference in opinion from my advice about breast-feeding duration and other aspects of childhood nutrition. Her husband was clearly upset by her decisions. Dan's father had made his own decision not to vaccinate Dan when Dan was born. They had very different ideas about raising their son, and I was not surprised when they divorced. The stress of taking care of a child with ASD makes the divorce rate in these families very high.

At nine months, Dan was not crawling. He scooted around on his butt at one year and had problems with constipation. At eighteen months, he was an extremely finicky eater and seemed tired a lot. By the time he was two, he was playing alone. He would scream endlessly at night.

One day, at age two and a half, Dan was playing in the park with his dad. A psychiatrist who happened to be there approached Dan's father and said, "I think your son has autism."

Dan was tested and received an ASD diagnosis. His dad found him all the help he needed. He put him on a gluten-free diet. He introduced Dan to tennis, which they played for hours. At eleven, Dan had an IQ of about sixty, but he had a wicked backhand and could hit a seventy-mile-an-hour serve. He started playing in tournaments and did well.

When he is with his mother, his dietary restrictions go out the window. To his father's frustration, Dan loses language, and his game goes bad when he stops eating his special diet. At fourteen, he is six-four, a big, strong kid. He is a tennis champion and has a collection of trophies. USC has scouted him as a tennis player. Dan is an autistic child with a special gift.

Common Physical Problems

Children with ASD often have problems with digestion, including constipation, diarrhea, and reflux. Their decreased enzyme production may cause these problems, which is why I always prescribe probiotics for my patients with ASD. Probiotic supplements support the good bacteria in the intestines and balance the intestinal environment.

Central nervous system inflammation has been observed in most autistic children. This condition is caused in part by such hormonal disturbances as increased cortisol production. The resulting inflammation can lead to immune dysfunctions. Autistic children develop autoimmune disorders at very high rates.

As research intensifies, scientists are uncovering more and more pieces to the puzzle of autism. Putting those pieces together to complete the picture is proving to be challenging. ASD is so complex that it seems as if the pieces come from different puzzles. The key to solving the puzzle and discovering treatments might well lie in understanding the way the brain of someone with ASD works.

4

The Autistic Brain

Your baby's brain at birth is still a work in progress and remains so for the first two decades of life. The nerve cells in the brain before birth are like wires that need to be connected. Neural development is when those connections are made. Only the core of the brain, the spinal cord and the brain stem, is well-developed at birth. This part of the brain is responsible for kicking, grasping, crying, rooting, feeding, and sleeping. Since our brains take time to develop, the neural circuits that run body functions essential for survival—for example, breathing, heartbeat, circulation, and swallowing—are well-established at birth. The higher regions, including the cerebral cortex, are still immature and incomplete at birth.

The gradual brain development that continues once your baby is born allows experience and environment to shape his mind. The cerebral cortex, responsible for conscious thoughts, feelings, and memories, is very immature at birth. All the neurons in the cortex are produced before birth, but they are poorly connected at first. Only after birth are the connections, or synapses, formed during the "exuberant period," when the nerves make connections in a burst. At the peak of this intense period of growth, your baby's brain creates 2 million new synapses every second as he connects to his world. When your baby is two years old, her cerebral cortex has more than a hundred trillion synapses.

Clearly this period of mental development is a crucial time for your baby. A child's brain is very impressionable and very vulnerable. Neuroscientists refer to this ability to change as *plasticity*. Genes are responsible for the basic wiring plan for forming neurons and their connections, and experience and environment are responsible for fine-tuning those connections. Toxic chemicals have the potential to wreak havoc on brain development at this formative time.

Sometimes Abnormal Brain Development Can Be Corrected

The brain is very vulnerable during the first two years of life, but its ability to change has an upside. It is possible to correct abnormal development with the right therapies at the right time, as you can see in Jeremy's story.

Jeremy, age seven, was diagnosed with ASD at fifteen months. His parents and I had noticed delays in his language and motor skills. He had persistent intestinal problems, constipation, and diarrhea. We immediately got him started on biomedical therapies with an autism expert in addition to conventional language, behavioral, and occupational therapy at the regional center. In California, the state has set up twenty-one regional centers to help children with developmental problems and their families. All the therapists are coordinated in one building in each region, so that parents can get their children all the needed interventions without having to drive from one office to another. Jeremy was put on a gluten-free, dairy-free diet. He received a B-12 injection every other day and took digestive enzymes because he had absorption problems.

The good news is that the "unproven" treatments worked. Jeremy had begun to receive therapy when his brain was plastic enough to be affected by intensive therapy. By the time he was ready for kindergarten, he did not need a special school. He went to a mainstream kindergarten. I am happy to say that he is about to start at his local elementary school.

We were able to reverse Jeremy's developmental delays.

Brain Growth and Autism

As an infant's brain continues to grow, the head's circumference will grow four inches in the first year. It takes seventeen more years to duplicate that initial four-inch change. The brain actually doubles in size during the first year or two of life. During nine months *in utero* and the first two years after birth, there are many critical points when a baby's brain is particularly sensitive to toxic exposure, which are outlined in chapters 8 and 15. We have to do everything we can to protect our children at these key times.

Researchers have found an unusual pattern of brain growth in babies who are later diagnosed with ASD. Children who develop autism often have a smaller head circumference at birth than children who develop normally, though their body weight and height are in normal range. They have an unusual pattern of brain growth that starts one or two months after birth. Their brains undergo rapid growth during the first two years of life that exceeds normal growth. Though their heads were smaller at birth, autistic children had larger-than-normal head circumferences between the ages of six and fourteen months. This difference persisted through ages three and four years. Children with more severe autism had more rapid increases in head circumference after six months than children with milder ASD. These studies reveal that brain-growth patterns before birth and in the first two years of life are different in autistic children.

Some important conclusions can be drawn from these findings. The causes of autism could lie in factors that lead to a smaller head at birth followed by rapid brain growth. Those factors would shape the brain well before signs of autism are evident in a baby's behavior. Another interpretation could be that rapid brain growth is a precursor to ASD and that an additional trigger might be needed for the disorder to develop.

To be clear: differences in head size are not diagnostic of autism but are certainly an abnormality worth observing. If head-size difference is present with other signs that point to an ASD diagnosis, the level of concern increases.

Toxins and Brain Development

Genetics may play a role in this abnormal growth pattern, but we cannot ignore the toxins that are known to affect the pace and the pattern of brain development in animal studies or that interfere with mechanisms that control brain development. The use of these toxins has increased dramatically during the same thirty-year period that autism has grown to epidemic proportions. I believe there is a real connection between these increases. A few of the major culprits, which I will cover in greater depth in chapter 6, are:

- **Bisphenol A (BPA).** This chemical is found in plastic and activates genes that regulate brain growth. BPA was used in making baby bottles. Of all things, baby bottles should always be non-toxic, and manufacturers have eliminated this toxin from most new bottles. Old baby bottles, however, almost definitely contain BPA and should be safely discarded.

- **Polybrominated flame retardants.** These are present in mattresses, bed linens, and children's sleepwear, and have been found to alter brain growth in mice. We should not have to defend kids from their own pajamas!
- **Perchlorate.** This is used in rocket fuel and disrupts the action of the thyroid in directing brain development. This substance is in the drinking water of more than 20 million people in the United States. What kind of inept government agencies allow rocket fuel ingredients in our drinking water?

By the time you finish reading this book, you will know all about these toxins and many more that damage our bodies and interfere with our children's development.

Seeing Brain Differences

Aside from differences in brain growth and size, scientists are discovering connections between brain biochemistry and structure and autism. It has become clear that normal brain physiology is disrupted in those with ASD. Something went wrong during development.

Newer imaging technology allows us to see how the brain of a person with ASD works and to observe the differences between them and someone with a normal brain. The scans are very different from one child to the next but are consistent in showing that the areas of the brain that process feelings, facial recognition, and social skills "light up" very differently in the brains of children with autism spectrum disorders.

MRI now reveals what structures of the brain are involved in the disorder. The region of the brain that stores social knowledge normally lights up on PET scans when a person processes another person's face. This function is impaired in the brain of a person with ASD. The emotional center of the brain, the amygdala, is less active in autistic people. The prefrontal cortex plays a role in empathy—it is normally active when a person is trying to figure out what someone else is thinking or feeling. This brain region is less active in a person with ASD. Nerve cells in another area of the brain light up when a person or animal looks at you and the cells normally send messages to the amygdala to figure out what is going on in the other's mind. This pathway is missing or incomplete in an autistic mind.

There are differences in the sizes of a number of brain regions. For example, the cerebellum is smaller in the autistic brain than in a normally developed brain. The reduced size of this part of the brain can lead to motor, cognitive, and social problems. The reduction of the number of specialized cells in the cerebellum is known to affect the pruning of neural connections in the brain. This might explain the rapid increase in brain size in the early development of autistic babies described earlier.

The wiring of the ASD brain is also different. Neurons in a single region are overconnected within that region and underconnected to other areas of the brain. This abnormality reduces communication from one part of the brain to another and creates problems with processing. Healthy connections between certain areas are key to regulating social behavior and interactions.

Exciting New Findings

Scientists have gone even further to look for what could be causing the disordered communication in the brain of a person with ASD. More than 200 genes have been linked to the way brain cells work and communicate with one another. These 200-plus genes have been found to work at a lower level in autistic brains. The 235 genes connected to immune and inflammatory responses are expressed more strongly with ASD. Scientists are beginning to identify how the expression of certain genes is responsible for autistic traits. This knowledge opens new paths for research.

A protein recently discovered in an animal study at Duke University may be an important key to understanding autism. This protein may trigger ASD by stopping effective communication between brain cells. Research like this study will uncover important clues to possible causes and treatments for autism. We can expect scientists to work out a model of the systems most affected by autism in the next five to ten years. Current research is pointing very strongly to inflammation as a common pathway in many brain disorders, including autism.

To understand what causes the characteristics of autistic brain differences discussed in this chapter, we have to consider genetic vulnerability and environmental influence. Genetic research has come a long way in identifying genetic markers that are associated with ASD. Chapter 5 explores the genetic roots of ASD and introduces you to epigenetics, a field of study that is already linking environmental toxins to autism.

5

The Genetic Factor

Studies of identical twins produced evidence of a genetic factor in ASD. The findings of a number of studies show that if one twin has ASD, from 60 to 90 percent of the time the other twin will, too. In the balance of subjects—10 to 40 percent of those studied—something happened in the womb or after birth to produce one child with ASD and one without. These twins share the same genes, but one has ASD and one does not. In those cases, there may have been damage to the growing brain. We have to conclude that environmental factors are responsible for autism in one twin and not the other. Whether a baby who inherited a genetic predisposition to autism develops ASD or not would seem to depend on environmental factors early in life.

Nature vs. Nurture

Stanford University conducted a study in 2011 of 192 pairs of twins in which one twin was autistic and one was not. Scientists found that genetics accounts for 38 percent of the risk of autism, and environmental factors account for 62 percent.

The findings of this study suggest that the causes of almost two-thirds of autism are environmental.

Twin Differences

Phoebe and Teddy's parents were older than many first-time parents. The twins' father was fifty, and their mother was in her forties when they were born. The twins are now twenty years old. They are both autistic.

They were diagnosed at the age of three. Their speech was atypical, their language delayed, their social skills off. They were remote and unconnected.

Teddy's autism is more severe than Phoebe's. At thirteen months, he was normal. At sixteen months, he had two words, at eighteen months, only three to five words. His developmental delays were so apparent that he went to UCLA for therapy.

Phoebe's delays were not as pronounced, but she did have social problems. She, too went on a biomedical regimen. Teddy remains severely autistic. Phoebe is in better shape, but she will never live an independent life.

Susceptibility Genes

A single gene does not cause autism. Hundreds of genetic variations have been associated with the increased risk of autism. Some genes make the child more susceptible, others affect brain development and the way brain cells communicate, and others may determine the severity of ASD. The complex interaction of many genes underlies the disorders. Scientists have been attempting to identify "susceptibility genes" and have located regions on three chromosomes that may contain some answers. Though hundreds of genes linked to autism have been found, the combination of genetics, biochemistry, and other environmental factors that produce autism remains unclear.

One route for genetic research studies families who have more than one member with ASD. Scientists looked for shared genetic markers, a sequence of genes. Once common areas were found, scientists tried to identify specific genes, and then the proteins those genes produce. Our bodies' cells become specialized to do certain jobs because different sets of genes are turned on or off at different stages of cell development. The types and amounts of proteins produced affect the way cells grow and act.

Overactive and Underactive Genes

A recent study has made an intriguing discovery. Scientists at the University of Southern California have found a gene (MSNP1AS) that suppresses the production of a particular protein. That gene is twelve times more active than normal in the brains of people with ASD. Proteins direct the development and biological activity in the brain and body. The protein suppressed by this gene is important to early brain development and immune functions. Work is intensifying in this important area to examine how genes and proteins interact in autistic brains. Finding well-defined, shared patterns could hold the key to pinpointing the genetic origins of ASD.

Some studies show that autistic children and their mothers have a high rate of a genetic deficiency in the production of glutathione, an antioxidant and one of the body's primary means of detoxifying heavy metals. Some experts believe that high levels of toxic metals in children are strongly correlated with the severity of autism. Low levels of glutathione combined with high production of homocysteine, an amino acid, greatly increase the chances of a mother having an autistic child, some say thirtyfold.

Genetic Mutations and ASD

A number of independent research teams have identified several gene mutations or changes that sharply increase the chance that a child will develop autism. We all have gene mutations, and most are harmless. Significant mutations are more common in autistic kids, and the effects are more severe. Hundreds of gene variations could disrupt brain development enough to cause social delays. Science is searching for patterns and explanations for what goes wrong.

In trying to learn what causes these mutations, scientists are looking at genetic material from parents who have no signs of autism but who give birth to a child who develops ASD. This allows

New Test for Sixty-five Genetic Markers for ASD

Autism Speaks announced a cheek swab test, known as ARISk Autism Risk Assessment Test and developed by Integragen, to screen infants as young as six months old and toddlers for sixty-five genetic markers associated with ASD. Though no single one predicts autism, a child who carries several mutations has a higher risk.

More and more tests of this kind will be available over the next few years.

scientists to spot spontaneous mutations that appear in the genes of the children but not in their parents. Researchers believed that these gene changes occur in the sperm and eggs before conception or during early development of the embryo in the womb. Only recently have scientists found that the genetic risk of complex developmental problems originates in sperm, not eggs. The sperm from an older father is more likely to have random, small genetic "glitches" that can affect brain development. The speculation is that older fathers have been exposed to environmental toxins longer, which has affected their sperm. You will learn more about this in chapter 7 when we discuss risk factors.

There can be changes in gene activity that do not involve alterations in the gene itself, but which still get passed down to at least one generation. *Epigenetics* is the study of chemical markers that alter gene expression but are not part of the DNA. These alterations are superimposed on genes to direct them to be active or inactive. Epigenetics can change a genetic profile. Environmental and lifestyle factors can affect your epigenome by making an imprint on your genes that causes them to behave differently.

Though many genes and gene mutations have been associated with autism, only a minority of people develop ASD purely from genetics. Science is proving that most cases of ASD result from a combination of autism risk genes and environmental factors. Preliminary research has shown that environmental factors might change the function of genes that control brain growth and brain cell communication.

The title of chapter 6, "Genetics Loads the Gun, but the Environment Pulls the Trigger," says it all. When you read about the more than eighty thousand untested chemicals that permeate almost every aspect of our lives, you will be alarmed by the lack of regulation of these known toxins. The rise of the chemical age that began in the late 1940s parallels the rising autism numbers.

6

Genetics Loads the Gun, but the Environment Pulls the Trigger

The title of this chapter was taken from a National Institutes of Health poster. The slogan is now part of the culture. It is becoming increasingly clear that the concept applies to ASD. In the twentieth century, we have seen the invention and production of more than eighty thousand new chemicals and millions of combinations of these man-made substances. Almost none of them have been tested for their effects on people. Many of these chemicals—industrial solvents and pesticides, for example—are toxic by design. These toxins are compromising the stability of the environment and are destroying the health of people, plants, and all living things. These chemicals pervade just about every aspect of our lives, and almost all of them have never been tested. To put the statistics that follow in perspective, pregnant women and their children have a hundred times more chemical exposure today than they did fifty years ago.

- Of the three thousand chemicals produced in the highest volume, only twenty to thirty have been tested using the Environmental Protection Agency's protocol for measuring the effects of toxins on developing nervous systems. These chemicals are found in a wide array of consumer goods, cosmetics, medications, motor fuel, and building materials. They are routinely detected in air, food, and drinking water.
- Each year an additional two to three thousand new chemicals are introduced in the United States with no systematic study of the hazard of exposure.
- Our bodies do not encounter single chemicals in isolation, but a number of chemicals that interact in unpredictable ways. To test how these chemicals interact in combinations of three would require 85 billion tests.
- These tests do not take into account at what age the exposure to an environmental trigger happens, how it happens, the size of the person exposed, or a baby's particular genetic vulnerability.

We simply do not have reliable information about the effect of most chemicals on the developing human body and brain. Manufacturers have free rein and answer to no one. The Toxic Substances Control Act is more than thirty years old. Since 1976, the burden of proving that chemicals are dangerous has fallen on the Environmental Protection Agency. The law has built-in confidentiality privileges for industry, allowing companies to withhold information about how substances are made and their known effects. In August 2008, the Food and Drug Administration reviewed BPA, a chemical used to harden plastic, and ruled it safe. The report was criticized by the FDA's own science review board because the decision relied almost exclusively on studies funded by industry.

In late July 2012, the U.S. Senate Environment and Public Works Committee passed the Safe Chemicals Act, sponsored by

Senator Frank Lautenberg of New Jersey, to replace the Toxic Substances Control Act. The new act reverses the burden of proof on chemical safety. In addition, the act requires chemical companies to provide fuller health and safety information about their products and gives regulators more authority to remove harmful substances from the market. Though this act is promising, it is only the first step to the bill's becoming a law. There is a political split over whether chemical reform should be strengthened. The burden is expected to remain on the EPA through this year. Bipartisan support is necessary for the bill to advance.

In *Legally Poisoned*, author Carl Cranor contends that laws put us all at risk to exposure to legal toxins. We are being contaminated by untested substances. He makes an important point. Medical and pharmaceutical research must follow stringent ethical guidelines, but industry gets a pass when it comes to making and selling potentially toxic chemicals. That seems very wrong. I have a personal mission to mobilize parents to challenge industry's right to poison us. Our babies are being born into a world that is increasingly unsafe for them to grow and thrive.

The potential list of autism's environmental triggers is long. Many studies show higher rates of autism with greater exposure to flame retardants, plasticizers like BPA, pesticides, endocrine disrupters in personal care products, heavy metals in air pollution, mercury, and pharmaceuticals such as antidepressants. Chemicals that are endocrine-disrupting change hormonal processes and disrupt the function of the endocrine glands, particularly the thyroid and sex glands. These disruptions throw off the body's intricate balance. Toxic chemicals can also affect the nervous system by altering the transmission of messages among the neurons and the formation of neural networks. From reading about the autistic brain in chapter 4, you already know that abnormality in brain development is found with ASD. Other convincing studies have shown an increased risk associated with power plant emissions. For every ten miles' distance from an industrial source or power plant, the incidence of autism decreased about 2 percent. Putting individual genetic risks aside, I find it hard not to believe there is a connection.

Toxins, Toxins Everywhere

Lead, methylmercury, PCBs, arsenic, and toluene are known to cause neurodevelopmental disorders and brain dysfunction. Exposure to these chemicals during early fetal development can cause brain injury at doses that are much lower than what would affect adult brain function. Two hundred more chemicals are known to have neurotoxic effects in adults, and many additional chemicals have been shown to be neurotoxic in laboratory models. There has been little to no systematic testing of how these chemicals affect the developing brain.

The following list is from "Developmental Neurotoxicity of Industrial Chemicals," published in the *Lancet*. I have reproduced the entire long list for shock value—to make you aware that you are surrounded by chemicals that we know can damage you and your baby.

And there are thousands more that have never been tested for safety. This chart represents just the tip of the iceberg.

Chemicals Known to be Neurotoxic to Humans

Metals and Inorganic Compounds	Organic Solvents	Other Organic Substances
Aluminum compounds	Acetone	Acetone cyanohydrin
Arsenic and arsenic compounds	Benzene	Acrylamide
Azide compounds	Benzyl Alcohol	Acrylonitrile
Barium compounds	Carbon disulphide	Allyl chloride
Bismuth compounds	Chloroform	Aniline
Carbon monoxide	Chloroprene	1,2-Benzenedicarbonitrile
Cyanide compounds	Cumene	Benzonitrile
	Cyclohexane	Butylated triphenyl phosphate

(continued)

Chemicals Known to be Neurotoxic to Humans *(continued)*

Metals and Inorganic Compounds	Organic Solvents	Other Organic Substances
Decaborane	Cyclohexanol	Caprolactam
Diborane	Cyclohexanone	Cyclonite
Ethylmercury	Dibromochloropropane	Dibutyl phthalate
Fluoride compounds	Dichloroacetic acid	3-(Dimethylamino)-propanenitrile
Hydrogen sulphide	1,3-Dichloropropene	Diethylene glycol diacrylate
Lead and lead compounds	Diethylene glycol	Dimethyl sulphate
Lithium compounds	N,N-Dimethylformamide	Dimethylhydrazine
Manganese and manganese compounds	2-Ethoxyethyl acetate	Dinitrobenzene
Mercury and mercuric compounds	Ethyl acetate	Dinitrotoluene
Methylmercury	Ethylene dibromide	Ethylbis(2-chloroethyl)amine
Nickel carbonyl	Ethylene glycol	Ethylene
Pentaborane	n-Hexane	Ethylene oxide
Phosphine	Isobutyronitrile	Fluoroacetamide
Phosphorus	Isophorone	Fluoroacetic acid
Selenium compounds	Isopropyl alcohol	Hexachlorophene
Tellurium compounds	Isopropylacetone	Hydrazine
Thallium compounds	Methanol	Hydroquinone
Tin compounds	Methyl butyl ketone	Methyl chloride
	Methyl cellosolve	Methyl formate
	Methyl ethyl ketone	Methyl iodide
	Methylcyclopentane	Methyl methacrylate
	Methylene chloride	p-Nitroaniline
	Nitrobenzene	Phenol
	2-Nitropropane	p-Phenylenediamine
	1-Pentanol	Phenylhydrazine
	Propyl bromide	Polybrominated biphenyls
	Pyridine	Polybrominated diphenyl ethers
	Styrene	Polychlorinated biphenyls
	Tetrachloroethane	Propylene oxide
	Tetrachloroethylene	TCDD
	Toluene	Tributyl phosphate
	1,1,1-Trichloroethane	2,2',2"-Trichlorotriethylamine
	Trichloroethylene	Trimethyl phosphate
	Vinyl chloride	Tri-o-tolyl phosphate
	Xylene	Triphenyl phosphate

This chart has been reprinted with permission from "Developmental Neurotoxicity of Industrial Chemicals" by P. Grandjean and P. J. Landrigan and published in *Lancet*, December 16, 2006, 368(9553): 2167–78.

The Toxic Load

Persistent organic pollutants (POPs) have been present in the air we breathe since the 1950s. There are hundreds of hazardous air pollutants, including heavy metals, and particulate and volatile organic compounds all known to harm human health. Dioxins and polychlorinated biphenyls (PCBs) are released during burning and plastics processing. Harmful chemicals outgas from plastics, fire retardants, and countless products that are a part of everyday life. Scientists believe that airborne exposure to chemicals could contribute to postnatal abnormal neural development because inhaled particles or heavy metals are delivered directly to the brain through the olfactory bulb. Very little is known about the action of very low doses of POPs and their effects on the developing brain during the prenatal and postnatal periods when the nervous system is developing and is very sensitive to hormonally active chemicals.

For decades, we have been surrounded by BPA, used to harden plastics, in every aspect of our lives, from food storage containers to plastic wrap to baby bottles in states where BPA use has not yet been limited. BPA breaks down when plastic is washed, heated, or stressed. The Centers for Disease Control found BPA in the urine of 93 percent of Americans over six years of age. A recent animal study inspired an Op-Ed column in the *New York Times* by Nicholas Kristoff entitled "Big Chem, Big Harm." It is encouraging that mainstream writers are paying attention to the work of dedicated scientists who are trying to get to the roots of autism. The study showed that if pregnant mice were exposed to low doses of BPA, there were immediate and long-lasting effects. The brain development of the offspring was affected. They displayed social behavior that resembled autism. These effects appeared in the next three generations. BPA, an endocrine disrupter, affected gene expression and the way certain hormones were processed. The researchers found that BPA interfered with vasopressin and oxytocin, hormones responsible for trust and warm feelings. The discovery of this mechanism is significant in understanding the physical roots of autism.

This study underscores the damaging interaction between genes and the environment. Even more troubling, the findings reveal that the epigenetic effect can persist for several generations.

Time magazine reported on a study in which scientists found that BPA and some phthalates cause in vitro cells to switch from connective cells to fat cells. This finding makes me speculate if these chemicals might contribute to the obesity epidemic in children, along with factors like bad eating habits and sedentary lifestyles. In the past year, new laws have banned BPA and phthalates. Despite this positive step, they have been replaced by other chemicals without proof of their safety.

Our toxic load comes from more than emissions in the air. If pesticides are designed to kill pests, it stands to reason that they are poisons that have a destructive effect on our bodies as well. The use of pesticides has increased dramatically. From the mid-1960s to 1980, the annual use of pesticides went from 400 million pounds to more than 800 million, mostly in the form of chemical herbicides used in industrial farming. We consume pesticides when we eat commercially grown food, but pesticides leach into soil and our water supply as well. The balance of this book discusses specific toxins in detail and explains how you can reduce your family's exposure to them. The following chart is an overview of the major toxins that are damaging the health of our children.

A Rogues' Gallery of the Top Toxins

Toxin	Use	Found In	Adverse Effects
Pesticides	Commercial farming, household and garden use	Air, soil, water, food	Disrupts neural transmission and formation of new networks
Lead	Stabilizes plastic molecules	Lead-based paint, household dust, soil, toys and dishware from outside the U.S.	Neural disruption often leading to aggression and hyperactivity
Mercury	Coal-fired power plants, cement manufacturing,	Air pollutant that leaches into water and contaminates	Disrupts neural and brain development, promotes

Toxin	Use	Found In	Adverse Effects
Mercury *(continued)*	trash incinerators, gold mining, vinyl production	fish and shellfish; used in some vaccines as a preservative	oxidative stress
Arsenic	Wood preservative, used to manufacture paints, dyes, metals, drugs, soaps, semiconductors	Outdoor play sets, decks, furniture made from pressure-treated wood	Damages DNA and disrupts brain development
Dioxins	Industrial emissions, fire	Plants and animals	Causes reproductive and developmental problems, damages immune system, disrupts hormones
BPA (Bisphenol A)	Harden plastic	Water bottles, plastic wraps, food packaging, baby bottles, canned food and beverages	Disrupts hormones, damages eggs
PCBs (polychlorinated biphenyls)	Lubricants, coolant, insulators, plasticizers	Food and consumer packaging, shampoo, dental floss, televisions and appliances	Carcinogenic, decreases sperm counts, disrupts hormones and neural development
Phthalates	Soften plastic	Leaches into soil and water; used in vinyl shower curtains and flooring, IV bags, cosmetics, plastic toys	Disrupts hormones and reduces sperm count
PFCs (perflourinated compounds)	Make products stain- and stick-resistant	Non-stick pots and pans, fabric finish	Disrupts hormones
PBDEs (Polybromiated Diplenyleters)	Flame retardants	Pajamas, furniture, mattresses, pillows, carpeting, electronics, appliances	Attaches to thyroid hormone transporters and receptors during critical periods of brain development
Parabens	Synthetic preservatives	Hair care and shaving products, moisturizers	Hormone disrupter
Perchlorate	Oxidant in rocket fuel	Drinking water, milk, some vegetables	Thyroid hormone disruption

Our Vulnerable Children

The damage begins before a baby is born. Last year, researchers at the Environmental Working Group tested blood from the umbilical cords of ten newborn babies for 413 pollutants, industrial compounds, and other chemicals. All of us live with hundreds of toxins or chemicals that our bodies have absorbed from the environment. The study was designed to find if any environmental toxins were transferred from the mother to the developing fetus. They found that 287 chemicals—more than half the number tested for—had passed from mothers to their newborns through the umbilical cord before birth. The chemicals they found in umbilical cord blood are linked to brain and nervous system damage, birth defects, developmental delays, and cancer.

This study found that harmful chemicals are already present in the fetus before birth. I always talk to my patients about putting the risk of exposure in perspective. A 2-ounce fetus, a 7-pound baby, and a 180-pound man all get the same amount of exposure. Do we need scientific proof to say that these toxic chemicals are going to harm a developing child more than a grown man? It is common sense to believe they do.

Children are at greater risk for harm from environmental exposure to toxins. Infants spend more time close to the floor where heavy air pollutants and dust settle, and they spend more time outdoors in the "fresh" air. Children eat, drink, and breathe far more per pound of body weight than their parents, which concentrates the effects of the toxins that threaten their bodies. Their immune systems are immature, and their defenses may have a harder time fighting off the negative effects of exposure.

Research will not find just one trigger that causes the neurological changes associated with autism to develop. As you read in chapter 5, some children are born with a susceptibility to developing autism. Exposure to harmful chemicals can cause a cluster of unstable genes to interfere with brain development. Preventing that exposure just might change everything.

There is a growing sense among researchers that repeated low-dose exposure to toxins and certain infectious agents contributes to ASD. This is how it works: Genes provide instructions for various bodily processes. At the same time, the body is constantly reacting to the environment. Certain man-made chemicals are bioactive. They interact with chemical processes going on in the body that are governed by genes. When environmental chemicals interfere with the balance of body processes, there can be serious consequences.

The direct effect of toxins on the developing nervous system is not the only route to autism. Environmental agents can affect other systems—the immune or endocrine systems, for example—during development that can lead to downstream effects that are passed on to future generations. The change in the way genes are expressed may appear in later generations. This sort of downstream effect has linked smoking to childhood asthma in the next generation. The toxic exposure parents have experienced for the past thirty years could contribute to the rising incidence of ASD in the next generation.

Determining the safety level before exposure becomes toxic is difficult. Even very low doses can disrupt hormones and neurotransmitters, the body's messengers. A major medical scandal is brewing because manufacturers are still allowed to use known hormone disrupters in the production of toys and other children's products. We all know that lead is hazardous, but we are still finding it in paint used on toys, especially those imported from China. Even worse, plastic toys are full of powerful hormone disrupters.

Understanding how our environment interacts with our genes is at the root of knowing how changing environmental factors can prevent disease, including ASD. This scientific knowledge is evolving and about to reach a critical mass. We cannot afford to wait. We have to take steps now to provide an environment for our babies and children that supports their good health. Children cannot make choices about their environment. It is up to us to make the right decisions to insure that their exposure to toxins is reduced and that they are protected.

PART TWO

Protect Your Baby before Birth

PART TWO

Protect Your Baby before Birth

7

Risk Awareness

When I meet with new parents in my practice toward the end of their pregnancy, I gather as much information as I can about their family history, and much more. I look very hard for a history of autism or very early heart disease. If a family has a history of heart disease, I make diet recommendations and pay special attention to cholesterol levels. Monitoring my patients' development may be the most important thing I do during my office day. If I identify autism risk factors in a family history, I must give that family specific advice that pertains to their situation. We work together to plan risk reduction strategies and to identify any developmental delays that might occur.

I want to make it clear that a risk factor for autism does not always mean that a child will automatically develop delays, but risk factors do raise a baby's chance of developing ASD. Risk factors are common characteristics that researchers have identified in

Reality Check

Please do not panic about risk factors. We are talking about statistics. If we say the chances double, it means, for example, instead of one in a hundred, it is two in a hundred; a 50 percent increase means one and a half in a hundred. Statistics can be frightening, but you have to put them in perspective.

Risks are cumulative. We do not know how they interact with other risk factors. Helping you to eliminate those risk factors under your control in preparing for pregnancy, during pregnancy, and after your baby's birth is my goal in *Preventing Autism.*

significant numbers in autism. Studies have found many parental, prenatal, pregnancy, and childbirth conditions that are associated with neurological and psychological disorders, including ASD. Scientists are zeroing in on specific autism risk factors. This chapter covers the most current findings.

Girl or Boy?

The obvious first consideration is the sex of the baby. Boys are at a greater risk than girls. Male babies are five times more likely to develop ASD. It starts with this basic factor.

Existing Conditions at Birth

Certain medical conditions are associated with a higher-than-average risk of ASD. Fragile X syndrome, which is inherited, Tourette syndrome, and epilepsy create a higher risk of ASD.

Autism Runs in Families

The primary known risk factor for autism is family history. If one child in a family has ASD, a younger brother or sister has an 18 percent risk of developing the disorder—nearly one in five, much higher than previously thought. When a family has multiple cases of ASD, the risk is even higher. A history of autism in other close relatives is also a risk factor.

If a baby has a sibling with ASD, I will often recommend genetic testing of both parents and the baby to see if any autism markers are present. With a look at the genetic picture, I am more vigilant about development and environmental exposure. The set of genetic tests we need is not ready yet, but the state of the science is changing rapidly. This testing will become more precise in the near future. My website, www.drjaygordon.com, features an updated list of available genetic tests.

Family Resemblance

Anyone who has an autistic child should listen to the warnings. If you have more children, it is important to check their development early and often. One family with an autistic son came to me for a prenatal visit for their second child. Corey, their firstborn, was receiving thirty-two hours a week of applied behavior therapy at home. They avoided toxins. They cleaned up the house and adopted a clean diet.

An occupational therapist spent a lot of time at the house working with Corey. The therapist noticed that Brian, their baby, was showing some signs of developmental delays. The parents became actively engaged in intervention. At three, Brian was eating a gluten-free, casein-free, sugar-free diet.

At seven and a half, Brian is now fully independent in first grade. He has no language or motor problems. Since the family dug in early to provide him with the therapy he needed, he moved off his diagnosis. Corey is at a special school, doing quite well, and continues to have biomedical therapy.

As with so many medical conditions, early diagnosis and treatment of ASD symptoms make all the difference in the world. Doctors and parents must leave denial behind and make the tough decisions to open up a very difficult discussion to facilitate this early care.

It is not unusual for parents and relatives of an autistic child to have problems with social and communication skills themselves. Relatives of autistic children often have language and neurological problems. Studies have found that some emotional disorders—such as bipolar disorder—occur more often in the families of people with ASD. A family history of schizophrenia, depression, or obsessive-compulsive disorder has been identified as an autism risk factor.

Autoimmune disorders appear more often in the relatives of children with ASD. You should know if members of your family have type 1 diabetes, adult rheumatoid arthritis, hypothyroidism, or lupus. The overactive immune system that produces the inflammation at the core of these diseases could affect brain development to increase vulnerability. When a pregnant woman has an autoimmune disease, her chronic inflammation could disrupt her baby's development.

Fathers over Forty

The risk of ASD rises with the age of the father, especially fathers over forty. The risk of autism increases twofold with each ten years in paternal age. Having an older father has been associated with schizophrenia as well as cleft lip and palate in children. We know that paternal age is an important risk factor in autism. As we discuss in chapter 5, mutations are more common in older sperm. After puberty, spermatocytes divide every sixteen days. By the time a man is thirty-five, there have been approximately 540 spermatocyte cell divisions. Genetic mutations and defective DNA repair mechanisms accumulate with advancing paternal age. Studies have found that the number of DNA changes was higher in children of older fathers.

Nature published a ground-breaking study in August 2012. The findings were such a breakthrough that the *New York Times* reported on the study in a lead front-page story. What was newsworthy about the study is that the researchers were able to quantify the genetic changes in the sperm of young and older men and to demonstrate the link between paternal age and autism. The researchers studied seventy-eight couples in Iceland who had children with autism but did not have ASD themselves. The goal was to find the new genetic mutations that could be responsible for the children's autism.

The scientists were able to identify an average of twenty-five random mutations in the children born to a twenty-year-old father that could be traced to the father's DNA. They found that the number of mutations increased by two mutations for each year of age of the father. Children of the forty-year-old men averaged sixty-five mutations passed on by the fathers' genes. The average number of mutations coming from the mother was fifteen regardless of age. In contrast to sperm, egg cells are relatively stable.

Since 50 percent of active genes play a role in neural development, random errors in DNA are more likely to affect brain and neural development than other systems. We can conclude that the genetic risk for complex developmental problems originates more commonly in sperm than in egg. The implications of this study from Iceland are that genetic changes in sperm could be responsible for 20 to 30 percent of all cases of ASD.

Noting the Risk Factors

The histories of Bobby's parents caught my attention. His father was fifty-two when Bobby was born. His mother, a physician, had an autistic niece. We watched Bobby's development carefully. At fifteen months, he was normal. His language skills were so good, and he was bilingual. At his eighteen-month visit, he was still talking. His parents had noticed that he only occasionally followed commands at that point. He was not on a standard vaccine schedule because his parents did not want him to receive that many shots at one time. Bobby gradually lost language over the next six months. We set him up immediately at the regional center, and he also began a biomedical program to address his developmental problems. He took glutathione and ate a gluten-free and casein-free diet known to improve ASD symptoms. His parents did everything they could to deal with environmental issues. Their efforts have had a positive effect. Bobby has improved, and his prognosis is good.

Mothers over Thirty-five

We know that mothers over thirty-five are more likely to have children with Down's syndrome or dyslexia. A woman is born with all the eggs she will ever have. The longer those eggs are exposed to toxins, the more likely they will have undergone genetic changes. For a mother older than thirty-five, the risk of genetic changes is 50 percent higher. That said, egg cells are more stable than sperm. New sperm are produced all the time, and mistakes can be made in copying genetic material. The study published in *Nature* cited on page 55 has found that genetic changes in sperm could be responsible for 20 to 30 percent of all cases of autism. What is important about advanced maternal age is that an older mother has an increased risk of pregnancy complications, which are risk factors for ASD. Research has made it clear that parental age and difficult pregnancies and births are major risk factors for ASD.

The Prenatal Environment

Aside from genetics, epigenetics, and environmental toxins, we have to consider what affects the environment of the womb after conception. It is in your power to control many of those risk factors. To do so, you need to know the critical times during your pregnancy when your baby is vulnerable. Scientists are studying what happens during pregnancy that compromises the prenatal environment and affects brain development. We know that the fetal environment in which your baby grows has significant impact on his neurological status later in life. Factors that can make the environment less than optimal include:

- Smoking
- Drinking alcohol
- Medications
- Infections
- Diet
- Stress

We all know that pregnant women should not smoke or drink alcohol. Prenatal exposure to cigarette smoke can increase the incidence of ADHD, and alcohol exposure can result in fetal alcohol syndrome. We know that both can impair neurological development. Smoking causes metabolic changes in the body and increases oxidative stress, which creates an excess of damaging free radicals, and consequent inflammation, which has been found in higher levels in people with ASD. Since oxidative stress makes a body more vulnerable, it increases the background risk of impaired brain development. I cannot emphasize this enough. You have to stop smoking and drinking if you want to have a healthy baby—but more on that later.

Three main medications have a proven effect on a developing fetus and are linked to autism:

- Valproic acid (VPA) is an anti-epilepsy drug and mood stabilizer. It has been shown to alter gene exposure and increase oxidative stress. The fetal brain is very susceptible to inflammation during critical windows of development.
- Thalidomide is an antinausea drug that used to be prescribed during the first trimester. The drug caused congenital malformations and is associated with impaired neurological development. Thalidomide is virtually never used anymore.
- Misoprostol is used for the prevention and treatment of gastric ulcers. The medication's effects on the uterus are so powerful that it is used for medical abortions.

It is shocking to know that over-the-counter medications that contain acetaminophen, such as Tylenol, have been linked to an increased risk of ASD. Terbutaline, a fast-acting bronchodilator used to treat asthma, has been implicated as well. Terbutaline has been used in the past to stop premature labor to allow a baby's lungs to develop. With the new findings, this usage is no longer recommended. If terbutaline is suggested for you, you can ask for an alternative treatment. Discuss this with your obstetrician well before your delivery date so you can get his or her opinion and consider alternatives.

Other medications, and perhaps viral illness, may increase your child's chance of autism spectrum disorder. My simple advice to moms-to-be is to stay as healthy as you can and to travel less than usual to diminish exposure to large crowds of people.

There is a higher frequency of hormone use among mothers of autistic children, and some studies have shown that infertility treatments can affect brain development in very early stages. Geneticists really dislike IVF, ICSI, and all other methods of bypassing natural conception. They argue that we are bypassing the natural selection process for viable, healthy embryos. This is not an absolute recommendation against assisted pregnancies, but potential parents should understand the risks and unknowns so they can have the best possible discussions with fertility experts.

The use of psychoactive drugs, which act directly on the brain to treat depression, anxiety, and other disorders, is thought to interfere with fetal brain development during pregnancy.

Maternal infections can raise the risk of ASD. German measles, also known as rubella, is known to produce birth defects and brain damage. Herpes or cytomegalovirus infection can affect a growing fetus or a baby being born. Severe viral or bacterial infections that require hospitalization are risk factors. The viruses and bacteria do not directly damage the fetus. Instead, the mother's inflammation response to rid her body of the invaders appears to be the problem.

I have to mention one nutritional deficiency here that is linked to ASD—vitamin D, which is actually a hormone, not a vitamin. Mothers of autistic children often have reduced levels of vitamin D in their bloodstreams. Vitamin D can influence many biological processes. It acts as an anti-inflammatory agent on the brain and affects the DNA repair process. Since we are all so careful about using sunscreen, many of us are not getting enough of this very important vitamin. Living in a city, at high latitudes, or in areas with a lot of rain decreases sun exposure and can put you at risk of a vitamin D deficiency.

Finally, maternal stress of all sorts can disrupt early development and may be a route to ASD. We usually think of stress as psychological, but when it comes to fetal development it takes many forms: infections, oxidative, and physical. Prenatal stress combined with genetic variances in the mother can lead to developmental problems. There is even some evidence that maternal and paternal stress before conception can cause genetic mutations.

One study that surveyed many others broke down the prenatal windows for autism risk. The following chart lays out the windows of vulnerability for a number of factors:

Prenatal Windows of Vulnerability

First Trimester (Weeks 1–12)	Second Trimester (Weeks 13–28)	Third Trimester (Weeks 29–40)
VPA	Generalized maternal stressors	Vitamin D deficiency
Thalidomide	Respiratory viral infections	Terbutaline
Misoprostol	Severe bacterial infection (requiring hospitalization)	Herpes simplex in birth canal
Severe viral infection (requiring hospitalization)		
Rubella (first 16 weeks of pregnancy)		
Herpes simplex		

Adapted with permission from "Environmental Risk Factors for Autism" by Rodney R. Dietert, Janice M. Dietert, and Jamie C. Dewitt from *Emerging Health Threats Journal*, 2011, 4:10, 3402.

Pregnancy and Birth Complications Heighten the Risk

Studies have identified a long list of pregnancy and birth complications that may raise the risk of autism. In addition, researchers have discovered a link between the degree of difficulty of a pregnancy and birth and the severity of ASD. I want to discuss the complications, but urge you not to overreact if you experience any of these events. Pregnancies rarely go smoothly, without a single problem. Autism is not an inevitable outcome of a single or even many obstetric complications.

Some of the obstetric conditions associated with increased risk of ASD include:

- Pregnancy-induced hypertension
- Excessive maternal bleeding during pregnancy and delivery
- Gestational diabetes
- Cesarean births
- Low birth weight for gestational age

- Prematurity—less than thirty-five weeks' gestation.
- Low Apgar score at five minutes—the Apgar score is an index used to measure a newborn's general health done one minute and five minutes after birth. A low score at five minutes can suggest that the baby had problems getting adequate oxygen during the pregnancy or at birth. The index is from one to ten. A score of seven or above is generally normal.
- Hypoxia, a major risk factor for ASD, is a set of conditions that causes oxygen deprivation to the fetus.
- Presence of congenital malformations—ear anomalies are more common in babies with autism. These malformations indicate abnormal development very early in gestation.

Troubled from the Start

Benjamin, the son of an actress, spent time in the neonatal ICU. He was a preemie, and his Apgar scores were borderline. He showed decreased muscle tone at six weeks of age, was not growing well, and had trouble breastfeeding. I wanted to refer him to a neurologist. His mother did not want any interventions, even though speaking delays became obvious as Benjamin grew. She was in denial. She thought Benjamin would grow out of it, but he did not. Benjamin is severely autistic.

As her doctor, I should have worked harder to shake her loose from the denial that prevented earlier treatment. This highlights a tremendously difficult problem. At what point should a doctor insist that a child receive special testing for autism? With severe medical illnesses, the court will intervene to get a child diagnosed and treated expeditiously. There is nothing that clear in the world of ASD diagnosis and treatment.

There is no need to worry about a single factor. It is a rare pregnancy that does not have one or two of the complications listed above. So keep this list in perspective. As you can see, birth and newborn complications do not occur in isolation. Understand that my point is to encourage you to change the things you can to prevent the accumulation of many possible and probable risk factors that increase the chance of autism even a very small amount.

It is natural to consider these risk factors as conditions that lead to the development of ASD, but there is another point of view we should consider. The complications during pregnancy, birth, and the early life of a child might occur as a result of an existing autistic condition.

This chapter is an overview of the risk factors science now associates with the impaired brain development of ASD. Educating yourself about the risks will help you make adjustments to avoid those risk factors in your control. If you are not yet pregnant, you and your partner can take steps to prepare your bodies before conception. If you are already pregnant, you have time to clean up your act—both with your body and in your home.

Read on.

8

Get Started the Minute You Think about Having a Baby

From the time you begin to think about becoming a mother or a father, you should prepare your body for a healthy pregnancy. The best way to do that is to clean your body as you would your house. Your aim is to rid your body of potentially damaging chemicals as well as to reduce your exposure to those toxins. As you have read in previous chapters, many toxins that have been related to the increased risk of ASD act during the first eight weeks after conception. You might not even know you are pregnant during that crucial time. ASD can originate very early in your baby's development. You and your baby will benefit immeasurably if you and your partner clean up the internal and external toxins that can affect your eggs or sperm and have an impact on your unborn child.

Everything you experience when you are pregnant—the air you breathe, what you eat and drink, the chemicals to which you are exposed, your emotions, the stress you feel—is shared with the baby you will be carrying. Your baby's future health depends on creating an optimal environment for growth. Preconception planning is so important. Depending on how much you have to do to get your body ready, it can take time to make healthy changes. For example, if you have been using birth control pills, your doctor might recommend being pill-free for a few months before you try to conceive. During that time, your hormones will balance as you go through several normal cycles. This delay has the additional upside of helping you to determine more precisely when you ovulate, so that calculating your expected due date will be more accurate. Birth control pills can deplete folic acid, vitamins B-12 and B-6, and magnesium. You will have to replenish these very important nutrients.

Preparing for pregnancy requires time, because some habits are hard to break and some health issues need to be dealt with. There is no better time for you and your partner to cut out any habits that might harm your baby. Limit alcohol consumption, stop smoking, reach and maintain a healthy weight, control chronic health problems, and build moderate exercise into your life. These are just a few of the things you and your partner may need to work on. Getting both of your bodies into prime health before trying to have a baby is almost as important as maintaining a healthy pregnancy. You have to take the time to rid the toxins from your body and to build up your health to give your baby the best possible home for the nine months of pregnancy.

Red Flags

One couple drove from a long distance—more than an hour—for a prenatal visit. They were very concerned about ASD because they had a nephew with autism.

Hearing their history, I reacted the way I would have if they had told me that both of their fathers had heart conditions. Hearing that even one father had heart pains in his forties and a heart attack in his fifties would alert me to specific medical attention their child would need. If I were asked if I had any specific diet and lifestyle recommendations for this child and family, I could only answer, "Yes! Your child will be a vegan with a soccer ball at his feet well before his first birthday."

The same is true with autism. When the family history includes a number of risk factors for autism, I observe the development of that baby very carefully and do not hesitate to recommend therapy if there are developmental delays.

Prepregnancy Consultation

A visit with your obstetrician will help you to evaluate what you need to do to prepare for pregnancy. You are at the start of an extraordinary experience. You should consult with an obstetrician at least three months before you begin trying to conceive. Do your best to schedule the appointment at a time when both you and your partner can be there, so that you have a clear path and shared goals. You will discuss your diet, lifestyle, the family history of both partners, and any health problems that could affect the pregnancy.

Be prepared for this consultation. Have a list of prescription drugs, over-the-counter drugs, and supplements you both use. Herbal preparations must also be considered. During the consultation you will discuss health problems that could possibly affect your pregnancy. The prescription medications you take may need to be altered in dose or type, or gradually stopped. Your doctor may want to change some of your medications. We know that the children of women taking certain antidepressants have a higher risk for ASD. You will consider if your work environment or hobbies expose you to high levels of toxins or could put you at risk for developing viruses or infections that could harm your baby. If your job requires you to use a cash register, be aware that BPA is found in cash register receipts. Potters should avoid the lead in ceramic glazes and colors. If you are a painter, know that there are toxins in pigments, formaldehyde in acrylic paint, and chlorinated hydrocarbons in varnish and paint removers. Even rubber cement contains toxins. Check the labels on art and hobby materials and make certain the room in which you work is well-ventilated.

If ASD and social problems are present in your family tree, your doctor should know about it. Talk to your families about health problems you might not be aware of. There may be illnesses you do not know about. Your families may have forgotten to tell you or you do not remember your grandmother's diabetes, your "strange" uncle who never left home, or the manic depression that afflicted a cousin and was kept quiet.

After discussing your family history, your doctor might recommend that you see a genetic counselor trained to interpret your genetic information. The genetic counselor will discuss background medical information for you and your partner, your family history, and any previous pregnancies. You will review your family tree going back three generations, or as far as you are able. This consultation can help you to examine genetic factors that might place you at a higher risk for having a baby who develops ASD, a hereditary disease, or birth defects. The counselor can help you determine if you want to pursue further genetic testing. The process will help you to understand and deal with any inherited risks.

Are Your Immunizations Current?

Your doctor will check to see if you are up-to-date on your vaccinations. A simple blood test can determine whether further immunization is needed. If you do not have immunization to rubella, you cannot get the vaccine during pregnancy. It is important to know whether you are immune to chicken pox, because chicken pox

Skip the Friendly Skies?

Janine was pregnant with her second child. Her first child, Larry, had autism. While Janine was expecting Larry, she had to travel frequently for business, logging many air miles. She is convinced that exposure to airplane chemicals and radiation, which are considerable, caused his ASD. She plans to stay on the ground until after her new baby is born.

during pregnancy is very dangerous. Chicken pox can cause severe fetal harm or a miscarriage, If possible, get that vaccine before you are pregnant.

Discuss relevant immunizations with your obstetrician. I have a unique view about vaccines—I emphasize avoiding diseases. By that I mean that even though rubella and other dangerous viruses are very rare in the United States, they may be much more common in other countries. I ask mothers to limit travel during certain weeks of their pregnancy, particularly between weeks twelve and sixteen. You should discuss travel limitations with your obstetrician.

Folate and Prenatal Vitamins

I recommend that you start taking prenatal vitamins before you conceive to make certain you are getting the proper nutrients for pregnancy. Your doctor will give you a prescription. You should take folate, also known as folic acid, starting three months prior to getting pregnant, continuing through your twelfth week of pregnancy and as directed by your obstetrician all through your pregnancy. All women of childbearing age should make sure they get adequate amounts of folic acid, because many pregnancies are unexpected. Taking folate before conception is the best way to prevent problems in the development of the brain stem and the spinal cord, known as the neural tube, which are formed during the first month of pregnancy. Folate deficiency has been directly linked to spina bifida, a condition in which the spinal cord is not fully encased in the backbone.

Though folate is important for normal brain development, some studies have associated increased levels of folate in pregnant women with the rising autism numbers. Discuss folic acid with your doctor and obstetrician. Depending on your history, your doctor may want to change the dose or the length of time you take folic acid. You can instead eat foods that are rich in folic acid to safeguard your baby.

New information has come forward involving a connection between calcium supplements and heart attacks. The research is showing that people who take calcium supplements may actually be more prone to heart attacks. The speculation is that when the

Food Sources for Folic Acid

Folic acid is an important nutrient for early brain development, but scientists are taking a close look at the possible link between maternal levels of folate and ASD. I suggest that you make sure your diet includes foods that contain folic acid when you start to think about getting pregnant. It won't be a chore, because folic acid is found in many delicious foods, including the following:

- Spinach
- Broccoli
- Brussels sprouts
- Asparagus
- Berries
- Avocado
- Beef
- Eggs
- Bran flakes
- Chickpeas
- Soybeans
- Oranges
- Grapefruit

Iodine Is Essential for Healthy Brain Development

Insufficient dietary iodine can affect your thyroid function, which affects the developing fetal brain during pregnancy. Iodine is found in pearl millet, cabbage, cauliflower, kale, rutabaga, kohlrabi, lima beans, and sweet potatoes.

proper dose of calcium is obtained naturally from foods, the blood level is constant, correct, and protective. When large doses are taken all at once in pill form, the blood level spikes too high, which is not safe. The same thing may be true of other nutrients like folate. Get as many of your vitamins and other nutrients as possible from healthy foods, not from pills.

Healthy eating before pregnancy means that your body has adequate stores of vitamins and minerals to support the growth of your baby. Poor nutrition will also make you more susceptible to environmental exposures, a condition you definitely want to avoid. I outline a simple plan for nourishing yourself and your baby in chapter 9.

See Your Dentist

Studies have linked periodontal disease to an increased risk of pre-eclampsia, or high blood pressure with elevated levels of protein in the blood, during pregnancy. You do not want to develop high blood pressure during your pregnancy; the condition is another probable risk factor for ASD. Make sure your teeth and gums are healthy before you get pregnant. Another incentive to keeping a clean mouth is that once pregnant, your use of anesthetics and painkillers will be minimized. That should motivate you to have work done on your teeth before you conceive.

Lose That Weight before You Get Pregnant

There is an obesity epidemic in the United States and in most of the world. One in three women of childbearing age in the United States is obese. More than 60 percent of women of childbearing age in the United States are overweight. Sixteen percent have metabolic syndrome, a dangerous mix of obesity, diabetes, and high blood pressure. A new study published in the *Journal of Pediatrics* found that women who are obese and have diabetes are 67 percent more likely to have a child with ASD or developmental problems than women of normal weight. The researchers speculate that obesity and poorly controlled maternal diabetes might reduce the nutrients that reach the fetus by reducing the body's ability to use insulin. The fetal brain could be suffering from a lack of oxygen, a known risk factor for ASD. Children with ASD of obese mothers with type 2 diabetes were more disabled than autistic children whose mothers' weight was normal. It makes no sense to train for a marathon by sitting on the couch eating potato chips, and it makes no sense to get ready for pregnancy and delivery by doing the same thing.

Maternal diabetes can hurt a developing fetus. When a mother's glucose is poorly regulated, the fetus is exposed to elevated glucose levels. That exposure raises fetal insulin production, which requires greater use of oxygen. The result is the depletion of the oxygen supply of the fetus. Diabetes can also cause fetal iron deficiency. The combination of a depleted oxygen supply and an iron deficiency can seriously affect fetal brain development. Diabetes and hypertension not only increase insulin resistance but also contribute to chronic inflammation. With inflammation, certain proteins produced by the immune system can cross the placenta to the fetus and disturb brain development. As you already know, inflammation is a common characteristic found in the brains of people with autism. Recent research has identified maternal inflammation as one of the causes of autism.

You and your baby will do so much better if you are at a healthy weight at the time you become pregnant. If you are overweight but do not have diabetes or hypertension, you might develop these diseases with the weight you gain when pregnant. You should seriously consider postponing pregnancy until you lose the extra pounds. You will have to build in time to take off excess weight sensibly.

Set your goal for the weight you want to be in consultation with your doctor and try to achieve it before you conceive. The health of your baby should be a strong motivation. Do not go on a crash diet, which could alter your metabolism and deprive you of important nutrients. Your doctor might recommend a diet specialist.

Do the best you can. Try to control or cut back 300 calories a day in your diet. Three hundred calories is equal to one hour of moderate exercise or one sandwich. If you get a half-hour of exercise and only eat a half sandwich, you will lose weight and maintain the loss. If you change your eating habits, follow the nutritional advice in chapter 9, and increase your fitness, weight loss will be a natural byproduct. Crash diets do not work. They are just not sustainable.

Break Those Habits

It is hard to ignore the warnings against drinking and smoking while pregnant. Alcohol is a teratogen, known to cause birth defects. Alcohol crosses the placenta and enters the body of the fetus, stunting growth and brain development. Cutting out all alcohol consumption is the best choice. You want to be alcohol-free at the time of conception. I have never agreed with some obstetricians who advise their moms-to-be that a glass of wine here or there is okay. It is not.

Secondhand Smoke Can Affect Your Baby

Tommy had a normal birth, but he was not an easy breastfeeder. His father, who worked on a tech crew at a television studio, continued to smoke after Tommy's birth.

At twelve months, Tommy did not seem to have problems. I did note that he had a junk food diet, and loved chicken nuggets and sugary foods.

At eighteen months, he had what we call in my office a "difficult exam," which is not uncommon for a child his age. He was scared. He yelled and kicked. He could not communicate what was wrong.

At two years, he was not just a routine picky eater. He refused anything except greasy or sugary foods. His parents were experiencing some marital problems, and one parent or the other would give in to his demands.

At two and a half years, Tommy got an extremely bad case of hives when he ate cashews. Even though Tommy was developing allergies, his father could not stop smoking. Never underestimate the effects of secondhand smoke.

At three, Tommy developed fears. Dogs scared him. So did wind. Later that year, he no longer made eye contact and had behavioral problems.

Tommy is now receiving hours of daily therapy.

I am not saying that his father's smoking alone is responsible for Tommy's developmental problems, but it certainly added to his toxic load—along with his fast-food diet.

The health hazards of cigarette smoking are printed on every pack of cigarettes. Smoking during pregnancy accounts for 20 to 30 percent of low-birth-weight babies and 14 percent of preterm deliveries. Secondhand exposure to smoke can cause lower birth weight. Smoking marijuana increases the chance of miscarriage, low birth weight, prematurity, developmental delays, and behavioral and learning problems. It seems obvious to say that you will have to stay away from all illegal drugs for your health and for your baby's.

This is the time to clean up your act. If you have trouble giving up any of these substances, you must get professional help to assist you. Joining a support group might make the process easier.

Stress Takes a Toll

Stress can depress your immune system, raise your blood pressure, and throw off your hormonal balance, all of which should be avoided. It can also affect your fertility. Environmental contaminants like air pollution, automotive exhaust, pesticides, and food additives stress your body on a cellular level, causing oxidative stress. In essence, you rust.

Before your body begins to undergo all the changes that accompany pregnancy, you should try to manage the stress in your life. Take the time to identify what causes you stress. Simplify your life. Learn to say no. Avoid people and activities that sap your energy and waste your time.

Exercise is one of the best remedies for stress, and you should incorporate physical activity into your life before you are pregnant. Walking only thirty minutes a day will help reduce tension.

Stress can also keep you from getting a good night's sleep, which is essential for your body to run optimally. If you have trouble sleeping, avoid caffeine, take up meditation, relax in a warm bath, create a bedtime ritual. This is a time to take great care of yourself. Knowing you have done what you can to prepare yourself for a healthy pregnancy should go a long way to alleviating your worries, allowing you to enjoy the months leading up to the birth of your baby.

Men Need to Make Some Changes, Too

Men have to focus on their preconception health just as much as women do. During the critical months of preparation for pregnancy, the job of future fathers is to insure the health of their sperm. Studies have shown that during the past four decades, the quality and quantity of men's sperm has decreased significantly. A major reason for this change is the presence of estrogen mimickers in everything from plastics to pesticides. DDT, PCBs, PVCs, phthalates, and perchloroethylene all mimic estrogen. These chemicals find their way into the bloodstream and act like estrogen, the female hormone, in the body. What results is a hormonal imbalance that leaves men with abnormal levels of estrogen and testosterone, which affects the quality of sperm.

Men have biological clocks, too. Men make sperm every day, and the process is less than perfect. It takes about three months for sperm to develop fully. Individual sperm cells divide every fifteen

Toxins Are Hazardous to Sperm Health

There is mounting evidence that paternal exposure to toxins can have a negative effect on fetal and postnatal development and that this damage can be carried on to future generations.

There are many toxins that can damage sperm cells. Here are just a few:

Pesticides	Glycol ethers
Chemical fertilizers	Petrochemicals
Lead	Benzene
Nickel	Perchloroethylene (used in dry cleaning)
Mercury	
Chromium	Radiation

If you know you are exposed to toxins at work or at home, be as safe as you can. Wear protective clothing and equipment and avoid skin contact with chemicals. Remember that you might take home contaminants on your work clothes that could affect your partner.

days. During that time factors like heat, toxic chemicals, recreational and prescription drugs, and infections can negatively affect the production of healthy sperm.

Sperm quality decreases gradually as men age. The high turnover rate of sperm production increases the chance that errors will occur in the genetic code that will be passed on to their children. As we discussed in chapter 7, women who become pregnant by older men, who have more lifetime exposure to environmental chemicals, have a higher risk of having children with autism. One of the reasons this is true is that the older you are, the longer you have been exposed to environmental chemicals. Cadmium, nicotine and toxins found in tobacco smoke, lead, and radioactive elements circulate in the blood and reach the testes, affecting the quality of the sperm produced.

Making Sure You Have Healthy Sperm

It is safe to say that anything that is not good for your overall health will have a negative impact on your sperm. You can protect your sperm by following this list of dos and don'ts:

- **Don't smoke.** The toxins will reach your testes.
- **Limit alcohol intake.** Too much alcohol will reduce your zinc levels. A zinc deficiency lowers your sperm count and affects the quality of your sperm.
- **Stay away from illicit drugs.** They can cause sperm to become misshapen.
- **Lose weight if you need to.** Obesity has a negative effect on the health of sperm.
- **Stay cool—literally.** The testes are located out of the body because sperm does better in temperature lower than 98.6°F. Heat from hot tubs, saunas, heating pads, electric blankets, and hot showers of thirty minutes or more can be harmful to your sperm. Men who hold laptops on their laps are likely to elevate the temperature of the scrotum, which affects sperm quality. Use your laptop on a desk or other surface.

The friction created by cycling or very hard workouts will also increase the temperature of the scrotum.
- **Stay cool—figuratively.** Manage your stress to avoid hormonal imbalance.
- **Clean out your medicine cabinet.** With the help of your doctor, eliminate as many medications from your routine as possible.

Medications Known to Affect the Health of Sperm

Several commonly prescribed medications can damage sperm. Knowing that a father's age is linked to autism because of increased likelihood of genetic changes in his sperm, you should not risk exposure to prescription drugs that are known to interfere with healthy sperm production. The list that follows contains a handful of the medications we know about. Others just have not been studied adequately. The drugs to watch out for are:

- Tagamet for reflux, abdominal pain, ulcers
- Sulfasalazine for arthritis and colitis
- Nitrofurantoin, an antibiotic prescribed for ulcers, gastrointestinal problems, and urinary tract infections
- Steroids for asthma, arthritis, and skin conditions
- Calcium channel blockers or calcium antagonists for high blood pressure, angina, irregular heartbeat, and migraines
- Chemotherapy and radiation

When you and your partner have your preconception consultation, bring along a list of the medications you take so that your doctor can make substitutions or changes in dosage.

Preconception Supplements for Men to Strengthen Sperm

Aside from eating a diet that is rich in antioxidants, a number of vitamins and minerals will boost the health of your sperm.

- **Zinc.** More than 70 percent of men do not get the minimum daily requirement of zinc. This mineral is necessary for all aspects of male reproduction, including sperm formation and the manufacture and repair of DNA. Zinc is found in meat, whole-grain cereals, seafood, eggs, and baked beans.
- **Coenzyme Q10.** The ability to produce the antioxidant coenzyme Q10 (CQ10) decreases with age. CQ10 is active in the testes where it fights the effects of oxidative stress on sperm production. Taking 200 to 300 mg of CQ10 a day has been shown to increase the quality of sperm.
- **Vitamin C.** This very important antioxidant improves sperm quality by preventing sperm from clumping together. You need to take vitamin E to activate vitamin C. These antioxidants protect you from free radicals that can damage sperm cells.
- **Selenium.** A deficiency of selenium can lead to deformed sperm. Brazil nuts, meat, seafood, mushrooms, and cereals contain selenium. Selenium is a little controversial, so you will need to discuss the best doses with your doctor. Some studies have linked selenium to cancer and heart disease.
- **B-12.** This essential vitamin helps the body to produce DNA and RNA.
- **Folate.** Just as women need to take folate before conception, men do, too. A recent study found that men with reduced levels of folic acid had more chromosomal abnormalities in their sperm. Another study showed a link between high levels of the nutrient in men's diet and the genetic quality of their sperm. Taking folic acid is particularly important for men over forty.

Having a baby will be one of the most momentous events of your lives. You will not regret making the effort to prepare yourselves for a healthy pregnancy. Isn't it worth it to give your baby the best start possible? Do what you can to incorporate the suggestions I make in this chapter in your lives in the months leading up to

Preconception Supplements for Men

Recommendations for vitamin consumption change often because of new information provided by ongoing studies. We were all advised to take calcium supplements. Then research found that taking calcium supplements can increase the risk of heart attacks. Too much vitamin E has now been linked to heart failure.

I believe it is best to get your vitamins and minerals from eating wholesome, fresh food. That said, the following supplements are currently recommended to enhance sperm production:

- Zinc (100 mg/day)
- CQ10 (200–300 mg/day)
- Vitamin C (250mg/3 times a day)
- Vitamin E (400 I.U./day). Check with your physician on the effects of vitamin E if you are on any medications. The recommendations for the best daily dose seem to change every year. You will need to discuss this nutrient with your doctor.
- Selenium (200 mcg/day). This mineral is controversial; you will need to discuss it with your doctor.
- L-carnitine (1 gram/day)
- B-complex (once a day)
- Folic acid (400 mcg/day). Folic acid is also available as folate.
- General multivitamin with minerals (once a day). Do some research online before you select one or consult with your doctor.

The quality of dietary supplements varies greatly. Though some companies research, manufacture, and sell their own products, most dietary supplements are produced by a few dozen companies and repackaged by other companies with their own labels.

Supplements do not have to be expensive to be high-quality. You can learn about the quality of supplements by checking the labels and the packaging. Dietary supplements are not regulated. The content of the pills could differ from what is listed on the label. The word *natural* is meaningless on a label because every supplement is derived from processed food. A vitamin's natural state is the actual food from which it is derived. Eating vitamin-rich food seems a better bet to me.

your pregnancy. You will be protecting your baby from ASD and other medical problems from the moment you decide to have a child.

While you are making these changes, you have to nourish yourself with fresh, unprocessed food. Chapter 9 is about eating with the health of your baby in mind. As you change your eating habits even before you are pregnant, you will look and feel so much better that eating clean will become a way of life that you will pass on to your children.

9

What to Do When You Are Expecting

Finding out that you are pregnant is one of life's most intense and thrilling experiences whether you have been planning the pregnancy or you suddenly discover you are going to have a baby. Even after all the years I have spent taking care of newborns and watching them grow, it remains a miracle to me. If you and your partner have had months to prepare for the pregnancy, you have a head start on protecting your baby from developmental delays, learning disabilities, and ASD. If your pregnancy is a happy surprise, you can set your baby's growth on a healthy course by following the Top Ten Rules of Healthy Prenatal Development, which focus on detoxing your inner environment to support healthy neurological development. See an obstetrician if you have not already. Each month that prenatal care is delayed after conception increases the risk of autism by 29 percent.

Top Ten Rules of Healthy Prenatal Development

1. **Take a prenatal multivitamin right away** so that your body functions at peak level. Talk to your doctor about taking folic acid (folate) the first twelve weeks of your pregnancy to protect your baby's developing brain.
2. **Drink filtered water.** Eliminating toxins from your diet is one of the themes of this chapter, and drinking plenty of water will help to flush those toxins from your body. You will need additional fluids while you are pregnant and breastfeeding. During pregnancy, you should drink ten cups of toxic-free fluid a day. While breastfeeding, increase your fluid intake to thirteen cups a day. Avoid tap water, which is loaded with chemicals.
3. **Stop drinking alcoholic beverages, smoking, or using recreational drugs.** Alcohol crosses the placenta rapidly, and the baby's blood alcohol level becomes similar to the mother's, but it takes much longer for the alcohol to clear from the baby's bloodstream. The chemicals in cigarette smoke and illicit drugs act the same way.
4. **Reduce or eliminate caffeine consumption.** Too much caffeine can lead to prematurity and low birth weight, risk factors for developmental delays and ASD.
5. **Eat unprocessed foods.** Preservatives, additives, and colorings have been linked to disrupted neurological development.
6. **Eat organic whenever possible.** Pesticides found in our food and leached into our water are among the most harmful toxins for your baby before birth.
7. **Avoid unsafe levels of mercury,** particularly from eating contaminated fish.
8. **Do not take aspirin, Advil, or Motrin.** Recent studies have implicated Tylenol as a neurotoxin. It is best to avoid painkillers during pregnancy, but if you have to take a painkiller, acetaminophen has the lowest risk.

Food Recommendations from a Vegetarian Doctor

This chapter contains many discussions about avoiding foods that contain pesticides, heavy metals, artificial colors, preservatives, and other toxins. I have been a vegetarian since finishing medical school. I think it is easier to avoid contaminants while eating a plant-based diet. Since most families eat meat and fish, I offer lots of guidance for all family nutrition choices. In this chapter, you will find my recommendations for the safest, cleanest sources of produce, fish, and meat for your family.

9. **Review your prescription medications with your doctor.** Antidepressants and a number of asthma medications have been linked to an increase in autism. Your doctor will be able to suggest healthier substitutes or change your dosage.
10. **Do not stop exercising.** Begin a regular routine if exercise is not part of your life. Talk with your obstetrician about what works best for you. Your doctor will help you decide what an appropriate program is for you. You do not want to overdo it. Remember, many toxins leave the body through sweat glands.

Following these rules will put you on track to have a smooth pregnancy, an uncomplicated delivery, and the healthiest newborn possible. Your obstetrician will undoubtedly have additional guidelines to supplement my top ten, which are a strategy for reducing the risk of developmental delays.

What You Eat Affects Your Baby's Genes

The *New York Times* reported on research done at Duke University that found that a mother's diet can permanently change the functioning of her baby's genes. *Methylation* is an epigenetic process, a way that the environment tweaks gene expression. The process acts like a gas pedal or a brake, turning gene expression up or down and on or off. Methylation plays a critical role in controlling the genes involved in prenatal and postnatal development. The atoms that are responsible for methylation are derived from the foods you eat, particularly vitamin B-12, choline, and folic acid. Scientists know that what a mother eats is very important, but they do not know exactly how this process works. They speculate that the modern American diet, full of fats and sugars, could be having epigenetic effects on future generations. To support healthy methylation in yourself and in the baby growing within you, you should eat a diet rich in foods from the following list:

- **Superveggies:** broccoli, cauliflower, Brussels sprouts, kale, cabbage, and bok choy
- **Folic-acid-rich foods:** egg yolks, dried beans, lentils, split peas, almonds, nuts, wholegrain breads, whole-wheat flour, potatoes, sweet potatoes, spinach, beetroot, asparagus, superveggies, bananas, oranges, and peaches
- **Antioxidant-rich foods:** red beans, kidney beans, pinto beans, black beans, blueberries, cranberries, blackberries, raspberries, strawberries, Red Delicious apples, Granny Smith apples, pecans, cherries, plums, dried prunes, russet potatoes, and cooked artichoke hearts
- **B-12-rich foods:** beef sirloin, lamb, chicken, fish, whole eggs, milk, cheeses, yogurts, fortified breakfast cereals. (I am a vegetarian, and I get my B-12 from tempeh, a fermented soy product, and a vitamin supplement. I do not think it is healthy to eat a lot of meat or fish.)
- **Choline-rich foods:** eggs, lettuce, and peanuts
- **Clean and Green:** organic fruits and vegetables

As you know by now, exposure to chemicals in the womb can cause serious damage when a baby's organs and systems are developing. The best way to reduce your body's chemical load during pregnancy is to eat fresh, unprocessed, preferably organic food.

Pesticides are found in commercially grown fruits and leach into the soil, then into our water supplies. Additives, preservatives, and artificial colors are key ingredients in processed food. Flavorings, fragrance, and artificial colors are used in processed foods to make them more appealing to the senses. Many of these chemicals are derived from petroleum and coal tar. Preservatives like BHT nitrates, sulfites, BHT, and BHA can raise blood pressure and can provoke allergies.

Food additives have a cumulative effect. They gradually build up in the body. Safety levels are based on average adult intake. The effects of these chemicals on a fetus, a newborn, and a child have not been adequately studied. If you consider dose and body weight, a child eats several times more additives than the acceptable daily intake. Imagine what this means for an unborn baby. Even a newborn has a limited capability to detox, because the liver is not yet mature. Almost all processed food contains chemicals that are not good for your baby.

Caution: Fast Food Can Be a Health Hazard

Tony's father was forty-seven when Tony was born. At sixteen and a half months, Tony's development was normal. When I saw him six months later, he was off track. He spoke in a singsong voice and was not making progress in efforts to speak. I referred him to a speech therapist. When Tony was twenty-six months, I had even greater concerns about his development. He had no expressive language, and he didn't make eye contact.

When I communicated what I had observed to his parents, we discussed their lifestyle. The family was not very food conscious, and Tony ate fast food all the time.

At three years, we did an intensive evaluation with a

pediatric developmental specialist and changed Tony's diet. The family shifted to a vegan diet, and Tony took probiotics to help with his digestion. His parents simply changed everything they could because of love, logic, and looking for the very best health. It worked. Tony, now five, is in preschool with an aide.

We consume additives in combination, which means that the chemicals have a more potent effect on nerve cells. One study showed that a toxic cocktail of common food additives and colorings disturb nerve cell growth and signaling. The flavor enhancers MSG and aspartame, a sugar substitute, were tested separately with blue and yellow food colorings. Brilliant blue was the most potent inhibitor of neural growth, followed by MSG, and yellow food coloring. The researchers found that mixing MSG with the blue food coloring had four times the power to derail neural growth; mixing aspartame with the yellow food coloring had seven times the effect. When you study the label of processed foods, you will find a long list of chemicals. The easiest rule of thumb is not to eat anything with ingredients you cannot pronounce. Fresh, natural food is the way to nourish yourself and your family all the time. I love to talk to kids about this and explain that the ingredients in an apple are . . . the apple! They laugh, but they seem to understand it better than the average American adult supermarket shoppers buying fried apple chips.

More than four hundred chemical pesticides are routinely used in conventional farming. Residues remain on non-organic food even after washing. These pesticides are endocrine disrupters that linger in your body and remain there long after you eat. Studies have linked pesticide exposure in the womb to autism. The active ingredients of synthetic pesticides, which are derived from petroleum, combine many chemicals, including chlorine, fluorine, and bromine. Why would you knowingly expose your unborn child to poison?

Washing all fruits and vegetables—even organic produce—thoroughly prevents exposure to listeria, a bacteria known to cause birth complications. You need to do more than a quick rinse. Keep a vegetable brush at the kitchen sink to give produce a good scrub.

This following list gives you an idea of the comparative chemical load common fruits and vegetables carry from worst to best. It begins with those that contain the most pesticides and continues to those that contain the least.

Pesticide Levels in Fifty-three Fruits and Vegetables

1. Apple
2. Celery
3. Strawberries
4. Peaches
5. Spinach
6. Nectarines
7. Grapes
8. Sweet bell peppers
9. Potatoes
10. Blueberries
11. Lettuce
12. Kale/collard greens
13. Cilantro
14. Cucumbers
15. Grapes
16. Cherries
17. Pears
18. Nectarines
19. Hot peppers
20. Green beans
21. Carrots
22. Plums
23. Blueberries
24. Raspberries
25. Green beans (imported)
26. Summer squash
27. Oranges
28. Broccoli
29. Green onions
30. Bananas
31. Cantaloupe (imported)
32. Honeydew melon
33. Cauliflower
34. Tomatoes
35. Papaya
36. Cranberries
37. Plums (domestic)
38. Winter squash
39. Mushrooms
40. Grapefruit
41. Sweet potatoes
42. Watermelon
43. Cabbage
44. Kiwi
45. Cantaloupe
46. Eggplant
47. Mangoes
48. Sweet peas (frozen)
49. Asparagus
50. Avocado

51. Pineapple
52. Sweet corn
53. Onion

Certain fruits and vegetables, spices, and meats are exposed to radiation to destroy microorganisms, bacteria, and viruses, to delay ripening, and to increase juice yield. Irradiation of food might not be good for you. The irradiation may create molecular changes in the foods' protein, and we have no idea what that might mean for nutrition and health. The jury is out, but why not be pure?

Many of you irradiate food every day without knowing it. Warming food in a microwave irradiates it and alters the structure of the molecules. Irradiated fats form free radicals that combine with existing chemicals to form new chemicals unknown to your body. My advice is to get rid of your microwave or refrain from using it during pregnancy.

Fishy Business

Fish and seafood used to be called "brain food," a good source of protein, omega 3 fatty acids, vitamin D, and iodine. But today mercury and other heavy metals are found in fish in varying degrees. The concept of brain food takes on a new, negative meaning, because the mercury in fish is harmful to health and brain development. We have not treated our waterways well, and fish and seafood have been contaminated. I recommend that you not eat fish and seafood for three months before you conceive, while you are pregnant, and while you are breastfeeding. If you cannot live without fish while you are pregnant and nursing your baby, severely limit the type of fish and the number of servings you eat a week.

Mercury occurs naturally in air, water, and food. The element is found in nature in various forms: organic, inorganic, and metallic. Organic mercury is the most hazardous. In water, inorganic mercury is converted into a toxic organic form called methylmercury by the microorganisms found in the sediment of sea beds. It accumulates up the food chain in fish and shellfish. Large, predatory fish at the top of the food chain live longer and so contain higher levels of mercury.

When a pregnant woman eats contaminated fish, mercury enters the bloodstream and can cross the placenta to the fetus. The severity of the neural damage depends on how much mercury is in the system. Mercury is stored in fat tissue, the brain, and the bones. Ridding your body of mercury takes several months. Its half-life is about eighty days. That is why you should limit your consumption of seafood and fish *before* you are pregnant. Babies born with high levels of mercury in their systems are at risk for neurological and developmental problems. We do not yet know the magnitude of the possible harm, but I have no intention of waiting for conclusive data proving that harm to warn against mercury exposure.

Mercury Levels in Fish and Shellfish

I do not recommend eating fish during pregnancy. If you do eat fish, try to cut way back.

The American Pregnancy Association has rated the mercury levels in a comprehensive list of fish, which I have adapted for you below. The Natural Resources Defense Council (NRDC) has released a more extensive list that you can view on their website www.nrdc.org/health/effects/mercury/guide.asp. You can check with your state or local health department for the mercury levels of locally caught fish and shellfish.

Do not eat any fish from the highest and high mercury lists. If you have to eat fish, select from the last two lists.

Highest Mercury	**High Mercury**
King mackerel	Bluefish
Marlin	Chilean sea bass
Orange roughy	Grouper
Shark	Mackerel (Spanish, gulf)
Swordfish	Tuna (canned, white albacore, yellowfin)
Tuna (ahi and bigeye)	

Lower Mercury

Bass (striped, black)
Carp
Cod
Croaker
Halibut
Lobster
Mahi mahi
Monkfish
Perch (freshwater)
Sablefish
Sea trout
Skate
Snapper
Tuna (canned, chunk light)

Lowest Mercury

Anchovies
Butterfish
Catfish
Clams
Crab
Crayfish
Croaker
Flounder
Haddock
Hake
Herring
Mackerel (North Atlantic, chub)
Mullet
Oysters
Perch (ocean)
Plaice
Salmon (canned, fresh)
Sardines
Scallops
Shad
Shrimp
Sole
Squid
Tilapia
Trout (freshwater)
Whitefish
Whiting

Organic vs. Conventional

Organic food is said to be an average of 25 percent more nutritious than conventionally grown food with higher levels of beta-carotene; vitamins C, D, and E; polyphenols; antioxidants; flavinoids; essential fatty acids; and minerals. The levels of trace minerals in industrially grown fruit and vegetables fell by up to 76 percent between 1940 and 1991. The introduction of synthetic fertilizers and pesticides during that time had a lot to do with the decline. The level

Shopping Advice from My Chef Wife

Meyera, my wife, is a wonderful cook. She used to own a vegetarian restaurant in Santa Monica. She is a serious foodie. Her contributions to this chapter will make your shift to eating more wholesome foods easy, quick, and fun. Meyera has a lot to say about ingredients:

> When I wrote my first cookbook in 1994, I had a hard time finding organic produce that looked good. Most stores across America had nothing. Now almost every market has at least some packaged greens, potatoes, and seasonal vegetables.
>
> If you can't find what you want, ask for it. Most likely you are not the only customer who has inquired. The more people who let the store know what they want, the more likely you are to have a variety of choices. Another reason to stay away from processed and canned goods is that their packaging just fills up landfills.
>
> Explore the multitude of farmers' markets that the locavore movement has made so popular across the country. They are a fabulous source of organically grown and freshly picked produce that has a very small footprint because of the usually short distance from field to food stand.
>
> At the supermarket, always start out in the produce department. Doing without cookies, chips, and snacks laden with preservatives, salt, and sugars might seem difficult at first. Later in this chapter, I share some recipes for healthy meals and snacks that taste so fresh and good and are so easy to prepare that you will not miss the junk food.
>
> —Meyera Robbins

of antioxidants in milk from organic cattle is between 50 and 80 percent higher than in non-organic milk. Organic wheat, tomatoes, potatoes, cabbage, onions, and lettuce have 20 to 40 percent more nutrients.

Organic food is usually 20 percent more expensive than chemically grown food. In weighing the price difference, you have to consider the costs of the damage to your family's health, to the climate, and to the environment. With its superior nutritional value, organic produce is equivalent to eating an extra portion of fruit or vegetables a day, so you actually have to eat less for the same nutritional benefits. The size difference between conventionally fertilized produce and organic produce is mostly due to water content. Aside from these nutritional benefits, organic food tastes better, because plants and animals are allowed to mature at their own pace. Less expensive food ends up being more costly because it is estimated that each one of those $1.49 hamburgers ends up costing five to six

Pesticides Implanted in Genetically Modified Crops

A recent study from the University of Sherbrooke Hospital Centre in Quebec found that 93 percent of blood samples from pregnant women and 80 percent of samples from umbilical cords tested positive for traces of toxins from genetically modified food. Toxins that had been implanted into genetically modified food crops to kill pests had reached the bloodstreams of pregnant women and their unborn babies. The built-in toxins protect crops and allow for the use of higher levels of pesticides. These toxins can get into the human body as a result of eating meat, milk, and eggs from farm livestock fed genetically modified corn. Big agriculture has argued that any toxins we eat from genetically modified food are destroyed in the process of digestion. The Quebec study proves that assertion wrong.

healthcare dollars to repair the damage fast food contributes to obesity, heart disease, cancer, and more.

When you are eating for two, the benefits of organic food are especially important. Conventional produce is grown with pesticides and herbicides to protect the crop. Synthetic fertilizers are used for bigger yields and better-looking produce. Hormones, steroids, and antibiotics are used to raise beef, chicken, and pork. Growth hormones are used so that animals grow bigger in a short time. The result is that kids today are maturing and growing at a very different pace than in the past because of all the endocrine disrupters they ingest in their food. Antibiotics prevent the spread of disease in the cramped quarters of livestock, but the amount of

When Buying Organic Is Essential

You can lower your pesticide intake by buying organic for only the twelve most contaminated fruits and vegetables. This list was created by the Environmental Working Group, whose website, www.ewg.org, is a treasure trove of information.

The Dirty Dozen

Try to buy the following items organic. They have the highest levels of pesticides and other toxins. If you buy organic food selectively, these are the items that need to be organic. Try to avoid commercially grown fruits and vegetables from this list.

1. Apples
2. Celery
3. Strawberries
4. Peaches
5. Spinach
6. Nectarines (imported)
7. Grapes (imported)
8. Sweet bell peppers
9. Potatoes
10. Blueberries (domestic)
11. Lettuce
12. Kale/collard greens

The Clean Fifteen

These fruits and vegetables have the lowest levels of pesticides. If you have to make a choice, these are the items you can buy conventionally grown.

1. Onions
2. Sweet corn (in the United States some sweet corn sold for human consumption is produced from genetically modified seeds)
3. Pineapples
4. Avocado
5. Asparagus
6. Sweet peas
7. Mangoes
8. Eggplant
9. Cantaloupe (domestic)
10. Kiwi
11. Cabbage
12. Watermelon
13. Sweet potatoes
14. Grapefruit
15. Mushrooms

antibiotics used has bred resistance into bacteria. We are consuming so many antibiotics in our food and water that bacteria might build a resistance to antibiotics when we really need them. We now have great concern about superbugs—bacteria that have been exposed to so many antibiotics that hundreds of infections are much more dangerously resistant than they have ever been. Avoid antibiotics and other chemicals in your food.

Organic farming is good for the planet, for wildlife, and for the environment. It results in less pollution and waste, and fewer global warming gasses than does conventional farming. And buying organic protects animal welfare.

I do want to discuss genetically modified food briefly. Scientists are able to change the genes within an organism or to transfer a gene from one organism to another. They alter the blueprint and characteristics of that organism in order to transfer desirable qualities from one organism to another. Genetically engineered crops are designed to resist disease better, decrease spoilage, increase yield, and lengthen lifespan. Sixty to seventy percent of processed foods on your grocery shelves have been genetically modified. The crops and products most often modified are soybeans, maize, cotton, rapeseed oil, field corn, high-fructose corn syrup, and canola oil.

Genetically modified foods are inherently unsafe. Currently, science does not know enough to evaluate the possible environmental effects of tinkering with Mother Nature. I believe the risk outweighs the benefits. The good news is that organic farmers do not use genetic engineering to "improve" their product.

If the additional expense of buying organic food will put a strain on your budget, you can be selective and buy organic just for the fruits and vegetables with the heaviest toxic load. Some conventionally grown produce is safe to eat. Remember, eating conventionally grown produce is far better than not eating fruit and vegetables at all.

Eating Defensively

I have compiled an at-a-glance chart of foods to avoid or that require special attention when consuming during pregnancy. You might want to copy this chart and post it on your refrigerator.

Foods and Drinks to Avoid during Pregnancy	Avoid	Prescription
Drinks		
Tap water	May contain pesticides, hormones, antibiotics, bacteria, and rocket fuel	Always filter water or drink bottled water.
Beverages that contain caffeine	Can contribute to low birth weight	Have no more than one cup of coffee or two cups of tea daily.
Alcohol	Can contribute to birth defects and abnormal neurological development	Try to avoid alcohol completely.
Unpasteurized juice or cider	Contains *E. coli*, pesticides, additives	Drink pasteurized juices made from organic fruits and vegetables.
Dairy and Eggs	May increase tendency to allergies	

Food and Drinks to Avoid during Pregnancy	Avoid	Prescription
Soft cheeses—Brie, Feta, Camembert, Roquefort, or soft blue-veined cheese and all unpasteurized cheeses	Contain *E. coli* or listeria	Eat hard cheeses like cheddar or Swiss. Check all cheese labels to be certain the cheese is made from pasteurized milk.
Unpasteurized milk	Contains *E. coli*, listeria, salmonella, camplylobacter	Drink only pasteurized milk.
Eggs and unpasteurized egg products, including mayonnaise	Undercooked or raw may contain salmonella	Cook eggs until yolks are firm. Any dishes containing eggs should be cooked to 160–167° F. For eggnog and homemade ice cream, use a pasteurized egg product.
Meat and Poultry		
Conventionally raised beef, veal, lamb, pork, and poultry	Contain *E. coli*, hormones, antibiotics	Cook all meat to 160–167° F. Eat only organically raised meat and poultry.
Liver, liver products, and fish liver oils	Contain levels of vitamin A that may be harmful	
Precooked and processed meat products, like hamburgers, sausages, hot dogs, and cold meat cuts	Contain listeria, hormones, antibiotics, additives, preservatives	Reheat meats to 160° F or steaming hot. Eat meats that do not have preservatives and additives. Cooking may create "co-carcinogens." Increase plant-based protein and stay away from S.A.D., the standard American diet.
Prepared salads, like chicken or seafood	Contain listeria, hormones, antibiotics, mercury	Make salads at home using organic ingredients.
Fish and Seafood		
Swordfish, shark, king mackerel, tilefish, and tuna	Contain mercury	Limit consumption of lowest-mercury fish to two six-ounce servings a week.
Raw or undercooked fish and shellfish, like sushi, uncooked clams, oysters	Contain mercury, parasites, bacteria	Cook fish to 145° F.
Vegetables and Fruits		
Conventionally grown vegetables and fruits	Contains pesticides, genetically modified, salmonella, *E. coli*	Eat organic produce whenever possible. Always wash and dry thoroughly before eating.

One More Reason to Eat Clean

As you have learned, chronic inflammation of the mother's body can affect your baby. The everyday stress of modern life can promote a state of hormonal imbalance that promotes inflammation. Inflammation is the first response of your immune system to infection. Chronic inflammation can result in asthma, allergies, muscle and joint pain, and cardiovascular disease.

With autoimmune diseases, an overactive immune system can create severe inflammation and free radical damage. Inflammation can be a by-product of oxidative stress. If your body does not have sufficient antioxidants to neutralize free radicals, oxidative stress occurs. Free radicals are unstable molecules that interact aggressively with other molecules and create abnormal cells. This lack of balance results in massive cell damage and a weakened immune system.

The good news is that you can reduce inflammation by avoiding certain foods and eating others. Eating junk food, high-fat meats, sugar, and highly processed foods is guaranteed to promote inflammation. The clean eating I have recommended all through this chapter will help you to bring inflammation under control. Certain foods are proinflammatory, including:

- Omega 6 fats are used in processed and fast foods. These unhealthy fats are found in corn, safflower, sunflower, peanut, and soybean oils.
- *Trans* fats are created in an industrial process that adds hydrogen to liquid vegetable oils to make them more solid. Another name for *trans* fats is "partially hydrogenated oils." They are highly inflammatory. Though manufacturers and fast-food chains are under pressure to eliminate the use of unhealthy *trans* fats in their products, *trans* fats are still widely used in processed and fried foods.
- Refined flour, sugar, and foods high on the glycemic index elevate glucose and insulin levels, which increases proinflammatory messengers.

- Food allergies or sensitivities to wheat and dairy can set off an inflammatory cascade.

The first step to reducing inflammation is to change the way you eat in these ways:

- Reduce your consumption of *trans* fats and saturated fats by avoiding red meat, processed foods, and high-fat, process meats like bacon and sausage. The nitrates found in hot dogs and some cold cuts also cause inflammation.
- Replace refined white flour in bread and pasta with whole grains.
- Don't eat anything white—rice and potatoes are high glycemic index foods.
- Avoid presweetened cereals, sodas, pastries, cookies, cakes, candy, and rich desserts.

Anti-Inflammatory Foods

If you eat from the following list of foods, you will enjoy managing whatever level of inflammation you might have:

Vegetables: arugula, asparagus, bean sprouts, bell peppers, bok choy, broccoli rabe, Brussels sprouts, cabbage, cauliflower, chard, collards, cucumber, endive, escarole, garlic, green beans, kale, leeks, mushrooms, onions, olives, radishes, radicchio, romaine lettuce, scallions, shallots, spinach, sweet potatoes, and zucchini

Fruits: apples, avocados, blueberries, cantaloupe, cherries, clementines, guavas, honeydew, kiwifruit, kumquats, lemons, limes, oranges, papayas, peaches, pears, plums, raspberries, rhubarb, strawberries, tangerines, and tomatoes

Animal proteins (organic, free-range, grass-fed, or wild): skinless and boneless chicken breast, turkey breast, anchovies, cod, halibut, herring, mackerel, oysters, rainbow trout, sablefish, salmon, sardines, shad, snapper, striped bass, and whitefish

Meyera's Healthy Pantry

I keep a minimum of products in my pantry, which affords me the opportunity to buy organic: maybe some pancake mix, whole-wheat pasta, brown rice, tea, oils and vinegars, mustards, organic ketchup (even Heinz makes organic ketchup these days!), and dried herbs and spices, including granulated garlic, basil, tarragon, dill, oregano, mace, nutmeg, thyme, marjoram, coriander, and cumin. I always have a supply of healthy, whole-grain crackers, baked pita chips, and organic corn chips for dips and spreads.

Always keep on hand the following items: onions, carrots, celery, mushrooms, fresh tomatoes, avocados, apples, bananas, berries (frozen if out of season), broccoli, cauliflower, bell peppers, potatoes, yams, beets, greens (plenty of lettuce, spinach, arugula), and an assortment of dried beans and soybeans (also known as edamame, found in the frozen food section).

Although using canned beans can be more convenient, I do not recommend it because of the plastic that lines the cans. Canned beans are also much more expensive than dried beans. It takes a little planning, but it is well worth starting from scratch. If you are pressed for time, organic beans from BPA-free cans work. Make sure you rinse them well before using.

You can stock up on other fruits and vegetables when they are in season and at the peak of their flavor.

My family is vegetarian. If you eat meat, try reducing the portions and making the vegetables as important and more abundant in your meals.

—Meyera Robbins

Nuts and seeds: almonds, flaxseeds, hazelnuts, sunflower seeds, walnuts, and pumpkin seeds
Oils: extra-virgin olive oil and virgin coconut oil
Herbs and spices: ginger, oregano, turmeric, cayenne, basil, parsley, rosemary, and thyme
Drinks: green tea, ginger tea, acai/blueberry juice, pomegranate juice, and apple juice

You can control what you eat. You can make food choices that will protect your baby from the harmful effects of eating food that is not pure and fresh. Shop the outer rim of the grocery store where the fresh food is sold. If your store does not have a good selection of organic products, ask for them. If the demand is there, your supermarket will stock organic food. Go to your local farmers' market. Eat a rainbow of fresh fruits and vegetables. You will look and feel great and be happy knowing you are giving your baby all the nutrients necessary for healthy development.

From Meyera's Kitchen

I like to make soups. They can be simple and diverse, and you can develop a multitude of meals from them. Not only are they versatile, but if you make a large quantity, you can freeze some in meal-size containers, preferably glass, to defrost and warm up for another time when you don't feel like cooking. The next recipe will create plenty of leftovers. Serve the soup with a salad and warmed whole-wheat bread with a crispy crust for a delicious, satisfying meal.

Meyera's Basic Bean Soup

Makes about 16 cups

When making this soup, you have to start the night before because the dried beans have to soak overnight.

4–5 cups dried beans—you can use kidney, navy, white beans, black beans, or any combination. Lentils and split peas do not need to be soaked overnight, so hold off on these for another recipe.
2 medium-size onions, chopped
4 medium-size carrots, peeled and chopped
1 bunch celery, chopped
2 cups either yams or potatoes, or some of each, peeled and chopped
1 red pepper, seeded, cored, and chopped
1 large parsnip (discard after cooking)
2 tablespoons granulated garlic (Using garlic in this form saves time.)
1 tablespoon marjoram
1 teaspoon ground pepper
¼ cup reduced sodium soy sauce
3 bay leaves
4 cubes or ½ cup powdered vegetarian bullion or ½ cup vegetarian stock

1. Soak beans overnight in water in a large covered pot, not in the refrigerator. The water level should be about an inch above the beans, covering them completely.
2. The next day, rinse the beans through a strainer.
3. Refill the pot with the beans and enough water to cover the beans. Bring to a boil.
4. Add the other ingredients and enough water to cover all the vegetables and bring back to a boil.
5. Reduce heat and simmer for 2 hours, adding more water or broth if needed.

— — —

Now is the time to be creative: You can thicken the soup by pureeing a cup or two in a blender or food processor and then returning it to the unblended soup.

The soup makes a great sauce either pureed or as is. You can steam broccoli or carrot slices or anything else that is in the refrigerator and serve over a bed of brown rice with the pureed soup as a sauce.

Here are some variations on the basic soup recipe:

BURGER

Additional ingredients

¼ cup quick oats
1 tablespoon cooked rice
Olive oil

1. With a slotted spoon, take out the beans and vegetables. You can use the broth you have left behind for a rice dish.
2. Combine the vegetables in a bowl with the quick oats and cooked rice.
3. Form the mixture into patties.
4. Cover the bottom of a frying pan with a little bit of oil.
5. Cook over medium heat, flipping to brown both sides, about three minutes a side.

RICE AND BEANS

Serve soup that has not been pureed over a bed of rice.

About Rice

Rice lasts for days. Make enough for soup and rice one night. The next night, mix the rest of the rice with the beans and vegetables from the soup, leaving out the liquid, to make burgers. You can freeze broth and use it to cook rice next time you make it.

Organic short grain brown rice is the healthiest of the rices. Quick or "minute rice" will give you way more calories than nutrition. Long-grain and basmati rices will be flavorful changes for meals.

TOMATO-RICE SOUP

To a cup or two of the soup, add either:

2 cups tomatoes, chopped, or 1 16-ounce can
of organic chopped tomatoes

At this point you can either puree or not. Add a cup of cooked rice before serving.

MUSHROOM SOUP

2 cups mushrooms, chopped

1. Sauté the mushrooms—season them as exotically as you like—and add them to the soup.
2. Serve pureed or not.

STEW

If you want to add tofu, chicken, or meat, they all work with Meyera's Basic Bean Soup recipe to create a stew that you can serve over short grain brown rice.

POTATO SOUP

Adding more potatoes changes the flavor of the basic soup.

2 cups white potatoes, chopped

1. Place potatoes in a separate pot of water.
2. Bring water to a boil.
3. Allow to simmer until potatoes are soft and add to Meyera's Basic Bean Soup.
4. Puree with bean soup by blending some soup and cooled potatoes, pulsing on and off for a few seconds.

YAM SOUP

Yams are so tasty that I don't even peel them for soup. Follow the Potato Soup recipe above, substituting yams for potatoes.

LENTIL AND SPLIT PEA SOUP

Makes about 20 cups

Here is a variation on Meyera's Basic Bean Soup that does not require soaking the legumes overnight. The cooking time is shorter, too.

2 cups red or green lentils or split peas
1 cup carrots, peeled and chopped
1 cup celery, chopped
1 cup onions, chopped
1 parsnip, remove after cooking
1 cup small chunks of potato (any kind)
2 bay leaves
Soy sauce to taste
Fresh ground pepper to taste

1. Place ingredients in a big pot. Add enough water to cover the vegetables.
2. Bring to a boil; simmer for about an hour.

This soup will thicken when cooled.

By now you're probably wondering what to do with this generous amount of soup.

Vegan Chopped Liver

Makes about 2 cups

This is a great appetizer served with crackers or crudité. It can also be used as a sandwich spread.

2 tablespoons olive oil
1 cup onion, chopped
2 cups mushrooms, chopped
4 cups parsley, chopped
½ teaspoon dried thyme
1 cup cooked green beans, cut into ½ inch pieces
1 teaspoon soy sauce
Pepper to taste
⅓ cup walnut pieces

1. Heat olive oil in a saucepan.
2. Add chopped onion and sauté for 5 minutes.
3. Add mushrooms, parsley, thyme, green beans, soy sauce, and pepper and stir for 6 minutes.
4. Remove from heat and allow to cool.

5. Put mixture into a food processor with the walnut pieces.
6. Pulse on and off a few times—just enough to combine all the ingredients.

Dips and Spreads

We always kept a variety of dips and spreads in the refrigerator along with bags of cut-up vegetables and fruit. Baked pita chips and corn chips work, too.

The simple recipes that follow can be part of a main meal.

Guacamole

Makes about 2 cups

4 or 5 ripe avocados
¼ cup mild salsa

1. In a bowl, mash together the avocados and the salsa.
2. If you plan on keeping this dip in the refrigerator, keep one avocado pit in the guacamole and cover with plastic wrap pressed into the top of the guacamole so it doesn't turn brown.

Green Tahini Spread

Makes about 2 cups

2 tablespoons olive oil
1 teaspoon granulated garlic
1 tablespoon lemon juice
1 teaspoon reduced-sodium soy sauce
1 cup spinach or arugula, chopped
2 tablespoons parsley flakes
2 cups tahini
Salt and pepper to taste

1. Combine all the ingredients except the tahini and salt and pepper in a food processor and pulse on and off until smooth.
2. Add tahini.
3. Season to taste with salt and pepper or more tahini if needed.

Bean Tahini

Makes about 2 cups

1 cup cooked white beans

Follow the Green Tahini Spread recipe, but substitute 1 cup cooked white beans for the greens, or just add the beans and a bit of their liquid to the Green Tahini Spread recipe.

Greek Potato Spread

Makes about 4 cups

2 cups potatoes, boiled and cubed
1 cup cooked white or navy beans
2 tablespoons lemon juice
¼ cup parsley, chopped
½ teaspoon granulated garlic
1 tablespoon soy sauce
⅓ cup chopped almonds or walnuts

Combine all ingredients and pulse on and off in a food processor until smooth but not runny (about 6 pulses).

Quickly Assembled Meals

Julienne (sliced in thin strips) any combination of vegetables you like:

Carrots
Broccoli
Celery
Onion
Yams
Squash

1. Sauté them in a small amount of oil.
2. Add your protein of choice—tofu, chicken, or shrimp, for example—and lower heat. Cook until tender (a few minutes).
3. Add cooked or drained canned beans, if you would like.
4. Experiment with different herbs and spices.
5. Shred some lettuce and chop some tomatoes, mushrooms, cucumbers, or peppers.
6. Lay out a tortilla, place a few spoonfuls of the hot ingredients, add beans, top with the cooled, chopped vegetables, and add salsa. Roll up that tortilla and enjoy!

ENCHILADA PIE

1. Repeat the above instructions using only the hot ingredients.
2. Roll up the filled tortillas and lay them side by side in a baking dish.
3. Top with tomato sauce and rice cheese. The Swiss Rice cheese is really good. My recipes are vegan, but if you want to use real cheese, go ahead.
4. Bake for about 20 minutes at 350° F.

CRISP TACOS

1. Brush one side of a tortilla with vegetable oil and lay it on a baking sheet.
2. Add the warm ingredients and roll it up.
3. Bake for 20 minutes at 350° F.
4. Serve with salsa, shredded lettuces, and seeded, chopped cucumbers.

WRAPS

There are so many exciting vegetable tortilla wraps to choose from—all colors, sizes, and tastes. So make a decision (or make two!): fill them with any and all wonderful chopped vegetables, rice and beans, slivers of your favorite protein, and top with hummus or salsa, and fold them over, tucking in the ends.

Salsa

1 cup cilantro, chopped
2 cups tomatoes, chopped
4 scallions, chopped
1 cucumber, chopped (optional)
Salt and pepper to taste
¼ to 1 teaspoon fresh jalapeño, chopped (if you like it hot)

1. Mix all ingredients, place in a jar, cover, and shake well.
2. Allow to sit for an hour or so for all the flavors to meld.
3. Chill.

VARIATION

Add corn kernels, black beans, minced squash, and minced garlic. You can puree before jarring.

One-Pan Dinners

A light sauté of fresh vegetables served over a bed of whole-grain noodles or rice can be a wonderfully tasty dinner. This is a basic recipe followed by a variety of options.

2–3 tablespoons olive oil
1 large onion
1 large carrot
2 celery stalks

1. Chop, julienne, or cut the vegetables into chunks, depending on how you like them.
2. Sauté until just shiny and glistening, in a pan large enough to hold an additional 2 to 3 cups of vegetables.
3. Here is where it gets interesting. You can add any or all of the following vegetables and toss them with the already cooked vegetables:

    1 cup mushrooms, sliced
    1 red pepper, sliced or diced
    1 cup broccoli, partially cooked
    ½ cup corn kernels
    1 cup asparagus spears, cut into 2-inch lengths
    1 cup cabbage or Bok Choy (Chinese cabbage), chopped
    1 cup Brussels sprouts, partially cooked
    ½ cup peas or snap peas
    ½ cup green beans, partially cooked
    1 cup cooked beans (frozen can be substituted)
    1 cup spinach (wash well)
    1 cup chard, chopped
    1 cup cauliflower, partially cooked

4. Get the idea? Anything you like or have on hand, just keep stirring until all is cooked.
5. Serve over rice, in a sandwich, or as a wrap.

Vegetable Pot Pie

Serves 6 to 8

This dish is somewhat labor intensive, but it serves a lot of hungry eaters, keeps well in the refrigerator for a few days, and can also be pureed for a toddler.

2 cups onion, chopped
2 cups celery, chopped
2 cups carrots, peeled and chopped
2 cups cauliflower, chopped
2 cups squash, chopped (I like butternut, but yellow crookneck is good, too)
2 cups turnips, peeled and chopped
2 cups rutabaga, peeled and chopped
1 large celery root, peeled and chopped
4 cups quick oats
¾ cup sesame seeds
½ cup soy flower
¼ cup olive oil
4 cloves garlic, minced
2 cups mushrooms, sliced

Step 1

1. Preheat oven to 350° F.
2. Put the first seven ingredients in a large pot, cover with water, and bring to a boil.
3. Turn heat down and simmer for 30 minutes.

Step 2

1. In another pot, cover celery root with water and bring to a boil.
2. Simmer for 20 minutes.
3. Puree cooked celery root in a blender with some but not all of the cooking water. Set aside.

Step 3

In a sauté pan, add a little olive oil and the garlic and mushrooms, stirring constantly for about 5 minutes.

Step 4: Assemble

1. Remove the cooked vegetables with a slotted spoon and put into an ovensafe serving dish. Leave the liquid in the pot.
2. Add the pureed celery root and fold into the vegetables.

3. Fold the mushroom mixture into the vegetables in the baking dish.

Step 5: Crust

1. In a bowl, combine the quick oats, sesame seeds, soy flour, and olive oil and mix until all ingredients are coated with oil.
2. Top the vegetables in the baking dish with this grain mixture.
3. Bake for 40 minutes.

Middle Eastern Stew

Serves 6 to 8

Here is a vegetarian version of a delicious stew. You can replace the tofu with chicken or meat. Note that you have to soak the chickpeas the night before you make the stew.

1½ cups dried chick peas
¼ cup olive oil
1 large onion, diced
1 cup celery, chopped
1 large yam, chopped
1 carrot, sliced on the diagonal
1 cup small button mushrooms, halved
2 cups tomato sauce
1 teaspoon ground coriander
1 teaspoon cumin powder
1 teaspoon chopped parsley
1 tablespoon granulated garlic
Dash of nutmeg or mace

1. The night before you plan on serving this meal, soak the chick peas in water to cover in a covered pot. The next morning, drain the soaking water and add fresh water to cover.
2. Bring to a boil and then simmer for almost 2 hours.
3. When the chick peas are almost done cooking, start the stew.
4. In a 1-gallon pot, sauté the onions in olive oil until they start to brown.
5. Add the remaining vegetables and toss.
6. Stir in the cooked chick peas.

7. Add the remaining ingredients and allow the stew to simmer for 20 minutes.
8. At this point, you can add protein if you would like to. We like a cup or two of lightly sautéed tempeh or tofu. Some meats take a little longer to cook well, so add a cup of water and increase stewing time, if necessary.
9. Serve over couscous or basmati rice, as per directions on package.

Black Bean Stroganoff

Serves 4 to 6

This is a vegetarian version of a famous dish. I have substituted soy yogurt or soy sour cream for regular sour cream.

- 2 cups of black beans
- ¼ cup olive oil
- 2 medium-size onions, cut into ½-inch pieces
- 2 cups celery, chopped
- 2 cups carrots, peeled and chopped
- 2 cups white potato chunks, about ½-inch cubes
- 2 cups mushrooms, sliced
- 1 Italian plum tomato, cored, seeded, and cut into small pieces
- 1 cup soy sour cream or soy yogurt

1. Soak the black beans overnight in 6 cups of water.
2. The next day, rinse the beans and put them in a large pot with enough water to cover generously.
3. Bring to a boil and simmer for 1½ hours or until soft enough to chew. This will grow into at least 3 or 4 cups of beans.
4. In a large pot, sauté the olive oil, onions, celery, carrots, and potato chunks. Keep stirring until the onions and celery glisten.
5. Stir in mushrooms.
6. Add the cooked black beans and the tomato.
7. Add whatever protein you wish at this point.
8. Add enough water to cover the vegetables and protein.
9. Simmer for about 40 minutes.

10. Allow stew to cool just enough to add the sour cream or yogurt. If the stew is too hot, the sour cream might curdle, so be patient.

— — —

This recipe can be prepared ahead of time and reheated slowly to avoid curdling the sour cream or yogurt. Serve this hearty stew over broad noodles like fettucini or parpadelle. Top with a dollop of sour cream and some finely chopped parsley.

Side Dishes

Rice Pilaf

Serves 4 to 6

Rice Pilaf is traditionally served with a fluffy rice, but I like to taste brown rice's nutty flavor.

2 cups organic, short-grain brown rice
2 medium-size onions, finely chopped
1 cup carrots, peeled and chopped
1 cup celery, chopped
2 cloves garlic, minced
½ cup parsley, chopped
2 tablespoons olive oil
½ cup frozen peas, or fresh when in season
1 cup corn kernels, fresh or frozen
Juice of 1 small lime or 2 tablespoons of lime juice
1 cup plum tomatoes, chopped and seeded
3 cups vegetable broth

1. Put rice in a pot with 4½ cups water and bring to a boil. Turn the heat down to keep the rice simmering and cover with a lid. The rice will be cooked in 40 minutes. Do not lift the lid to check it.
2. In a large frying pan, sauté the onions, carrots, celery, garlic, and parsley in the olive oil until the onions are shining—about 7 to 8 minutes.

3. Add the peas, corn, lime juice, tomatoes, and vegetable broth.
4. Simmer for about 10 minutes. To serve, pour the mixture over a bed of brown rice. Garnish with some chopped parsley.

Risotto

Here are two versions of this amazing Italian dish so you can vary it.

WILD RICE RISOTTO

Serves 4 to 6

2 cups long-grain brown rice
1 cup wild rice
1 medium-size onion, minced
2 cups mushrooms, sliced
¼ cup olive oil
6 cups vegetable broth
½ cup peas

1. Combine brown and wild rice.
2. In a large frying pan, sauté the onion and mushrooms in the olive oil for 5 minutes.
3. Add the rice and stir well.
4. Pour in 2 cups of vegetable broth and cover the pan tightly with a lid. Simmer for 15 minutes.
5. Add 2 more cups of vegetable broth and the peas and simmer covered for another 15 minutes.
6. Add the remaining vegetable broth, cover, and simmer for another 15 minutes.

— — —

Note: It is a good idea to check on the rice every 5 minutes or so and stir to combine the broth and the rice.

VARIATIONS: You can add steamed broccoli or asparagus when the rice is finished.

BROWN RICE RISOTTO

Serves 4 to 6

This recipe follows the same steps as for Wild Rice Risotto.

1 medium-size onion, minced
1 cup mushrooms, sliced
1 cup kale, chopped
¼ cup olive oil
2 cups brown rice
6 cups vegetable broth
1 cup spinach, chopped
1 cup chard, chopped

1. Sauté onion, mushrooms, and kale in the olive oil.
2. Stir in the rice.
3. Add 2 cups of broth at a time at 15-minute intervals, stirring often.
4. When you add the second 2 cups, add the spinach and chard.
5. When you add the last 2 cups, you can add any other chopped or diced fresh vegetables that you would like.

Barley and Rice Salad with Vegetables

Serves 6

This recipe is good in warm weather.

2 cups pearl barley (does not need to soak)
½ cup medium- or long-grain brown rice
Pinch sea salt
1 small red onion, diced small
1 stalk celery, diced small
1 to 2 ears fresh corn, kernels removed from cob
1 small cucumber, diced small
4 radishes, diced small
¼ cup parsley, minced

Dressing:

4 tablespoons olive oil
2 tablespoons umeboshi vinegar, found in the Asian section of the supermarket
Juice of 1 lime or lemon

1. Wash and drain the grains.
2. Place grains in a pot with 3 cups of water and bring to a boil.

3. Add salt, lower the flame, cover, and cook for 45 minutes. The grains should be tender, and the water should be absorbed.
4. Transfer to a bowl and let cool.
5. Sauté the red onion, celery, and corn in a little water for about 5 minutes.
6. Add the sautéd vegetables to the cooled grains along with the cucumber, radishes, and parsley.
7. In a small bowl, combine all the dressing ingredients and whisk until well blended.
8. Toss the dressing with the grain/vegetable mixture.
9. Allow the salad to marinate 30 minutes before serving.

Seared Green Beans

Serves 4 as a side dish; great as a snack

1 pound green beans, ends cut off
2 tablespoons olive oil
3 tablespoons sesame seeds
Pinch of salt

1. Bring 8 cups of water to a boil.
2. Carefully drop the beans into the water. Boil for 4–5 minutes.
3. Drain and run under cold water immediately to keep the beans green and stop them from cooking.
4. Heat olive oil in a pan. Add the beans and stir for about 2 minutes.
5. Add sesame seeds and a pinch of salt.

Seared Carrots and Asparagus

Serves about 4 as a side dish; great as a snack

2 carrots, peeled and cut into long strips
1 teaspoon soy sauce
2 cups asparagus spears, cut into 3-inch pieces
½ cup green onions, chopped
2 to 3 cloves garlic, chopped
2 tablespoons olive oil

1. Bring 8 cups of water to a boil.
2. Carefully drop the carrots and asparagus into the water. Boil for 5 minutes.
3. Drain and rinse with cold water. Set aside.
4. In a saucepan, sauté the green onions and garlic in the olive oil for 2 minutes.
5. Add the carrot/asparagus mixture and the soy sauce to the saucepan. Stir for a couple of minutes.

Roasted Potatoes

Serves 4

4 large or 6 medium-size white potatoes, peeled and cut into French–fry style strips
¼ cup olive oil
1 teaspoon salt

1. Preheat oven at 350° F.
2. Put potatoes in a large bowl and toss with the olive oil and salt.
3. Arrange the potatoes in one layer on one or two baking sheets.
4. Bake for 20 to 25 minutes.
5. You might want to season the potatoes with rosemary or other herbs. Cajun seasoning can be delicious.

Roasted Yams

Serves 4

4 medium-size yams, skin on, cut into chunks
3 tablespoons olive oil
Pinch of salt

1. Preheat oven at 350° F.
2. Toss the yams, olive oil, and salt in a bowl.
3. Spread them out on a baking sheet and bake for 15 minutes, turning them over and moving them around to roast evenly.

Roasted Greek Potatoes

Serves 4

4 white potatoes, cut into chunks
1 bulb fennel, sliced
3 tablespoons olive oil

1. Toss fennel with potatoes.
2. Follow recipe for Roasted Potatoes on page 115.

Roasted Fresh Vegetables

Serves 4 to 6

Roast whatever vegetables you like. As the seasons change, so will the fresh, local vegetables.

Any or all of the following:

1 large onion
2 carrots, sliced on a diagonal
3 stalks of celery
1 red pepper, cored and seeded, sliced
I yellow pepper, cored and seeded, sliced
1 green pepper, cored and seeded, sliced
2 medium-size zucchini, sliced ¼-inch thick on a diagonal
2 cups of cauliflower flowers (short sterns)
2 cups butternut squash, pattypan squash, or yellow crookneck, cut in chunks
¼–½ cup of olive oil

1. Preheat oven at 350° F.
2. In a large bowl, toss the vegetables in olive oil.
3. Put on a cookie sheet and roast in the oven, turning every 10 minutes, for 30 minutes.

Millet and Cauliflower Mash

Makes 12 servings

2 cups millet, washed and drained
7 cups water
2 teaspoons sea salt
1 head cauliflower, including stems, chopped

1. Place all the ingredients in a saucepan and bring to boil.
2. Cover and simmer for about 40 minutes or until the millet is soft and creamy and the cauliflower is very soft and falling apart.

Millet Bread

Makes enough to fill a 9 × 11 baking dish

1 cup millet, washed and drained
3 cups water
½ teaspoon sea salt
½ cup red onion, raw or lightly blanched (blanching creates a milder flavor)
2 tablespoons toasted black or tan sesame seeds

1. Toast the millet in a frying pan for about 5 minutes.
2. Place the millet in a pot with the water.
3. Bring to a boil, add the sea salt, cover, lower heat, and cook 40 minutes.
4. Stir the onion and sesame seeds into the warm millet. Cover and let set for 10 minutes.
5. Remove the millet mixture from the pan and press into a 9 × 11 baking dish.
6. Refrigerate about 30 minutes.
7. Cut into squares and spread vegetable jam or butter on top. Or you can drizzle tahini dressing on each square if desired.

This bread is good with Sweet Vegetable Jam (see the next recipe) or an herb or veggie butter.

Sweet Vegetable Jam

Yields 3 cups

2 cups onion, cut into ½- to 1-inch pieces
2 cups squash, cut into ½- to 1-inch pieces. (Sweet winter squashes like kabocha and butternut work best.)
2 carrots, peeled and cut into 1-inch pieces
1 cup parsnips or cabbage, diced (optional)
Pinch of sea salt
3 tablespoons roasted tahini (optional)
1–2 tablespoons umeboshi vinegar

1. Place the vegetables in a sauce pan. Add just enough water to cover the bottom of the pan.
2. Add the sea salt.
3. Bring to a boil, cover, and lower the heat. Simmer for 2 to 3 hours or until the vegetables have cooked down.
4. Add water as needed during cooking to prevent scorching, but only a little at a time so that the vegetables do not become too watery.
5. Mash the vegetables in the pot or puree with a hand or wand blender. Place puree back in the pot over a low flame.
6. Add the tahini and the umeboshi vinegar. (Note: Instead of using tahini or umeboshi vinegar, you can use a bit of sweet light miso.)
7. Mix well and cook another 5 minutes.

If you make this dish with just one vegetable such as onion, carrot, or squash, it will have the consistency of veggie butter.

Brown Rice Pudding

Serves 4

2 cups cooked short-grain brown rice
2 cups rice or soy beverage
2 tablespoons maple syrup
1½ cinnamon sticks
½ vanilla bean, sliced in half lengthwise
1 cardamom pod, split, and seeds removed (discard outer shell)
1 whole clove
¼ teaspoon sea salt
1 tablespoon raisins

1. Combine all the ingredients in a saucepan. Heat over a medium-high flame until the pudding is very hot, steaming but not boiling.
2. Lower the heat to a simmer, and cover the pan.
3. Cook, stirring occasionally until the pudding is thick and creamy—about 45 minutes. You may want to use a flame diffuser to keep the pudding from spilling out over the top of the saucepan.
4. Remove the whole clove, the pod of the vanilla bean, and the cinnamon stick.
5. When cool, refrigerate in a bowl or individual serving bowls.

You will enjoy preparing and eating this food. I know I do. Once you begin to add more vegetables and fruit to your diet, you will not believe how good you will feel. And you will carry over your good eating habits to your family. Your children will grow up healthier than if they had eaten the standard American diet, or SAD.

In this chapter, we have looked at what you can do to clean up your act from the inside out. In chapter 10, you will assess the toxicity level of your home. We will go from room to room, looking at the furnishings and cleaning products that contaminate the space in which you live. There is plenty of advice in that chapter about how to substitute safer products to improve your home environment.

10

Home Detox

As you make the shift to a clean diet to prepare for the birth of your baby, your home needs your attention, too. The Environmental Protection Agency did a five-year study that found much higher concentrations of twenty toxic compounds inside homes than outdoors. The air inside your apartment or house can be more toxic than the air in the most polluted cities. One study found that the concentrations of toxins linked to cancer inside homes were two hundred to five hundred times higher inside than they were outside. In light of these numbers, that fact that the average person in the United States spends 90 percent of their time indoors is alarming. There is a reason asthma rates have tripled in the last thirty years, with 30 million Americans affected. Modern construction, furnishings, and the chemicals in the cleaning products you use to take care of your home can damage your family's health.

In this chapter, I want to walk you through the rooms of your home to show you the sources of these health threats and the chemicals that can disrupt the development of your baby. Some things are beyond your control, but you can make changes to create a healthier environment while you are pregnant and after your baby is born. You can detox your home one step at a time. Start by replacing cleaning products that may be doing more harm than good. The actress Jessica Alba and her business partner Christopher Gavigan have founded one of my favorite websites, The Honest Company. Jessica has many cleaning products on her site, www.honest.com. I will recommend products from other sources throughout this chapter.

Detoxing Your Home Is a Strong Defense

Jordan is the son of an actress and a lawyer. At the age of two, he was having intense tantrums and did not have enough language. He was diagnosed with ASD at two and a half and saw a developmental pediatrician.

The family cleaned up the toxins from their house and started using healthy cleaning and personal care products. Then they improved their diet, understanding the importance of detoxifying what they could control in their environment.

Jordan is now in a mainstream kindergarten. His parents are dedicated to providing him with the best—the best diet; the most nontoxic house possible; the most consistent occupational therapists, language therapists, applied behavior therapists; and much more.

Carter, Jordon's younger brother, is now three. His language is delayed. He has not been diagnosed yet, but he will start getting intensive therapy immediately. His now very aware parents know what has to be done to help their son. I have to note how wonderful it is for these children that their family has access to all of this. That is not always the case.

The Age of Chemistry

A Chemical Age began during World War II with war-related research. Until then, a limited number of simple ingredients kept the house clean and odor-free. Different combinations of castile soap, vinegar, baking soda, ammonia, borax, alcohol, and cornstarch worked to wash clothes, pots, dishes, carpets, and floors, and to remove stains, disinfect, scrub, deodorize, and polish. Today, the average American uses forty pounds of toxic cleaning products each year. The chemicals in those products are absorbed through our skin. They make their way into the environment when they are flushed down the toilet, poured down the drain, tossed into the trash, or sprayed into the air. Eighty percent of the chemicals found in products used every day lack detailed toxic information. Laws in the United States exempt manufacturers from fully labeling products used for personal or household care. Less than 10 percent of these chemicals have been tested for chronic effects, even though more than 150 chemicals found in home care products have been connected to allergies and birth defects. No matter how often and in how many different ways I see these numbers, they amaze and disturb me every time.

Buildings of the past were made from wood, brick, stone, glass, cement, and plaster. Now our insulation contains formaldehyde, which damages DNA, and plastics. During the housing boom in the mid-2000s and the Hurricane Katrina rebuilding, drywall manufactured in China was found to be tainted with toxins that made almost five thousand homes unlivable. Vinyl building materials and PVCs, widely in use today, cause genetic changes and birth defects. In modern construction, PVC plumbing pipes outgas into tap water. To be fair, I should note that toxic materials like arsenic, lead, mercury, and asbestos were in wide use in the past. We got smart about those contaminants and have taken steps to limit our exposure to them. Now we have to restrict the use of these new toxins, which are so prevalent in our lives today. The growing use of these chemicals parallels the rising autism and allergy numbers.

A few years ago, I was skiing down a slope in Deer Valley, Utah. Spec houses were being constructed along the trail for very costly ski-on–ski-off homes. The materials used for these multimillion-dollar homes were far from the best. I saw pressed wood everywhere as well as that awful pink insulation. If you buy a new home, you have no idea what is outgassing, because the core building materials are not visible. Always speak to the builder about materials used in the construction and to finish the interior.

You should test your home for radon. Radon is a cancer-causing radioactive gas that you cannot see, smell, or taste. It is the second-leading cause of lung cancer, after smoking. Studies have found that children are especially sensitive to radon. The gas is produced from the decay of uranium, found in rocks, soil, groundwater, and well water. It moves up through the ground to the air above and into your home through cracks and holes in the foundation. According to the Environmental Protection Agency, nearly one out of fifteen homes in the United States has elevated radon levels. To learn how to test for radon and correct a problem, check "A Citizen's Guide to Radon" at http://www.epa.gov/radon/pubs/citguide.html.

Toxins are everywhere now—from the polyurethane we use to finish floors to the flame retardants in our mattresses, from the stain protection used on our carpets and upholstery to the water we bathe in. Furniture used to be made of solid wood. Now we use particle board, plywood, and pressed wood, which are all treated with formaldehyde and plastic. Rugs and carpeting used to be made of natural fabrics—wool, silk, or cotton. Now they are made of synthetic fabrics that did not exist in the past.

Four groups of people are most affected by indoor chemicals—developing fetuses, infants and toddlers, the sick, and the elderly.

They spend more time indoors, and their immune systems are weaker. Babies spend time crawling around and playing on the floor and put their fingers in their mouths and noses, ingesting toxins. They taste and chew everything. Children are often exposed to pesticides that are brought inside on shoes. The pesticides trapped in a carpet break down more slowly than outdoors in sunlight.

Common Household Toxins

Some of the toxins that are polluting your home come from ingredients in seemingly safe products that you use every day. These toxins can build up in your body over time. After you review the list that follows, you should be convinced to make some changes in your life. You can start by choosing natural cleaning and personal care products. When household items, such as carpets, couches, and mattresses, need to be replaced, buy the healthiest alternatives you can afford.

The Big 10 Common Household Toxins

1. **Arsenic** is found in treated lumber and in drinking water. It has been linked to developmental delays, lower IQ, and behavioral problems.
2. **Bisphenol A** is one of the most common chemicals in the world. Fortunately, it is becoming less common. It is found in some plastic water bottles, the lining of metal food cans, plastic baby bottles, reusable food containers, and electronic equipment. Every time you make a call on your cell phone or tap an email on your keyboard, put on your sunglasses, or run your tongue against a tooth filling, you may be in contact with BPA. The Centers for Disease Control and Prevention found BPA in the urine of 93 percent of the people it tested. This synthetic chemical is an endocrine disruptor that can affect the brain of fetuses, infants, and young children. The chemical has been linked to hyperactivity. New laws and regula-

tions are decreasing the use of this toxic chemical. This should have been done a decade ago.

3. **Chlorine bleach** is found in household cleaners. Chlorine is a highly toxic gas. Bleaches are often considered disinfectants, but are classified as pesticides under the Federal Hazardous Substances Act.
4. **Formaldehyde** is used as a disinfectant, a preservative, and a glue in the manufacture of pressed wood products. It is found in particle board, furniture, carpets, dishwashing liquids, carpet cleaners, permanent press fabrics, fabric softeners, adhesives, and glues. Formaldehyde outgases from these products and is found in cigarette smoke and car exhaust as well. Formaldehyde damages DNA and depresses the central nervous system.
5. **Perfluorinated chemicals** (PFCs) are used to make stain-repellents and nonstick surfaces like Teflon. They are found in carpets; scratch-and-stain-resistant material; waterproof, breathable fabric; cleaning products; and microwave popcorn bags. PFCs have been linked to developmental problems in children.
6. **Phthalates** are used to soften plastics and make them more flexible. They give lotions their texture. They are found in bottles, toys, storage containers, teethers, shower curtains, plastic bags and food wraps, cosmetics and personal care products, detergents, and vinyl flooring. Phthalates are hormone disruptors that have been connected to developmental problems in children. When phthalates have been banned or voluntarily discontinued, the chemicals used in their place are untested and might be even more dangerous to our children's health.
7. **Polybrominated diethyl ethers** (PBDEs) are used as flame retardants. They are found in televisions, computers, and furniture and mattress foam. PBDEs accumulate in dust and collect in our body fat. You can find toxic amounts of these chemicals without moving from your couch or getting your

child out of his PJs in the morning. Breastfeeding infants have the highest exposure to PBDEs, from their mother's milk.

8. **Polyvinyl chloride** is a plastic used to make a wide array of products, including shower curtains, bottles, flooring, window frames, window blinds, and pipes. PVCs have been linked to central nervous system problems.
9. **Triclosan** is an antibacterial found in liquid hand soaps, dish detergents, cleaning products, toothpastes, toys, and bedding. It can have a negative effect on the endocrine and immune systems.
10. **Volatile organic compounds** (VOCs) are gases and vapors that contain carbons that contribute to air pollutions. They are found in cleaning and personal products, carpets, paints, varnishes, air fresheners, and dry cleaning. They are linked to allergies, asthma, and neurological, developmental, and reproductive problems.

If a Product Has a Warning Label, Throw It Out

Extremely toxic substances must display a warning label. The warnings mostly refer to the hazards of ingestion, yet 90 percent of health problems are caused by inhalation of vapors and absorption of particles.

Go through all your household cleaning products to look for toxicity buzz words on the labels. If any of the following words and phrases appear on a product, get rid of that product safely.

- Caution
- Warning
- Danger
- Poison
- Keep out of reach of children

- Corrosive—rinse from skin immediately
- May cause burns on contact
- May cause skin irritation
- Flammable
- Protect eyes while using product
- Call physician immediately
- Do not induce vomiting
- Vapors harmful
- Carcinogens
- Neurotoxins
- Endocrine disrupters

In his book *Home Sweet Toxic Home*, Barry Jones suggests that any ingredient that ends in "-cide" is a long-lasting chemical. That's a good clue for determining the potency of the chemicals in a product.

Now that you are preparing your home to be a safe place during your pregnancy and after the arrival of your baby, you should follow this rule: A child should be able to drink anything under your sink. At some point in a child's life, he'll try to taste everything, and you'll want to have only nontoxic cleaners on hand. Kids chew on every shirt, blanket, and toy they own. I no longer taste my shirts before I buy them, but I do know what a shirt tastes like.

First Steps for Reducing the Toxicity of Your Home

There are simple changes you can make to reduce the harmful chemicals to which you are exposed in your home. If you manage to do anything from the list that follows, you will make good progress in reducing home pollution.

- **Let in the fresh air.** Open windows to circulate fresh air. Brand-new "safe, extremely energy-efficient" houses are the most dangerous. Everything is sealed as tight as a drum, and air does not circulate enough. Get rid of that stale air filled with toxic accumulations. Use exhaust fans that ventilate outdoors in bathrooms, the kitchen, and the attic. You might want to invest in an air-circulation system that brings in fresh air and replaces stale air throughout the house.
- **Remove your shoes when you enter your home.** You can track in harmful quantities of pesticides, lead, cadmium, and other chemicals on the soles of your shoes. When your baby begins to crawl around on the floor, ask guests to remove their shoes. Do not be embarrassed to start now. You are getting your house ready for your baby's arrival.
- **Use nontoxic cleaning products or make your own.** Later in this chapter, I recommend nontoxic products and give you recipes for natural cleansers you can make at home at a fraction of the cost of commercial products. You can use the money you save to buy organic food. I recommend you look at *Clean & Green: The Complete Guide to Nontoxic and Environmentally Safe Housekeeping* by Annie Berthold-Bond. This terrific book is filled with ideas for living free of hazardous household products.
- **Stop using aerosol sprays.** The propellants in sprays contain propane, formaldehyde, and methylene chloride, which are neurotoxins that depress the nervous system. When you use an aerosol spray, you are putting unnecessary volatile organic chemicals (VOCs) into the air. Aerosol sprays produce a fine mist that is more deeply inhaled than pump sprays do, increasing the toxic effect. Always choose pump sprays.
- **Use microfiber cloths to reduce your use of cleaning products filled with chemicals.** To make this untreated and reusable cloth, polyester and polyamide threads are spun into tiny wedge-shaped strands that are designed to penetrate and trap dirt. You do not need to use cleaning products

with microfiber cloths, and you will not use as many paper towels if you switch to cleaning with cloths.

- **Speaking of paper towels, it is a good idea to use unbleached paper products and diapers.** The chlorine used to bleach the wood pulp during the paper-making process produces dioxins, which persist in the environment for many years. Dioxins, which accumulate in the fat cells of animals and are passed on to us when we eat meat, cause developmental problems. The choice to use unbleached paper products will contribute to the health of the planet on which your baby will grow up.

Toxic Rental

Steve Greenwood had been offered an exciting job in California with the stipulation that he start immediately. Rather than leave his wife, Lily, and eighteen-month-old son, Andy, Steve decided to rent a house until they sold theirs. Steve did not want to miss a minute with his son at such a wonderful time in Andy's life.

The Greenwoods came to see me because they were alarmed by what was happening to Andy. Since they had moved into their rental a few months earlier, Andy had regressed. They witnessed their son gradually lose language and eye contact. His ability to play with friends was deteriorating rapidly. Lily attributed their son's regression to mold exposure. They had the house tested and found it infested from the drywall to the ductwork. They moved into a hotel to get away from the toxic mold.

They had very little family history that appeared to be risk factors for autism. Andy had not been vaccinated since their move. His regression was a red warning flag. The Greenwoods were ready to try aggressive treatments in an effort to help their son. I put Andy on the diet I often recommend: sugar-free, casein-free, gluten-free. I also suggested speech and occupational therapy. He responded well enough to attend a mainstream kindergarten with a shadow, or trained aide.

A Tour through the Hazard Zones in Your Home

A walk through a typical American home should open your eyes to the hidden toxins that surround you where you live. The more stuff you have, the more contaminated your home will be. I offer recommendations for reducing the toxic load and for replacing commercial cleaning products with organic, natural substitutes. You will find recipes for simple homemade cleansers that do the trick later in this chapter.

The Living Room

The centerpiece of most living rooms is the couch and other upholstered furniture. Beneath the upholstery, most furniture today is made from pressed wood, plywood, particle board, and fiberboard, all of which emit formaldehyde fumes for up to five years. If you are buying furniture, choose pieces that are made of solid wood, glass, metal, or chrome. Avoid new furniture that is coated with polyurethane or has polyurethane foam cushions. Polyurethane outgasses toluene, a potent toxin that affects the central nervous system and damages a developing fetus. Choose natural fabrics like wool and cotton for upholstery rather than synthetic fabrics with acrylic, polyester, and polyvinyl chloride. I will go into more detail about man-made fabrics in chapter 11. Fabrics that have been coated to be stain-resistant with products like Scotchgard contain PFCs, which have a half-life of eight years.

Tips on Couches

Furniture that is more than five years old that has not been refinished or reupholstered usually does not continue to outgas, so don't be so quick to replace that old couch.

If you buy new upholstered furniture, unwrap it from the plastic or cartons and keep it in the garage for several days to air out.

Carpets: A Trap for Toxins

Of the four hundred compounds in the family of VOCs (volatile organic compounds) family, two hundred are found in synthetic carpeting, which is treated with pesticides, fungicides, and non-stain coatings. Carpeting is made from petroleum-derived plastic fibers. The backing of carpets and the glue used to install them are also highly toxic. Dangerous fumes will be outgassed for five years from the time of installation. If you want to replace your carpeting before your baby is born, it is generally better to have wool, silk, or cotton area rugs than wall-to-wall carpeting. If you do not have hardwood floors, invest in carpeting that is made from natural fibers. Natural sisal rugs can be a less expensive alternative. Carpets and other floor coverings are most toxic when they are being ripped up or installed. It is best to make a change before you are pregnant. A growing baby spends a lot of time on the floor, playing, crawling, and gradually learning to walk. You do not want toxic gases from floor coverings to disrupt your baby's development. It helps to have a vacuum cleaner with a HEPA filter to catch small particles. Your baby will soon be crawling on that rug.

Electronic Poison

We all use computers, printers, cell phones, DVD players, and TVs, but we do not often stop to think that the electronic devices that are so much a part of our lives are a source of toxins. The government is gradually phasing out the flame retardants (PBDEs) that are present in TVs and other appliances, and plasma TVs being produced now are much cleaner than older electronics. Even so, more than a thousand materials, including chlorinated solvents, PVC, heavy metals, plastics, and gases, are used to make computers and other electronic products and their components. Greenpeace has been campaigning to reduce toxic pollution from electronics by publishing the chemical policies of companies on the web. Samsung, Nokia, and Puma have announced plans to phase out toxic chemicals in all their products. Sony is removing them from their TVs. Dell, HP/Compaq, Apple, and IBM have all refused to take this positive step as of this writing. I hope other large companies will be doing the right thing by the time this book hits the shelves. For an update, check the Greenpeace website, www.greenpeace.org.

Modern energy-efficient electronics and appliances, including computers and plasma TVs, produce electromagnetic fields that may be harmful to your health. There is controversial research about electronic fields and their effects on growing children. Minimize your child's exposure to electromagnetic fields and don't wait for research that proves that holding a cell phone next to your head is dangerous. Use your laptop on a table, not on your lap. Unplug any electronics you are not using.

One of the best things you can do is to be heard by the companies that continue to manufacture products with the potential to damage you and your family. The technology is there to make products safer. You can speak out by working through an organization like Greenpeace or by contacting the company directly. You can demand safer products from the electronic industry and the stores that sell their goods.

Cleaning the Living Room

To keep your living room fresh, you probably use furniture polish, window or glass cleaner, spot removers, and carpet cleaners. Furniture polish is made from petroleum and contains formaldehyde, turpentine, synthetic fragrance, and a number of other toxins. Commercial glass cleaner contains ammonia, which is a very strong irritant. Carpet cleaners and spot removers are highly toxic as well.

Recently, I saw what appears to have been a very severe reaction to carpet cleaners. I received a call from one of my patients saying that her best friend's daughter was in the hospital with heart failure. She asked if I would help to get in touch with a world-renowned cardiologist with whom I had studied in medical school. The four-year-old girl got sick after the carpeting in their house was cleaned. The symptoms piled one on top of another: fever, rash, swelling of the hands and feet, redness of the eyes, swollen lymph glands, and inflammation of the mouth, lips, and throat. The inflammation was internal as well, affecting the walls of the arteries throughout the body, including the coronary arteries. The diagnosis was Kawasaki syndrome, a rare condition that affects children younger than five. I was able to contact an expert on Kawasaki syndrome, with whom I had also trained. If not treated, the disease can cause an aneurysm or a heart attack in a child. After a few days in the hospital, this little girl was able to return home, but she did suffer some heart damage.

I am also familiar with a high-profile case of Kawasaki syndrome. A prominent person in Hollywood told me that when his son was about four, he had problems with vaccines. After the carpets were cleaned, his son had terrible seizures and developed Kawasaki syndrome. Was it a coincidence that carpet cleaning was a trigger for both cases? I don't think so. I have seen this condition only twice in my career, and both times an acute reaction followed carpet cleaning.

These stories show how powerful chemicals in cleaning products can affect a child's health. Imagine what chemicals and toxins can do to your unborn baby. If you use a professional service to clean your rugs and carpets, be certain that they use organic, nontoxic cleaners that are low in VOCs and irritants.

Some carpet cleaners use enzymes to break down stains. The enzymes remain in the carpet fibers after cleaning, and subsequent vacuuming can lead to prolonged exposure to the enzymes. Some enzyme cleaners contain the same harsh chemicals and preservatives found in standard cleaners, so be sure to read labels carefully. One product I recommend is Biokleen's Bac-Out Stain & Odor Eliminator, available online and at many grovery stores or by calling 800-378-4786.

Here are some nontoxic recipes for effective cleaners for your rugs, carpets, and upholstery that you can make at home. They will not only keep your baby from harm, but they will also save you money:

- Clean spills right away with club soda. Always treat a spill as soon as possible.
- For red wine spills, rub a thick layer of salt on the spill, then sponge it up after the spill has been absorbed.
- Deodorize dry carpets by sprinkling with baking soda and vacuuming after fifteen minutes.
- A simple and effective pet-stain remover can be made with equal parts warm water and vinegar with a tablespoon of baking soda per cup of liquid. Apply with a spray bottle. Always work from the outside of the stain inward.

There are many good organic, nontoxic carpet cleaners available. Simple Green makes a line of products that are sold everywhere. You can find house carpet cleaners and other cleaning supplies at www.greenhome.com; or call 415-282-6400. I recommend more products on the pages that follow and have made a point to include the websites and phone numbers of the companies when available. There is no excuse to continue to use products with toxic ingredients. Even supermarkets and big box stores carry safer products now.

Homemade Nontoxic Furniture Polishes

- Mix 1 tablespoon lemon juice in 16 ounces of vegetable oil. Apply a small amount with a clean cotton cloth.
- Polish unfinished wood with a light vegetable oil.

- Wash painted wood with 1 teaspoon washing soda in 1 gallon hot water. Rinse with clear water.
- For dusting and polishing, combine a mixture of ½ cup white vinegar and 1 teaspoon olive oil. Use less olive oil if this ratio leaves your wood furniture too oily.

When you buy furniture cleaners and polishes, look for solvent-free products that use plant oils as the active polish. You can find Earth Friendly Furniture Polish at natural foods stores, or order online at www.ecos.com or by calling 800-335-ECOS.

The Organic Consumers Association recommends the following glass cleaners. The products may be found at natural foods stores or can be ordered online.

- Aubrey Organics Liquid Sparkle
  www.aubreyorganics.com
  800-282-7394
- BioShield Glass Cleaner
  www.bioshieldpaint.com
  800-621-2591
- Earth Friendly Window Kleener
  www.ecos.com
  800-335-ECOS
- Naturally Yours Glass & Window Cleaner
  888-801-7347

Homemade Glass Cleaners

Use a microfiber cloth with water or try the following:

1 quart water
½ to ¼ cup of white vinegar
1–2 tablespoons lemon juice (or rubbing alcohol)

Combine ingredients. Spray on glass surfaces and wipe clean with soft, lint-free cloth.

- Our House Works Shiny Surface Cleaner
  www.ourhouseworks.com
  877-236-8750
- Seventh Generation Glass & Surface Cleaner
  www.seventhgeneration.com

The Kitchen

The kitchen is often the heart of the house. Family and friends gather there while snacks and meals are prepared. You give a lot of thought about what you serve and spend time preparing healthy food. The last thing you want is to do is to contaminate the good food you make. Many of the products you use to cook, bake, eat, and store food may put your family's health at risk.

The cabinets and shelving in your kitchen can be as much of a source of toxins as the furniture in your living room. If they are not made of wood or stainless steel, they are probably made of fiberboard, which outgases formaldehyde. Countertops also can be a problem. Granite, the countertop of choice in modern homes, has been reported to emit the radioactive gas radon. Radon gas tends to accumulate at floor level, which makes it even more hazardous for young children. Other countertop materials, such as concrete, need to be sealed. It is important to use nontoxic sealants and dyes on countertops. Vinyl floors outgas as well. There are alternative products for everything. They may be more expensive, but it is worth stretching your budget if you can. If you install ceramic or marble tiles, make certain the glue is nontoxic. Chances are you have other things to focus on besides undertaking an expensive renovation of your kitchen during your pregnancy, but you can at least make certain you use safe pots and pans, plastics, and cleaning products in the kitchen.

Stick with Nonstick Only with Caution

Nonstick pans may seem to be time-savers and the answer for low-fat cooking, but they can be a threat to your health, especially if scratched or overheated. PFOA (perfluorooctanoic acid) is used to bond the nonstick coating to the pan. Studies have shown that PFOA is present in low levels in the bloodstream of nine out of ten Americans, and in the blood of most newborns. PFOA exposure is believed to have caused birth defects in babies born to mothers working at a Teflon plant in the early 1980s. The chemical has been linked to low birthweight.

Above certain temperatures—the point where food is burned or cooking oils smoke—the nonstick coating will break down and release toxic fumes. *Cook's Illustrated* magazine tested nonstick skillets and found that extreme temperatures could be reached simply by cooking some foods on high heat. The Environmental Working Group reported that nonstick coatings could reach 700 degrees F in as little as three to five minutes, releasing fifteen toxic gases. These fumes have been known to kill pet birds. Though pans without a nonstick coating are preferable, you can follow a few rules for using nonstick cookware safely:

- Do not preheat nonstick pans.
- Do not leave nonstick pans unattended on the stove.
- Do not cook at temperatures higher than 450 degrees F.
- Get rid of pots and pans with scratched nonstick surfaces.
- Do not use metal utensils, steel wool, or abrasive cleaners on nonstick cookware.
- Do not stack nonstick cookware, in order to avoid scratching.
- If you choose to have nonstick pans, switch to anodized aluminum pans, which are nonstick and will not release toxins.

While you are pregnant, I advise putting the Teflon pans away. Or better still, throw them out.

You should use caution with aluminum cookware as well. Aluminum is a soft metal that is highly reactive. It can migrate into food when used for cooking. Aluminum has been linked to brain disorders and behavioral problems. Anodized aluminum is dipped in a chemical bath to create a tougher layer to prevent leaching into food. The layer can break down over time, so aluminum is not the safest choice for cookware. The safest materials for cooking and baking are cast iron, porcelain, and stainless steel.

Which Plastics Are Safe?

When it comes to food and beverages, plastics should be avoided whenever possible. Hard plastics can contain harmful BPA that can transfer from the plastic into food and drinks. A recent study found that even BPA-free plastics contain synthetic chemicals that can contaminate your food.

What Do Those Codes Mean?

The recycling codes for plastic—those numbers inside the triangles on the bottom of plastic containers—are a good indication of the safety of the plastic in your kitchen.

#1: PETE or PET (polyethylene terephthalate) is used to make soft drink, water, ketchup, and salad dressing bottles and peanut butter, pickle, jelly, and jam jars. Bottles coded #1 are acceptable to use, but are not reusable.

#2: HDPE (high density polyethylene) is used in milk, water, and juice bottles, yogurt and margarine containers, cereal box liners, and grocery, trash, and retail bags. Generally considered safe.

#3: PVC (polyvinyl chloride) is used in food packaging, cling plastic wraps, and vinyl-lined lunchboxes. This type of plastic gets its flexibility from phthalates or untested replacement chemicals. These are to be avoided.

#4: LDPE (low-density polyethylene) is used in dry-cleaning bags, bread bags, frozen-food bags, and squeezable bottles. It is generally considered safe.

#5: PP (polypropylene) is used in food and medicine containers. This plastic is hazardous during production, but is not known to leach harmful chemicals.

#6: PS (polystyrene), also known as Styrofoam, is used in egg cartons, packing peanuts, disposable cups, plates, and cutlery. This plastic is not good for you. Benzene, a known carcinogen, is used in its production, and several of the ingredients of the plastic are harmful.

#7: Other (often PC, polycarbonate) is used in hard plastic sports bottles, baby bottles, and five-gallon water jugs. There are BPA-free products marked with the number 7 but not those containing PC.

Look for the number 2 or 4 inside the triangle at the bottom of the bottom for the safest plastics. Number 1 is conditional. Number 5 is safe, but production of this plastic damages the environment. Avoid using plastics labeled with the numbers 3, 6, or 7.

When it comes to food and beverages, I think you should avoid plastic whenever you can. If you do use plastic, make certain it is free of PVC and BPA; use containers numbered 2, 4, or 5. Do not heat plastic containers or plastic wrap in the microwave. When kitchenware is labeled "microwave safe," it means that the plastic will not melt in the microwave. However, the extreme heat generated by microwaving will release phthalates and other chemicals that will be transferred to your food. Do not store fatty or acidic foods in plastic. Hand-wash plastic kitchenware to lessen wear and tear. Do not continue to use badly worn, cloudy, or scratched plastic containers. Glass, stainless steel, and bamboo or wood with food-safe finishes are safer food-storage materials. Avoid hard plastic melamine dishes. Formaldehyde is used to make them. Plastic utensils for cooking can melt from extreme heat or wear down, allowing chemicals to transfer to food. Use wood, bamboo, or stainless steel utensils instead.

A Safe and Spotless Kitchen

We want our kitchens to be "spotless," but in keeping them clean we can unknowingly create problems. Commercial multipurpose cleaners, liquid dish soap, dishwasher detergents, metal polishes, disinfectants, scouring powders, and oven cleaners all contain toxins that can harm you and the environment. Just a few simple ingredients—soap, water, baking soda, vinegar, lemon juice, and borax—with a coarse sponge can take care of most household cleaning, provided you use a little elbow grease.

If you prefer the convenience and added power of commercial cleaners, you have to read the labels carefully to make certain you choose the safest products. Most cleaners do not list ingredients, but the warnings are important. Products labeled "Danger" or "Poison" are the most hazardous, "Warning" indicates moderately hazardous, and "Caution" indicates slightly toxic. Avoid them all. Labels sometimes list active ingredients. Look for irritating chemicals like ammonia, chlorine, or sodium hypochlorite. Evaluate the ecological claims: "Biodegradable in three to five days" is more significant than simply "Biodegradable," because most substances eventually break down. Claims like "No solvents," "No phosphates," or "Plant-based" are more meaningful than "Natural" or "Ecologically friendly." Do not be fooled by the label "organic" when it comes to cleaning products. In chemistry, "organic" means ingredients are carbon-based and are not any safer than other substances. If ingredients are listed, select cleaning products made with plant-based, not petroleum-based, ingredients.

ALL-PURPOSE CLEANERS

Some all-purpose cleaners contain the sudsing agents DEA (diethanolamine) and TEA (triethanolamine), which can react with nitrites, an often undisclosed preservative, to form carcinogens that your body absorbs through the skin. Cleaners contain harsh chemi-

Homemade All-purpose Cleaner

½ cup vinegar
½ gallon water
¼ cup baking soda
(or 2 teaspoons borax)

Mix ingredients and store. Apply with a spray bottle or sponge.

cals like ammonia or bleach. When mixed, these chemicals are highly toxic.

Most household cleaning needs can be met safely and inexpensively with a pure cellulose sponge and simple ingredients like water, liquid castile soap (Dr. Bronner's, for example), vinegar, lemon juice, or baking soda for scrubbing grease and grime. Most cellulose sponges sold in supermarkets are treated with triclosan, a synthetic disinfectant. Packaging claims such as "kills odors" or "odor resistant" are the giveaways. Stay away from them.

Since sponges are a perfect breeding ground for germs and mildew, boil sponges in water for three to five minutes or put them in the top rack of the dishwasher often.

Some all-purpose cleaners are safer for your health and the environment than others. Toxin-free cleaners are becoming more widely available in conventional grocery and home goods stores. At the supermarket, you can find Arm & Hammer Baking Soda and Super Washing Soda. 20 Mule Team Borax is another ingredient you should have in your pantry. Some of the best choices can be found only at natural foods stores or online or must be mail-ordered. They are just a phone call away.

- AFM SafeChoice Super Clean
  www.afmsafecoat.com
  800-239-0321
- Aubrey Organics Earth Aware
  www.aubreyorganics.com
  800-282-7394

- BioShield Vinegar Cleaner
  www.bioshieldpaint.com
  800-621–2591
- Dr. Bronner's Pure Castile (Liquid) Soaps
  Dr. Bronner's Sal Suds
  www.drbronner.com
  760-743-2211
- Ecover All-Purpose Cleaner
  Ecover Multi-Surface Cleaner
  www.ecover.com
  800-449-4925
- 1st EnviroSafety Cleaner/Degreaser
  www.1stenvirosafetyinc.com
  888-578-9600
- Honest Multi-Surface Cleaner
  www.honest.com
  888-862-8818
- Naturally Yours Product Line
  www.naturallyyoursclean.com
  888-801-7347
- Our House Works Sanitizing Surface Cleaner
  www.ourhouseworks.com
  877-236-8750
- Seventh Generation All Purpose Cleaner
  www.seventhgeneration.com
  800-456-1191
- Shaklee Basic H
  www.shaklee.com
  800-SHAKLEE
- Vermont Soapworks Liquid Sunshine
  www.vermontsoap.com
  866-SOAP4U2

DISHWASHING SOAPS

Most commercial dishwashing detergents are petroleum-based. Look for colorless, plant-based detergents. Dyes made from coal tar can be contaminated with arsenic and lead, which can remain as residue on dishes. Phosphoric acid is used in liquid dishwasher detergents and metal polishes. This corrosive chemical is toxic to the central nervous system. Formaldehyde and ammonia are found in liquid dish soap. This cleaning product that you use every day without a second thought is the leading cause of poisoning in the home for children under six.

Powdered detergents for automatic dishwashers can contain phosphates, a water-softening mineral that acts like fertilizer when it washes down the drain, causing an overgrowth of algae, which depletes the oxygen supply in water and kills fish and other organisms. Those made with chlorine can release chlorinated chemicals into the air when the dishwasher is opened at the end of the wash cycle.

To wash dishes by hand, use a liquid soap, like Dr. Bronner's. Add two or three tablespoons of vinegar to soapy water for tough jobs.

The following eco-friendly brands can be found at some grocery stores as well as at natural foods stores or can be ordered online.

- Bio Pac Dishwashing Powder
  www.bio-pac.com
  800-225-2855
- BioShield Dishwasher Concentrate
  www.bioshieldpaint.com
  800-621-2591

Homemade Dishwasher Soap

Mix equal parts borax and washing soda. You can buy Arm & Hammer Super Washing Soda at the supermarket. Increase the amount of washing soda if your water is hard.

- Cal Ben Seafoam Destain
  Cal Ben Seafoam Dish Glow
  www.calbenpuresoap.com
  800-340-7091
- Earth Friendly Dishmate
  www.ecos.com
  800-335-ECOS
- Ecover Dish Liquid
  Ecover Washing-Up Liquids
  Ecover Dishwasher Tablets
  www.ecover.com
  800-449-4925
- Honest Dishwasher Gel
  www.honest.com
  888-862-8818
- Life Tree Super-concentrated Herbal Ultra Dishwashing Liquid
  www.lifetreeproducts.com
  800-824-6396
- Naturally Yours Gentle Soap
  Naturally Yours Dishwashing Detergent
  888-801-7347
- Our House Works Dishwasher Complete
  www.ourhouseworks.com
  877-236-8750
- Seventh Generation Automatic Dishwashing Powder
  Seventh Generation Automatic Dishwashing Gel
  Seventh Generation Dish Liquids
  www.seventhgeneration.com
  800-456-1191
- Shaklee Basic-D Automatic Dishwashing Concentrate
  www.shaklee.com
  800-SHAKLEE

SCOURING POWDERS

Now that you have reduced your use of nonstick pots and pans, you might be using more scouring powders. Some scouring powders use silica as the abrasive scrubbing agent, which is harmful when inhaled. Others are made with chlorine bleach. You already know the risks associated with bleach.

For cleaning up grease, green cleaning expert Annie Berthold-Bond recommends the following recipe:

Homemade Scouring Powder

½ teaspoon washing soda
2 tablespoons distilled white vinegar
¼ teaspoon liquid soap
2 cups of hot water

Mix ingredients in a spray bottle. Wear gloves when working with washing soda.

The scouring cleaners listed next are safe to use. They can be found in grocery stores and natural foods stores or online.

- Bon Ami Cleaning Cake
  Bon Ami Cleaning Powder
  www.bonami.com
- Earth Friendly Cream Cleanser
  www.ecos.com
  800-335-ECOS
- Ecover Cream Cleaner
  www.ecover.com
  800-449-4925
- Seventh Generation Cream Cleaner
  www.seventhgeneration.com
  800-456-1191

OVEN CLEANERS

Oven cleaners are among the harshest chemicals in your house. The lye and ammonia they contain emit toxic fumes. If you are lucky, you have a self-cleaning oven. You should use this feature regularly. You can use any of the scouring cleansers mentioned earlier to clean an oven. Preventing spills from baking on is a good idea. Line the bottom of your oven with aluminum foil and clean up spills before they have a chance to dry and bake in.

Homemade Oven Cleaners

If you need to remove grease and baked-on spills, soak the surfaces of your oven overnight in a mixture of water, baking soda, and soap. The next morning, scrub the oven with baking soda and a soapy sponge. You can also use washing soda and water, but wear rubber gloves if you do.

METAL POLISHES

Metal polishes may contain nerve-damaging petroleum distillates or ammonia. Try the following nontoxic polishers:

Silver: To remove tarnish from silver, scrub with toothpaste.

Copper: For copper, rub on a mixture of 1 teaspoon salt and a cup of white vinegar or lemon juice with a cloth. Rinse with water.

Brass: Unlacquered brass can be cleaned with a paste of 1 teaspoon salt, 1 cup white vinegar, and 1 cup flour.

You can find the clean brand of metal cleaner listed here at hardware, home improvement, or grocery stores.

- Our House Works Minerals and Metals Cleaner
  www.ourhouseworks.com
  877-236-8750

From the core of the house, we will move on to the room in which all of us spend the most time—the bedroom.

The Bedroom: "The Most Important Room in the House"

You take about twenty thousand breaths a day, and more than half of those breaths happen in your bedroom. You spend so much time in that room—eight hours sleeping, I hope. Your body is regenerating and detoxing while you sleep, so the air should be as fresh as possible in your bedroom. If the room feels stuffy, open your windows. You might want to use a HEPA (High-Efficiency Particulate Air) air purifier in the bedroom to filter out harmful particles and air pollutants like pollen, mold, dust, and dust mites. Remember to change the filter every six months to be certain the air purifier operates at top efficiency. There are many air purifiers available at a range of prices.

Two online sources for air purifiers I recommend are:

- The Clean Bedroom
  www.thecleanbedroom.com
  866-380-5892
- Nirvana Sleep Haven
  www.nontoxic.com/airpura/airpurifiers.html
  800-968-9533

Mary Cordaro, a bau-biologist (an expert on the impact of built environments on health), writes, "Make sure your bedroom is as healthy as possible. It is the most important room in the house. And the most important piece of furniture in your house is your bed—where you spend one third of your life. We are most vulnerable when we sleep. Our bodies let down . . . regroup, and regenerate."

Try to stay away from anything synthetic in your bedroom. Your bed frame should be hardwood or metal. Avoid plywood or particle board in your headboard, night tables, and dressers. You should polish your furniture with oil and natural beeswax. The rugs should be made from natural fibers. Your bed linens should be made from untreated, undyed, unbleached, organic cotton. The closer you get to this pure state, the better. Your entire body is in contact with the materials you sleep in, and you inhale whatever is in those fabrics. Check the following websites for organic sheets and mattress pads:

- The Clean Bedroom
  www.thecleanbedroom.com
  866-380-5892
- Gaiam
  www.gaiam.com
  877-989-6321
- Nirvana Sleep Haven
  www.nontoxic.com
  800-968-9533
- No Feathers Please
  www.nofeathersplease.com
  619-741-8120
- PemAmerica, Jenny McCarthy Organic
  www.pemamericaoutlet.com/default.aspx
  888-368-5374

Your Mattress

We all consider comfort when we choose a mattress, but we should pay attention to the toxins we may be exposing ourselves to as we sleep. Investing in an organic mattress is worth the expense. Conventional mattresses are made from plastic foam products and polyesters filled with petrochemicals. Polyurethane foams emit toluene, a highly toxic solvent that can cause brain damage and is harmful to developing fetuses. Chemicals like fire retardants, stain-resistant solvents, harsh dyes, glues, formaldehyde, pesticides, and herbicides never completely dissipate. These toxins bind to house dust that you inhale while you sleep. Remember, a mattress gets more toxic as it gets older. Now that you are getting ready for your new baby and might be having trouble getting comfortable as your pregnancy advances, it could be time for a change.

When buying a mattress, look for high-quality, natural components. Rather than one made of foam, your mattress should be made of pesticide-free organic cotton, wool batting, and natural latex. Wool batting is actually a highly effective fire retardant. You can find organic mattresses at most furniture and department stores. The best online sources of organic mattresses are:

- Nirvana Sleep Haven
  www.nontoxic.com/
  800-968-9533
- The Organic Mattress Store
  www.theorganicmattressstore.com/
  866-246-9866

The Bathroom

Keeping the bathroom immaculate feels like a challenge. Using strong cleansers in your bathroom could do more harm than the germs you are trying to wipe out. You might worry less about germs once you know that studies have shown that your computer keyboard has more germs than your toilet seat. The first necessity is to keep the bathroom well-ventilated. The dampness produced by showers and baths creates the perfect atmosphere for mold to grow. Install an exhaust fan if the bathroom does not already have one, and keep the window open, particularly after bathing. Vinyl floor mats and shower curtains contain phthalates that are released into the air you breathe and can interfere with your baby's development. As for towels, go for organic cotton, free of pesticides and harmful dyes. Moist, warm skin gives toxins from towels easy access to enter your body.

Disinfectants and Antibacterials

Disinfectants are EPA-regulated pesticides that kill bacteria. They kill germs on surfaces temporarily. They cannot kill germs in the air, and they do not provide long-lasting disinfection. Some disinfectant cleaners contain APEs (alkylphenol ethoxylates), suspected hormone disruptors that do not biodegrade quickly. Along with throwing off the hormone balance in your body, they are harmful to fish and wildlife when they end up in water sources after going down your drain. Triclosan, the active ingredient in most antibacterial soaps, was detected in 57.6 percent of stream-water samples from across the United States in a study by the U.S. Geological Survey. A 2000 World Health Association report found that the heavy use of antibacterial soaps and other germ-killing products is contributing to a rise in antibiotic-resistant bacteria. Unless you have a compromised immune system or an illness that makes you especially vulnerable to infection, you probably do not need a disinfectant for most household needs.

If you want to purchase a nontoxic disinfectant, try Earth Power's Power Herbal Disinfectant, which is hospital-grade and EPA-registered. It is made from herbal extracts, deionized water, and denatured alcohol.

- Earth Power's Power Herbal Disinfectant
  www.earthpower.com
  712-647-2755

Homemade Disinfectant

This recipe is not an antibacterial formula.

2 teaspoons borax
4 tablespoons vinegar
3 cups hot water
¼ teaspoon liquid castile soap (optional)

Wipe on surface with a dampened cloth or use a nonaerosol spray bottle.

Bathroom and Toilet Bowl Cleaners

Along with very irritating corrosive ingredients, some toilet bowl cleaners contain sulfates, which can trigger asthma attacks, and hydrochloric acid that release strong vapors. Bathroom cleaners that contain sodium hydroxide, sodium hypochlorite (bleach), or phosphoric acid can irritate your lungs and burn your eyes and skin. Mixing acid-containing toilet bowl cleaners with cleaners that contain chlorine will form a chlorine gas that can make you pass out and can cause damage to your lungs. Your safest bet is to avoid both ingredients. Commercial mildew removers contain highly toxic formaldehyde and kerosene. Here are some homemade alternatives:

Strong Homemade Toilet Cleaner

1 cup of borax

¼ cup distilled white vinegar or lemon juice

1. Pour ingredients into the toilet bowl and let sit for a few hours.
2. Scrub with a toilet brush and flush.

Use baking soda to scrub soap scum and clean toilet bowls. To remove mildew and mold, scrub tiles with a toothbrush of baking soda-water paste or borax-water paste, then rinse with clear water. Or try this recipe:

Mold and Mildew Remover

1 cup lemon juice or white vinegar

2 cups of water

1. Mix ingredients in a spray bottle.
2. Spray the moldy areas and let sit for an hour.
3. Scrub the mold with a brush and rinse with water.

When scrubbing mold, make sure you remove all of the mold from hard surfaces. The cleaner helps to neutralize the mold, making it easier to break it away from the surface. Take care not to inhale any mold. If you have a big problem with mold in your home, you can learn about nontoxic mold removal online at http://www.ehow.com/way_5886734_nontoxic-mold-removal.html.

You can find safer, plant-based bathroom, shower, and toilet cleaners at natural foods stores. Some are only available online.

- AFM SafeChoice Safety Clean
  www.afmsafecoat.com
  800-239-0321
- BioShield Toilet Bowl Cleaner
  www.bioshieldpaint.com
  800-621-2591
- Bon Ami Cleaning Powder
  www.bonami.com
- Earth Friendly Shower Kleener
  Earth Friendly Toilet Bowl Cleaner
  www.ecos.com
  800-335-ECOS
- Ecover Toilet Cleaner
  www.ecover.com
  800-449-4925
- Naturally Yours Basin, Tub and Tile Cleaner
  888-801-7347
- Seventh Generation Bathroom Cleaner
  Seventh Generation Shower Cleaner
  Seventh Generation Toilet Bowl Cleaner
  www.seventhgeneration.com
  800-456-1191

Air Fresheners

Air fresheners work by using a chemical that interferes with your sense of smell by coating your nasal passages with an oily film that masks odor. Dichlorobenzene is found in most household deodorizers and room fresheners. It is also an active ingredient in mothballs. The chemical accumulates in the body. Researchers have found the chemical stored in the fat of 100 percent of people tested, and greater amounts are being stored at younger ages. When children are exposed to dichlorobenzene prenatally, the chemical can disrupt neural development.

Stay away from air fresheners in aerosol spray cans. They produce very small droplets that are easily inhaled and absorbed into the body. The propellants, usually butane and propane, are flammable. Synthetic fragrances should be avoided. Researchers at Bristol University found that aerosols and air fresheners might be

Homemade Air-Freshener Solutions

There are many safe ways to keep your house fresh-smelling by using natural ingredients. Watch out for potpourri that lists "fragrance" as an ingredient, because phthalates and PVCs are often added to lengthen the life of synthetic fragrances. Here are just a few ways to sweeten the air in your house naturally:

- Improve ventilation by opening windows and using fans.
- Baking soda is good at absorbing odors. Leave small dishes of baking soda around the house.
- Vinegar with lemon juice will remove odors.
- Spray lemon or any citrus fruit juice to freshen the air. Leave a spray bottle near the toilet.
- Put cedar blocks or balls in a dish or in drawers.
- Use pure essential oils or sachets of naturally dried flowers or herbs.
- House plants such as aloe vera reduce odors—and absorb toxins—in your home.

making pregnant women and children sick in their survey of fourteen thousand pregnant women. They found that in homes where aerosols and air fresheners were used frequently, mothers suffered from 25 percent more headaches and 19 percent more depression. Infants under the age of six months had 30 percent more ear infections and 22 percent higher incidences of diarrhea.

Scented candles may contain toxins. Here is a list of safe potpourris, candles, and essential oil dispensers:

- Aroma Naturals essential oils aromatic room mists
  www.aromanaturals.com
  800-462-7662
- EcoDaySpa Natural palm wax candles
  www.ecodayspa.com
  626-969-3707
- Greenridge Herbals' aromatherapy soy candles
  www.greenridgeherbals.com
  866-250-HERB
- Lavender Green
  www.lavendergreen.com
  703-684-4433
- Molly's Herbals
  www.fiascofarm.com/herbs
- The Scented Room Provence Potpourri
  www.scentedroom.com
  208-342-8504
- Vermont Soy Candles
  www.vermontsoycandles.com
  888-727-1903

The Laundry Room

Another designated place in the house to make things clean is the laundry room. You do not want to use laundry products that add to your toxic load. This is an easy part of everyday living you can control. Most detergents are made from petrochemicals. They may contain bleaches and chemical whiteners. Even "fragrance-free" detergents sometimes contain chemical fragrances. Detergent residues can irritate the skin and cause respiratory problems. If you need to change the products you use for your laundry, here is what to look for:

- Vegetable oil–based soap
- Biodegrades in days
- No phosphates
- No bleach, which degrades into long-lasting chlorine compounds that are stored in fat
- No brighteners that do not biodegrade
- No synthetic preservatives

Homemade Laundry Soap

This laundry cleaner is low-sudsing. The ingredients in the soap, not the suds, do the cleaning.

⅓ bar Fels Naptha,
or 1 bar Ivory,
or 1 cup Ivory Flakes

2 gallons hot water
½ cup washing soda
½ cup borax powder

1. Grate the soap into a saucepan.
2. Add 6 cups water and heat the mixture until the soap melts.
3. Add the washing soda and the borax powder and stir until they are dissolved.
4. Remove the saucepan from the heat.
5. Pour 4 cups hot water into a 2-gallon bowl or bucket.
6. Add the soap mixture and stir.
7. Add 1 gallon plus 6 cups of water and stir.
8. Let the soap mixture sit for about 24 hours until it sets up. It will be a watery gel.
9. Use ½ cup soap per load of laundry.

- No EDTA, which is used to improve stability in commerical laundry detergents and liquid soaps

There are many acceptable laundry detergents and soaps on the market. The following list highlights a few brands:

- Dr. Bronner's Sal Suds
  www.drbronner.com
  760-743-2211
- Ecco Bella Products
  www.eccobella.com
  877-696-2220
- Ecover Products
  www.ecover.com
  800-449-4925
- Life Tree Premium Laundry Liquid
  www.lifetreeproducts.com
  800-824-6396
- Nellie's All-Natural Laundry Soda
  www.nelliesallnatural.com
  888-984-7471
- Seventh Generation
  www.seventhgeneration.com
  800-456-1191

Bleach

Try to avoid using chlorine bleach. This chemical is believed to be a neurotoxin. Its main ingredient is sodium hypochlorite, a mixture of chlorine and lye. If you need to whiten your laundry, use a non-chlorine bleach that is oxygen-based.

- Ecover, The Alternative Bleach
  www.ecover.com
  800-449-4925
- OxiClean
  available everywhere

Home Remedies for Whitening and Brightening

- Use ¼ cup borax during wash cycle to whiten laundry.
- To brighten clothes, add 1 to 2 tablespoons of Epsom salts to the wash cycle.
- For graying whites, add ¼ cup white vinegar to the wash cycle.
- Add ¼ cup lemon juice to the wash cycle.

Fabric Softeners

The purpose of fabric softeners is to reduce static in synthetic fabrics. There is no reason to use fabric softeners with natural fabrics. Softeners contain compounds that are formaldehyde releasers. As you know, formaldehyde damages DNA. Fabric softeners contain coal-tar dyes, ammonia, and very strong scents. When the softeners are exposed to hot water and heat from dryers or ironing, the vapors produced can be inhaled deeply.

Fabric softeners work by leaving a residue on the fabric that never completely washes out. Dryer balls are a good option. Make sure they are PVC-free. They soften clothes, reduce drying time, and eliminate static cling without residue and scents.

- Gaiam Lavender Sticks and Dryer Balls
  www.gaiam.com
  877-989-6321
- You can find a wide selection of wool dryer balls at www.etsy.com.

Easy Homemade Fabric Softeners

- Add ¼ cup white vinegar to wash cycle.
- Add ¼ cup baking soda to wash cycle.
- Add ¼ cup or somewhat less borax to wash cycle.

A nontoxic fabric softener available online and in stores is:

- Ecover Fabric Conditioner
  www.ecover.com
  800-449-4925

A Clean Sweep

You should make the switch to natural cleaning products right away. You might not be able to make such big changes as buying a new mattress or couch, but you can change the cleaning products you use. My advice is to go through all the bottles, spray cans, cans, and boxes under your sink, in the laundry room and utility closet, and on the shelves in your garage and start over. Get rid of the industrial-strength cleansers and all the products filled with toxins and replace them with natural and gentle alternatives. Forego the pesticides if you have a garden. Your aim is to create an environment in which your baby will grow and thrive.

While you are getting your house in order, you can do more in another area to protect yourself and your baby. You need to evaluate what you wear, your personal grooming products, and your cosmetics. Chapter 11, "A Wardrobe Not to Die For," will reveal the hazards from the clothes you put on your body.

11

A Wardrobe Not to Die For

When you resolve to live in a healthier way, you probably do not think of your clothes. The fact is that the fabrics you wear can hurt you and your baby. Chemicals in the clothing you wear contribute to your toxic load. Your skin is the largest organ of your body. What goes onto your skin goes into your body. When toxins are breathed in or absorbed through your skin, they enter your bloodstream and travel to your liver. Think of your liver as the chemical processing plant of your body. The liver's job is to eliminate toxins. You release and absorb toxins through your skin each day. What your skin drinks in directly affects your baby when you are pregnant and when you breastfeed. This chapter will examine the hidden toxins in your clothing and explain how to avoid them.

You probably will need new clothes as your body grows with your baby. This is a chance to make changes in your wardrobe that will keep you and your baby safe from harm.

Dress for Success

Synthetic fabrics were not developed until the twentieth century. Rayon, which is made from wood pulp, was introduced in 1924. The first completely synthetic fiber was nylon, made from toluene. Wash-and-wear and wrinkle-free fabrics were introduced with acrylics and polyester in the 1950s. By 1959 spandex and olefin appeared on the scene and were used in bathing suits, sportswear, and thermal underwear. Olefin is produced by breaking down petroleum molecules into propylene and ethylene gases. Synthetic fabrics are hard to avoid now, but it is worth the effort, particularly when you are pregnant.

Synthetic fabrics are full of chemicals and dyes that can be absorbed or inhaled but cannot be washed out. Most synthetic fabrics are treated with chemicals before and after processing. For example, PFCs are added to clothing to make the fabric last longer and stay wrinkle-free. Producing manmade fabrics is a complex

Top Fabrics to Avoid

Try to stay away from the fabrics in the list that follows. Choose more natural options.

- **Polyester** is the worst fabric you can wear. It is made from synthetic polymers, which are toxic.
- **Nylon** is made from petroleum and has a permanent finish that is harmful.
- **Acetate** and **triacetate** are made from wood fibers called cellulose. Producing the finished fabrics requires extensive chemical processing.
- **Rayon** is recycled wood pulp that must be treated with chemicals like caustic soda, ammonia, acetone, and sulphuric acid to be strong enough to survive wearing.

process that requires chemical manipulation of raw materials. Chemicals are also part of the process to make natural fibers suitable for spinning and weaving. Formaldehyde is widely used to prevent shrinkage. It is trapped in the fiber with heat. Chemicals including volatile organic compounds (VOCs) and dioxin-produced bleach are commonly added to make clothing fire-resistant, softer, moth-repellant, and stain-resistant. Petrochemical dyes, made from oil, pollute water and stay in the body permanently. Dye fixatives used in fabrics are often produced from heavy metals.

Harmful Surprises in Your Clothes

The clothing industry routinely uses around eight thousand synthetic chemicals. Let's have a look at a few. Many of the chemicals on the short list must be familiar by now. These harmful chemicals are everywhere, and we have to do our best to reduce our contact with them.

- **PFCs** are used with dirt- and water-repellent finishes. Windproof clothing that is made to breathe has been treated with various coatings, which often are fluorine-based.
- **Formaldehyde** is used to prevent shrinkage and wrinkles and to fix dyes.
- **Phthalates** are used as softening agents in clothing. The pressed-on designs on T-shirts are made from phthalates.
- **Heavy metals like chrome and lead** can be found in clothing. Chrome is used in tanning leather. Lead is sometimes used in dyeing.
- **Nonylphenol ethoxylates** (NPEs) are used in washing and dyeing textiles. They break down to form nonylphenol, which has toxic, hormone-disrupting properties. The chemical is known to impair fertility.
- **Triclosan,** an antibacterial chemical, is used to prevent fabrics from absorbing odors. Antibacterial chemicals are used widely in sports clothes.

- **DMF,** a fungicide, is used to prevent mold in fabrics during transport. Fungicides are often present in the small bags you find in products that are labeled "antimold agent."
- **Azo** dyes give leather and fabric clear and strong colors. They are water-soluble and can transfer easily into our bodies. They are known to cause gene mutations. Azo dyes have been banned by the European Union.

Greenpeace did testing a few years ago that found traces of NPEs in products made by fourteen top clothing manufacturers. The group purchased seventy-eight different clothing samples from

Convenience Clothes Are Toxic

Do not buy anything labeled "Permanent press," "No-iron," "Stain-proof," or "Wrinkle-resistant." Convenience clothes are toxic. The chemicals that have been added to make them easy-care have *never* been tested.

Stay away from clothes that have these finishes and labels:

- Easy-care
- Wrinkle-free
- Shrinkage-free
- Anti-cling
- Anti-static
- Anti-shrink
- Waterproof
- Water-repellant
- Perspiration-proof
- Moth-proof
- Mildew-resistant
- Chlorine-resistant

In addition, check the label for antibacterial and fungicidal chemicals

For years, I bought wrinkle-free cotton dress shirts, even though my shirts were hand-laundered and hand-pressed. My research for this book made me change my ways. I picked up the phone and ordered shirts without that wrinkle-free promise.

eighteen countries, mostly from China, Vietnam, Malaysia, and the Philippines, and subjected them to scientific analysis. NPEs were detected in two-thirds of the samples tested, made by fourteen global clothing manufacturers, including Adidas, Calvin Klein, Uniqlo, H & M, Abercrombie and Fitch, Lacoste, Converse, Ralph Lauren, Phillips-Van Heusen Corporation, Nike, and Puma. Greenpeace found that all of these popular brands were linked to two manufacturers. Nike and Puma have since pledged to eliminate the use of hazardous chemicals in their products by 2020. Adidas and H & M are also cooperating. Most of the international brands said they were "cut-and-sew" customers, and they did not use the dye services at the two factories that were responsible for the hormone-disrupting discharges. The last Greenpeace report was in September 2011. I have been unable to discover if any of the other brands have promised to change their manufacturing processes.

How to Protect Yourself

When you are shopping for maternity clothes, avoid synthetic fabrics including acrylic, polyester, rayon, acetate, triacetate, and nylon. Nylon and polyester are made from petrochemicals, the production of which creates nitrous oxide, a potent greenhouse gas. Rayon is made from wood pulp that has been treated with chemicals including sulfuric acid and caustic soda. Petrochemical fibers suffocate your skin by shutting down the release of toxins. When the toxins are not able to escape, a toxic soup is cooked up. That mixture can be more powerful than the individual chemicals. Your body burden will grow, and you will pass those toxins to your baby.

Natural fabrics such as cotton, linen, wool, cashmere, flax, and hemp breathe better than synthetic fibers. They wick moisture from your body, which can prevent harmful chemicals from being absorbed through your skin because moisture is needed for absorption. Flax is one of nature's strongest fibers. Hemp grows without the need of fungicides or pesticides because it is naturally insect-resistant. Its fibers are four times stronger than cotton. Most wool available today is contaminated from pesticides used to kill parasites on sheep. The demand for organic wool is growing. If you look for it, you can find it. Alpaca, angora, camel, mohair, and ramie (which is made from plant fibers) are other options.

Even Natural Fibers Are Processed

If your clothing is not organic, it contains residues from processing. Getting from raw material to a conventional cotton T-shirt takes a lot of chemicals, as shown here:

- To grow the cotton for a cotton T-shirt requires almost the weight of the shirt in fertilizers and pesticides.
- Chemicals, including harsh detergents, are used to prepare fibers for spinning and weaving.
- Formaldehyde is applied with heat to prevent shrinkage. The toxin is permanently trapped in the fabric.
- Petrochemical dyes are used for color.
- Dye fixatives are derived from heavy metals.
- VOCs and dioxin-producing bleach are used.
- Chemicals are added to make clothing softer, wrinkle-free, stain-resistant, and moth-repellant.
- PFCs are used to make fabrics wrinkle-free and longer-lasting.
- Clothing treated with flame retardants emits formaldehyde gas.

After a few washings with organic detergent, the toxic residues from cloth processing and previous detergents can be reduced or eliminated. Always wash non-organic clothing at least once with organic detergents before wearing it.

It takes one-third of a pound of pesticides and fertilizers to grow enough cotton for just one T-shirt. The chemicals used for cotton production do not end with those used for growing the plants. Producing fabric involves bleaching, sizing, dyeing, adding odor resistance, and undergoing the other processes I have mentioned with synthetic fabrics. The fabric is washed many times with softeners and detergents that can leave residues. Try shifting to organic cotton, which accounts for less than 1 percent of the cotton produced worldwide. Organically produced cotton has few of the issues of conventionally grown cotton, so organic fabrics are the way to go. Cottonseed oil was used to fry potato chips and other junky snack foods because it is so inexpensive. Cotton is one of the most chemicalized crops, and as awareness of all those chemicals rose, even the manufacturers of the junkiest junk food diminished the amount of cottonseed oil they use in their products. Buying organic cotton is important.

As you are switching your wardrobe to natural fibers, start with the clothing you wear closest to your body—underwear, nightgowns, PJs, socks. Synthetic underwear can affect sperm production. Fabrics like polyester trap body heat, enable chemical absorption, and create static buildup, all of which can lower sperm count.

Natural fabrics usually do not have to be dry-cleaned. That is a plus, because most dry cleaners use the solvent PCE, or perc, which is highly toxic. Dry cleaners now are conscious of the problem. They face significant health risks themselves because of their long exposure to these chemicals. More and more are using less toxic solvent. Whenever you pick up dry cleaning, take it out of the bag and let it outgas outside or near an open window before you wear it.

Chapter 12 shifts attention from your clothes to your grooming products and cosmetics. As you can probably guess, there are some nasty surprises in your makeup bag.

12

Beauty Does Not Have to Hurt

Just as what you wear affects your baby through your skin, so can your makeup and toiletries. More than fifteen thousand ingredients are allowed for use in grooming products. According to a 2009 study, the average American woman uses 515 chemical ingredients on her body every day. Mineral oil and petroleum are derived from fossil fuels. They are the basic ingredients in conventional cosmetic products. Almost 90 percent of the chemical ingredients used in grooming products have never been tested for their health effects. The regulations for cosmetics are not as stringent as those that apply to other FDA-regulated products. Manufacturers can use any ingredient or raw material, except for dyes and a few prohibited substances, in cosmetics and toiletries without government regulation. Some of these ingredients threaten a developing nervous system.

Beauty by the Numbers

- Americans spend more than $189 billion a year on personal care products. For that kind of money we deserve safer products.
- The average American woman ingests four pounds of lipstick during her life. Lipstick contains lead and other toxins.
- The United States government has tested only 11 percent of the 10,500 ingredients used in grooming products.
- The use of 1,100 ingredients in cosmetics has been banned in the European Union.
- The Food and Drug Administration has banned only 10 ingredients from use in cosmetics.
- 1,4-dioxane, a by-product of manufacturing, contaminates 22 percent of cosmetics.
- One third of personal care products contain at least one chemical linked to cancer.

Toxic Beauty A to Z

I had planned to discuss the top ten toxic ingredients found in personal care products, but I decided that a more comprehensive account was important. You need to have a sense of just how many damaging chemicals you apply to your body. I want to motivate you to replace the grooming products you currently use with safer alternatives. The thought that these toxic chemicals are absorbed into your body and reach your developing baby should persuade you to make safer choices.

This following list is compiled from a number of sources, but I relied heavily on information provided by the Environmental Health

Association of Nova Scotia. They have an information-packed website, www.lesstoxicguide.ca, that is worth checking.

Acetone, found in nail polish remover, is a neurotoxic agent.

Alpha hydroxy acids (AHAs) and **beta hydroxy acids (BHAs)** are acid skin peels. The Environmental Working Group found that they were added to one out of every seventeen personal care products in the United States, including moisturizers, eye creams, and sunscreen. They can burn the skin.

Aluminum compounds are active ingredients in antiperspirants. They temporarily plug sweat ducts to keep sweat from coming to the surface of the skin. These compounds have estrogenlike effects.

Ammonium glycolate is a penetration enhancer found in body products that changes the skin's structure to allow other chemicals to be absorbed deeply. It increases the toxic load in your bloodstream.

Benzoic acid is used as a preservative in cosmetics. The chemical affects the nervous system.

Benzyl alcohol and **isopropyl alcohol** are used as preservatives, fragrance ingredients, and antifoaming agents for hand sanitizers, sunscreens, and lotions. These alcohols are neurotoxic, particularly in children younger than three.

BHA and **BHT** are preservatives and antioxidants that have been banned in other countries. They slow down the rate of color change and are present in lipsticks and many other cosmetics. There is evidence that they are hormone disrupters. They are suspected of causing metabolic stress, depressed growth, fetal abnormalities, hyperactivity, and other behavioral disturbances.

Coal-tar dyes are made from a petroleum product. They are used extensively in personal care products, including bubble bath, hair dye, and dandruff shampoo. They appear on ingredient lists as "FD & C" or "D & C." Each coal dye has different properties and health concerns.

Coumarin is used in the manufacturing of deodorants, shampoos, skin fresheners, and fragrances. It is the active ingredient in rat poison.

1,4 dioxane is a contaminant, not an ingredient, so it will not appear on a label. It can be formed during a manufacturing process used for many cosmetics. More than fifty-six cosmetic ingredients are associated with 1,4 dioxane. It has been found in shampoos, body wash, and children's bath products.

DMDM hydantoin, diazolidinyl urea, and **imidazolidinyl urea** are preservatives that can release formaldehyde. Theses neurotoxins and carcinogens are found in facial cleansers, shampoos, and conditioners.

Formaldehyde is used in grooming products as a disinfectant, germicide, fungicide, and preservative. It is found in soaps, shampoos, deodorants, lotions, shaving cream, mouthwash, and nail products. It is a neurotoxin and a carcinogen.

Fragrance is the most common ingredient found on the label of personal care products. The general term can stand for up to three thousand mostly synthetic ingredients. Exposure to fragrances can affect the central nervous system, causing hyperactivity, depression, and other behavioral changes. The Environmental Protection Agency found that all of the perfumes they tested contained toluene, which can damage a developing fetus. DEP is a solvent used in fragrances and can damage the DNA in sperm.

Glycolic acid alters skin structure to allow other chemicals deeper penetration. This neurotoxin affects the liver, kidneys, and gastrointestinal system. It is found in creams and lotions.

Lanolin, found in moisturizers, comes from sheep's wool. Diazonin, a neurotoxic pesticide, is found in lanolin.

Lead is a neurotoxin that can lead to learning and behavior problems. It is absorbed through the skin and accumulates in the bones. Lead can be a contaminant in such personal care products as foundations, sunscreens, nail polish, whitening toothpaste, and lipstick. Lead can be found in color additives as well.

Methylisothiazolinone and **methylchloroisothiazolinone** are preservatives used in shampoos, conditioners, dyes, cleansers, and body washes. Animal studies have found them toxic to the immune system and the developing nervous systems.

Nanoparticles are particles from known chemicals that have been manipulated to extremely small dimensions. They are used in lotions, moisturizers, and sunscreen and remain untested. Their small size allows them to penetrate cell walls. They are highly reactive, causing inflammation and damage to brain cells. To date, the original chemical is listed on ingredients list, but there is no requirement to indicate whether it is present in nano form. The European Union has ruled that "nano" has to appear in brackets after the ingredient.

Nonylphenol is an estrogen-mimicking chemical found in shaving creams, shampoos, and hair colors. It is created when chemicals break down. It can be a component of PVC.

Oxybenzone is a UV-light absorber as well as the active ingredient in most sunscreens and cosmetics that contain sunscreens. Evidence suggests that oxybenzone is a hormone disruptor and may be toxic to the nervous system. One study done by the Mount Sinai School of Medicine found that oxybenzone exposure to pregnant women was associated with low-birth-weight baby girls. The CDC found the chemical in 97 percent of people tested in the United States.

Parabens are preservatives with antibacterial properties used in many different types of personal care products, particularly deodorants. Parabens mimic estrogen and have been linked to breast cancer.

PEG (polyethylene glycol) and **ceteareth** are petrochemical compounds found in body washes, liquid soap, baby wipes, sunscreens, and shampoo. They are used to thicken, soften, carry moisture, and enhance penetration. They can damage the central nervous system. PEG and ceteareth may be contaminated with 1,4-dioxane and ethylene dioxide, both carcinogens.

PPD (phenylenediamine), a coal-tar dye, is used in permanent hair dyes, even in products marketed "natural" or "herbal." The darker the formula, the higher the concentration of PPD, which is a carcinogen.

Phthalates (pronounced "tha-lates") is an odd word that you have encountered many times in this book. In cosmetics, phthalates are used to enhance fragrances to make them last longer. The Campaign for Safe Cosmetics found phthalates in fifty-four of the seventy-two products they tested, including deodorants, fragrances, hair gels, mousses, hairsprays, and hand and body lotions. Phthalates disrupt the hormonal system and interfere with reproduction. A study published in *Environmental Health Perspectives* found that DEP, a common type of phthalate used as a fragrance ingredient, damages the DNA of sperm in adult men at current levels of exposure. Another hormone-disrupting phthalate, DBP, is used in nail polishes. In the United States, women of childbearing age have been found to have high levels of DBP.

Polysorbate 60 and **polysorbate 80** are used as emulsifying agents and fragrance ingredients. These chemicals may be contaminated with 1,4-dioxane.

Propylene glycol is used in skin products, including moisturizers, facial cleansers, foundations, and anti-aging products, as well as mascara and hair dyes. It is used as a moisture-carrying ingredient instead of glycerin, because it is cheaper and more readily absorbed through the skin. It is a recognized neurotoxin.

Retinal palmitate and **retinol** (vitamin A) can cause severe birth defects if pregnant women are exposed. When applied to skin exposed to the sun in products like sunscreens, lip products, and moisturizers, the compounds break down and produce free radicals that can damage DNA.

Selenium sulfide is an antidandruff and hair-conditioning agent found in shampoos, conditioners, and dandruff treatments. It is believed to be a neurotoxin and is classified as a possible human carcinogen.

Sodium lauryl sulfate (SLS) enhances allergic response to other toxins and allergens. It can build up in the heart, lungs, brain, and liver and cause damage. **Sodium laureth sulfate** (SLA) is also an endocrine disruptor. Used as a lathering agent and detergent, it is an ingredient in shampoos, body washes, bubble baths, skin creams, and toothpaste. The milder sodium laureth sulfate may form 1,4-dioxane, a poison.

Talc is a mineral that is carcinogenic when inhaled. Talc is found in blushes, face powders, eye shadows, foundation, and skin fresheners. Airborne talc in body powders and antiperspirant sprays can irritate the lungs, which is why I tell parents to avoid using talc on their babies. Women who regularly use talc in their genital area are at increased risk for ovarian cancer.

TEA (triethanolamine), **DEA** (diethanolamine) and **MEA** (monoethanolamine) are additives used in sunscreens, moisturizers, foundations, and hair dye. DEA and its related compounds are used to adjust the pH of products, to help to mix oil and water, and to work as emulsifiers. DEA and TEA are known to combine with nitrates to form nitrosamines, which have been classified as possible carcinogens. DEA applied to and absorbed by the skin was found to cause liver and kidney damage in animals. When absorbed through the skin, DEA is known to accumulate in our organs. TEA, which is used as a fragrance ingredient, is toxic to the respiratory and immune systems. These chemicals are restricted in Europe.

Thimerosal is a preservative that contains mercury. You have undoubtedly heard a lot about its use as a preservative in vaccines. It has been almost completely phased out of medical products, including vaccines. Mercury may cause allergic reactions, affect reproduction, and have adverse effects on the nervous system. Thimerosal is used as a preservative in eyedrops and contact lens solutions. Mercury is sometimes found in cosmetics. The *Chicago Tribune* did tests in 2010 and found a number of skin-whitening products containing high levels of mercury. Mercury is readily absorbed through the skin.

Titanium dioxide is used in toothpastes and other products to provide whiteness and opacity. It also protects the skin from ultraviolet light and is found in sunscreens. Many sunscreen manufacturers have chosen to use nano-sized particles of titanium dioxide or zinc oxide so that sunscreen appears clear instead of white. The health effects of nano-sized titanium dioxide are unknown. The few animal studies to date suggest serious concerns that the smaller particles may have greater risks.

Toluene is a solvent used in nail polish to suspend color and form a smooth finish. It can appear on labels as "methylbenzene" or "toluene." It is a reproductive toxin and may put pregnant women at risk of having a baby with birth defects or delayed development.

Triclosan and **triclocarban** are synthetic antibacterial chemicals added to soaps, toothpastes, mouthwash, deodorant, and shaving cream. They are antibacterial, not antiviral. That means that they have no effect on viruses and are not effective against colds and flu. Triclosan has been detected in human breast milk, and in 75 percent of human tissue samples taken. Studies show that triclosan and triclocarban may have endocrine-disrupting effects. In animal studies, triclosan was shown to reduce thyroid hormones, which are critical for normal development. When you wash your hands with an antibacterial soap that contains triclosan, the chemical can react with chlorine in the water to create chloroform, a highly toxic gas. An Advisory Panel to the United States Food and Drug Administration reported that there is no evidence that soaps with triclosan are any more effective in killing bacteria than plain soap and water. It causes bacterial resistance, which can interfere with the effectiveness of antibiotics.

After reading this list of hazardous chemicals in common use in personal care products, you might want to count the number you use each day. According to the Environmental Working Group, the average person uses up to twenty-five products a day. Each product contains many chemicals. From your body wash to your hand lotion, from your styling gel to your lipstick, you expose yourself to hundreds of harmful chemicals every single day. When you are pregnant, these toxins make their way to your baby. We know this is true, because, as I mentioned earlier, umbilical cord blood is loaded with toxic chemicals. You can reduce that toxic burden by using products that do not contain the chemicals listed earlier in this chapter.

Change Your Beauty Regimen

While you are pregnant and nursing, there are serious beauty don'ts. I know that many women continue to use questionable procedures and products without consequence, but I prefer always to err on the side of caution when it comes to developing babies. Take a break from all these beauty treatments and enjoy the natural beauty of being pregnant.

Heavy Fragrances

Many fragrances contain phthalates, which are not listed on labels. The chemical can imitate hormones that control the growth and development of your baby. It is dangerous to have even low levels during pregnancy. Buy all your toiletries fragrance-free.

Retinoids for Acne and Wrinkles

Avoid these vitamin A derivatives, which are found in anti-aging creams and acne medication. They are less damaging when used on the skin than when ingested. Reti-A, Avita, and Renova are treatments applied to the skin for acne, for improving skin appearance and wrinkles, and for hyperpigmentation. Hormone fluctuations during pregnancy often make acne worse. The jury is out on these products, but I suggest not using them when you are pregnant due to the possible risks. Oral retinoids like the acne medication Accutane are known to cause birth defects. If you are having a problem with your skin, check with a dermatologist for other medications.

To identify retinoids on the label, look for "Differin," "Reinta-A," "Renova," "Retinoic acid," "Retinol," "Retinyl Linoleate," "Retinyl palmitate," and "Tazorac."

Botox

Botox is a powerful neurotoxin that is produced by the same bacteria that causes botulism. Enough said.

Salicylic Acid

This mild acid is used to treat skin disorders, including acne, and is found in cleansers, toners, body wraps, and leave-on lotions. BHA is a form of salicylic acid used in exfoliants. High doses of the oral form have been shown to cause birth defects. My advice is to be cautious and do not even use the topical form. Salicylic acid is also identified as "Beta hydroxyl acid" or "BHA" on the label.

Teeth Whiteners

Peroxide is the active ingredient in teeth whiteners. If you swallow some during the bleaching process, it will not harm you, but not enough is known about how peroxide affects babies during pregnancy. I believe it is better to be careful during your pregnancy and while you are nursing. Use a whitening toothpaste instead. I suggest some in the product guide on page 181.

Sunscreen/Sunblock

Using sunscreen while you are pregnant is important, because your skin is more sensitive during this time. The ingredient to avoid is oxybenzone. It has been linked to low birth weight in girls. Look for sunblocks that contain zinc oxide or titanium dioxide, which block UV rays by sitting on top of the skin. It is best to use products that block the sun without being absorbed. And be sure to wear a hat and protective clothing. Some good sunscreens are listed on pages 190 and 191.

Nail Care

The *Nation* reported on the potentially toxic effects of chemicals in nail care products. There is anecdotal evidence that nail salon workers have a high incidence of stillbirths, birth defects, and developmental issues with their babies. No studies have been done to date, but the polishes, acrylics, and other products used in nail salons contain twenty chemicals that the Environmental Protection Agency has identified as having negative health effects.

Phthalate, formaldehyde, and toluene are the toxic trio in nail polish. A list of less toxic nail products appears on pages 201 and 202.

You could just buff your nails while pregnant, as it is best to avoid the fumes at nail salons during your pregnancy.

Self-Tanning/Spray-on Tanning

The FDA has approved DHA (dihydroxyacetone) for use in chemical tanning. DHA works by reacting with the dead layer of surface skin—like toasting bread. The DHA is not absorbed below the dead surface layer, so it is considered safer than getting a tan from the sun. But this does not take into account the risk of inhaling particles of spray. DHA may cause gene mutations and DNA damage, so skip the chemical tan.

Chemical Hair Removal/Laser Hair Removal

Avoid depilatories or cream hair removers because the chemicals seep into your pores to loosen hair follicles. The active ingredient is usually a form of thioglycolic acid, which reacts chemically with bonds in hair. No studies have been done about this chemical's prenatal effects. Since the chemical reaction is strong enough to affect hair follicles, it makes sense not to expose your baby to the chemicals.

Laser hair removal requires very powerful topical anesthetics, which can be absorbed into the bloodstream. Most laser hair removal spas will not treat pregnant women.

Put those products away or cancel those appointments. Shave while you are pregnant, even though doing so can be a challenge in the last trimester. See pages 184 and 185 for some nontoxic shaving creams.

Hair Dye, Extensions, and Keratin Treatments

The ammonia, peroxide, and coal-tar dyes found in hair dyes are toxic. You certainly should avoid coloring your hair during the first three months of your pregnancy. Some doctors say you should avoid hair dyes that cover your entire head because the chemicals saturate your scalp and can be absorbed. They believe getting highlights is fine. I recommend that you avoid conventional hair coloring when you are pregnant. I list some products on page 195 that are safe to use. Hair extensions without glue are an option. Keratin or Japanese smoothing procedures should be postponed. Very harsh chemicals, including formaldehyde, are used to straighten hair.

Skin Whitening/Lightening

The hydroquinone or glutathione in skin whiteners interferes with processes that lead to the production of melanin, which darkens the skin. Mercury has mostly been removed from whitening/

lightening products. The FDA has proposed a ban on over-the-counter sales of products containing hydroquinone because it is a carcinogen.

Pregnancy can induce darkening of the skin and can lead to a pigment mask on the face. My advice is to wait until after your pregnancy before using any skin-lightening treatments.

Tattoos

I recommend that you resist the urge to get a tattoo during your pregnancy. The pigments used for a tattoo are not controlled by the FDA. The numbing cream is absorbed through the skin, and an injectable anesthetic is also used.

Marketing Purity

Do not be fooled by labeling. The words "natural" or "all natural" are not regulated labels, and they appear on packaging to convince you that a product is good for you. The same goes for "hypoallergenic," "nontoxic," "doctor-tested," and "no synthetic ingredients." Products labeled "natural" and "organic" often contain synthetic ingredients and petrochemicals, with no certified organic ingredients at all. Toxic synthetic chemicals have become a big issue in the beauty community. As consumers express their concern and demand healthier products, the marketers grow more creative. These marketing claims are not regulated by law.

Make sure to read the labels on all personal care products. Companies can legally omit many chemicals from labels, including nanoparticles, ingredients considered trade secrets, and the component of fragrance. Tested fragrances revealed an average of fourteen hidden components, including hormone disruptors and phthalates.

There are many companies making pure grooming products that are accessible. What follows is a product-by-product guide to

Everything You Need to Know about Your Beauty Products

If you want to check the hazard level of the products you are using, take a look at the Environmental Working Group's Skin Deep Cosmetics Database at www.ewg.com. The website rates seventy-four thousand popular personal grooming and cosmetic products. All you have to do is type the name of a product into the search feature to find the hazard score of that product. The scores range from zero to ten, with ten showing the highest level of toxicity.

the safest brands and products on the market today. I used a number of sources, including the Environmental Working Group's database and the experience of my patients, friends, and family. I chose the least toxic products available with a rating below two in the Skin Deep database. The products are from a broad range of companies. I want to give you an idea of just how many good products are out there. Almost every company mentioned has a full product line. I include safe name brands that you can get anywhere. You can find some of the organic products in CVS, Walgreens, Walmart, Target, and other chains. You do not have to search for them, though. You can call or order these products online. Many companies offer free shipping if your order is above a certain dollar amount. Read about the products online. Experiment with them. Most of my patients never go back to conventional body care products.

Basic Grooming

Soap

Commercial soaps contain perfumes, dyes, mineral oil, and other petroleum-based chemicals. Antibacterial chemicals are often found in liquid hand soaps.

A wide range of high-quality natural soap is available. It is often produced by small artisanal businesses. You can find these soaps at local markets and health food stores.

Harmful Ingredients and Contaminants: antibacterial chemicals triclosan and triclocarbon, which disrupt hormones; fragrances, dyes, and petroleum-based chemicals

Bar Soaps

- A Soap for Goodness Sake Soap Bars
  www.soapforgoodnesssake.com
- By Valenti True Castille Organic (Olive Oil) Bar Soap
  www.byvalenti.com
- Jaydancin Inc. All Natural Soap, Unscented
  www.jaydancin.com
  519-775-2300
- Olivier Soapery 100% Castille Soap
  www.oliviersoaps.com
  888-775-5550
- Trader Joe's Oatmeal and Honey Soap
  www.traderjoes.com

Liquid Soaps

- Be Green Bath and Body Liquid Soaps
  www.shoptobegreen.com
  623-252-5470
- Loving Naturals 100% Organic Soaps
  http://loving-naturals-skin-care.webstorepowered.com
- Nature Clean Soaps
  www.naturecleanliving.com
  905-940-1107
- Rocky Mountain Soap Company
  www.rockymountainsoap.com
  877-679-2214

Homemade Toothpastes

Brush with plain baking soda or salt.
Brush with 2 parts baking soda and 1 part sea salt ground to a powder in a blender.

Toothpaste

The fluoride in toothpaste that prevents cavities is a neurotoxin. Antibacterials like triclosan are added, as are dyes and chemicals that produce foam.

Hazardous Ingredients and Contaminants: sodium fluoride, artificial sweeteners, dyes, sodium laurel sulfate, triclosan, and propylene glycol

- Anarres Natural Health Toothpaste and Powder
  www.anarreshealth.com
  416-535-9620
- Healing Scents Toothpastes
  www.healing-scents.com
  815-874-0924
- Miessence Mint Toothpaste
  http://miorganicproducts.com
  888-535-2226
- Solay Smile Natural Tooth Powders
  www.natural-salt-lamps.com
  847-676-5571
- Tom's of Maine Fluoride-Free Toothpaste
- Tom's of Maine Natural Antiplaque Toothpaste

Dental Floss

Most dental floss is made of nylon, a petroleum product, and coated with a chemical that is related to the coating on nonstick pots and pans. Unwaxed floss and floss made with beeswax or other natural wax coating are better choices.

Hazardous Ingredients and Contaminant: nylon and PTFE

- Dr. Collins Dental Work Flosses
  www.drcollins.com
  888-583-6048
- Eco-dent International Flosses
  www.eco-dent.com
  877-263-9456
- Tom's of Maine Naturally Waxed Antiplaque Flosses

Mouthwash

Conventional mouthwash is made with alcohol and fluoride. Alcohol can contribute to cancer of the mouth, tongue, and throat. You already know that fluoride is a neurotoxin. The products listed here do not use alcohol, fluoride, artificial colors, or sweeteners.

Hazardous Ingredients and Contaminants: alcohol, sodium fluoride, artificial sweeteners, synthetic flavors, fragrances, and colors

- Dr. Katz Therabreath Oral Rinses
  www.therabreath.com
  800-97-FRESH
- Healing Scents Mouthwashes
  www.healing-scents.com
  815-874-0924
- Jason Natural Cosmetics Powersmile Super Refreshing Mouthwash
  www.jason-natural.com
  888-659-7730
- Miessence Freshening Mouthwash
  http://miorganicproducts.com
  888-535-2226
- Tom's of Maine Natural Mouthwashes

Homemade Teeth Whitener

Brush your teeth with baking soda to remove stains once or twice a week. It will have a salty taste.

Teeth Whiteners

Bleaching products rely on hydrogen peroxide, a neurotoxin and endocrine disruptor. There have been no long-term studies done on the safety of teeth whiteners. It is best to avoid conventional brands. Using a safe whitening toothpaste is the best way to go.

Harmful Ingredients and Contaminants: hydrogen peroxide and artificial sweeteners

- Arganat All Natural Clay Toothpaste Whitening
  www.arganat.net
  514-941-6955
- Jason Natural Cosmetics Powersmile Whitening Toothpaste
  www.jason-natural.com
  888-659-7730
- Tom's of Maine Natural Antiplaque Plus Whitening Gel Toothpaste

Deodorants and Antiperspirants

Deodorants work by inhibiting the growth of odor-causing bacteria. Antiperspirants stop perspiration by blocking the sweat ducts. Some studies have made a connection between the aluminum compounds in antiperspirants and breast cancer. Triclosan is used as an antibacterial agent.

Crystal deodorants are an alternative to conventional products and are growing in popularity. They use aluminum salts that react differently than the aluminum compounds in conventional deodorants and are less likely to be absorbed.

Hazardous Ingredients and Contaminants: aluminum compounds in antiperspirant, triclosan, synthetic fragrances, phthalates, parabens, and talc

- Alvin Connor Ltd Natural Body Stick Deodorant
  www.alvinconnor.com
  800-083-4315
- Bubble and Bee Organic Deodorants
  www.bubbleandbee.com
  801-560-7899
- Innocent Oils Pure Himalayan Crystal Body Spray
  www.innocentoils.com
  44(0) 1473 622816
- Lafe's Natural Body Care Deodorant Spray
  www.lafes.com
  800-926-LAFE (5233)
- Miessence Aroma Free Roll On
  www.miorganicproducts.com
  888-535-2226
- Naturally Fresh Deodorant Spray Mist Deodorants
  www.naturallyfreshdeodorantcrystal.com
  800-653-4006

Shaving Cream

Shaving cream is full of potentially damaging chemicals. The following list contains soaps, creams, and gels that are safer alternatives.

Hazardous Ingredients and Contaminants: TEA, PEG, 1,4-dioxane, propylene glycol, BHA, fragrance, and colors

- Aubrey Organics Shaving Cream
  www.aubrey-organics.com
  800-876-8166
- Dr. Bronner's Magic Shaving Gels

- Nurture My Body Shave Cream
  www.nurturemybody.com
  866-440-8137
- Plantlife Foam Soaps
  www.plantlife.net
- Soap for Goodness Sake Shaving Soaps
  www.soapforgoodnesssake.com

Bubble Bath/Bath Salts

Aside from the toxic chemical cocktail in bath products, soaking in hot water with bubble bath, bath salts, or bath oils makes your skin more permeable to those toxins. A relaxing bath can be a joy when you are pregnant, but make sure you use safe products.

Hazardous Ingredients and Contaminants: formaldehyde, DMDM, 1,4-dioxane, sodium lauryl sulfate, synthetic fragrance, dyes, and parabens and other preservatives

- Aveeno Soothing Bath Treatment
- Best Bath Store Bath Bombs
  www.bestbathstore.com
  888-366-2284
- Big Tub Botanicals Tub Bubbler
  www.bigtubbotanicals.com
  506-640-0001
- The Body Shop Aloe Comfort Oil
- EO Bubble Bath
  www.eoproducts.com
  800-570-3775

Skin Care

Eye-Makeup Remover

To remove your eye makeup gently, you probably use an eye makeup remover that contains a variety of toxins. The products listed next are among the least toxic on the market.

Homemade Eye-Makeup Remover

1 tablespoon castor oil
1 tablespoon light olive oil
1 teaspoon vegetable oil

Mix ingredients, pat the remover around the eyes, and wipe off gently with a cotton ball.

Hazardous Ingredients and Contaminants: mineral oil, sodium laureth sulfate, DEA, PEG ethylene dioxide, 1-4 dioxane, parabens, methylisothiazoline, methylchloroisotheizoline, TEA, colors, triclosan, phthalates, and synthetic fragrance

- Face Naturals Organic Eye Makeup Remover
  www.facenaturals.com
  877-885-0162
- Nothing Nasty Tender Eye Makeup Remover
  www.nothingnasty.com
  845-450-8982
- Real Purity Eye Makeup Remover
  www.realpurity.com
  800-253-1694
- Salon Naturals Eye Makeup Remover
  www.salonnaturalsonline.com
  800-985-3121

Cleansers and Makeup Removers

Conventional cleansers and makeup removers remove dirt and clean the skin with alcohol and petroleum products, which are absorbed by your skin along with other toxins. Your skin might be cleaned, but the effects are harmful.

Hazardous Ingredients and Contaminants: polyethylene glycol and ceteareth, ethylene oxide, 1,4-dioxane, DMDM hyantoin, formaldehyde, propylene glycol, coal-tar colors, parabens, and synthetic fragrance

- Herbal Choice Mari Makeup Remover
  www.herbalchoicemari.com
  888-417-1375
- Non Toxic Skin Care Cleansing Oil
  www.thenontoxicshop.com
- Nurture My Body Cream Cleanser Fragrance Free
  www.nurturemybody.com
  866-440-8131
- Organic Essence Certified Organic Shea Cream
  www.organic-essence.com
  707-465-8955

Homemade Makeup Removers

FEELING YOUR OATS CLEANSER

1. Put rolled oats in a blender and process until fine.
2. Massage wet skin with a small amount of the oats and rinse.

TANGY CLEANSING MILK

½ cup plain yogurt
2 teaspoons lemon juice
1 tablespoon oil
essential oil (optional)

1. Blend the yogurt and lemon juice in a blender. Slowly add the oil with the blender running.
2. You can add a drop or two of an essential oil, if you would like, for fragrance. Massage into skin and rinse.
3. Store in a jar.

- Rocky Mountain Soap Company Transformative Cleansing Oil
  www.rockymountainsoap.com
  877-679-2214
- Zosimos Botanicals Makeup Remover and Cleanser
  www.zosimosbotanicals.com
  877-889-9969

Astringents and Toners

These products are designed to remove traces of cleanser, dead skin cells, and excess oil. Toners are supposed to balance the skin's PH and close pores. Commercial toners produce that tight feeling by using PVPs. Astringents have higher levels of alcohol and anti-

Homemade Astringents and Toners

LEMON TONER FOR ALL SKIN TYPES

¼ cup lemon juice
½ cup distilled water
⅓ cup witch hazel

Blend all the ingredients together and store in a glass jar.

HERBAL TONER FOR DRY SKIN

¼ cup rose water
¼ cup aloe vera gel
1 drop chamomile essential oil
1 drop jasmine essential oil

Blend all the ingredients together and store in a glass jar.

WATERMELON TONER FOR OILY SKIN

Puree 1 cup of watermelon chunks in a blender
2 tablespoons distilled water
2 tablespoons witch hazel

Blend all the ingredients together and store in a glass jar.

septic ingredients. Nontoxic alternatives use witch hazel, aloe vera gel, or rose water.

- The Body Shop Aloe Calming Toner
- Non Toxic Skin Care Calming Toner
  www.thenontoxicshop.com
- Nuvo Floral Waters
  www.nuvocosmetics.com
  608-515-8131
- LaRoche-Posay Thermal Spring Water
  www.laroche-posay.us
  800-560-1803

Lotions, Creams, and Moisturizers

Lotions are a mixture of water and oils with an emulsifier added to keep them from separating. Preservatives and thickeners are also added. Hand lotions are often thicker versions of facial moisturizers. Plant-based lotions and moisturizers are the healthiest choices.

Hazardous Ingredients and Contaminants: mineral oil, petrolatum, propylene glycol, 1,4-dioxane, polysorbate 60 and 80, TEA, DMDM hydantoin, formaldehyde, parabenslycol, lanolin, PEG, retinyl palmitate, and fragrance

- Coastal Classic Creations Sea Strand Hand Cream
  www.coastalclassiccreations.com
- Garden of Eden Organic Apothecary Skin Care Products
  www.gardenofedenstores.com
  800-405-5545
- Healing-Scents Whipped Body Butter
  http://healing-scents.com
  815-874-0924
- Herbal Choice Mari Hand and Body Lotions
  www.herbalchoicemari.com
  888-417-1375

- Naked Skin Care Moisturizer
  www.nakedskincareproducts.com
  800-411-4066
- Purple Prairie Botanicals Skin Care
  www.purpleprairie.com
  320-558-9010
- Soap for Goodness Sake Unscented Shea Butter Crème Moisturizer
  www.soapforgoodnesssake.com

Sunscreen

The Environmental Working Group examined sunscreens and found that most conventional products offered poor protection from sun damage and contained toxic ingredients. They recommend using a sunscreen with the active ingredients zinc oxide, titanium dioxide, or Mexoryl SX. Buying a sunscreen with an SPF over 50 does not buy you added protection. The water-resistant claims are real, so use a water-resistant sunscreen for the beach or pool. Lotions work better than sprays and powders.

Hazardous Ingredients and Contaminants: oxybenzone, retinyl palmitate, cinnamates, and nanoparticles

- Aubrey Organics Sunscreens
  www.aubrey-organics.com
  800-282-7394
- Badger Sunscreens
  www.badgerbalm.com
  800-603-6100
- Eco Logical Skin Care All Natural Sunscreens (SPF 30+)
  www.ecologicalskin.com
  949-218-2665
- Honest Sunscreen
  www.honest.com
  888-862-8818

- Loving Naturals Clear Body Sunscreen (SPF 30+)
  http://loving-naturals-skin-care.webstorepowered.com
  603-509-3158
- Sunology Lotion
  www.sunology.com
- True Natural Cosmetics Sunscreens
  www.truenatural.com
  877-515-8783

Hair Care

Shampoo

You subject yourself to a full complement of toxins every time you wash your hair in a steaming shower. Fortunately, there are so many pure-ingredient shampoos available that making the switch will not be difficult.

Hazardous Ingredients and Contaminants: formaldehyde-releasing preservatives, DMDM hydantoin, parabens, sodium lauryl sulfate, sodium laureth sulfate, ethylene dioxide, 1,4-dioxane, TEA, propylene glycol, methylisothiazoline, methylchlorothiazoline, and coal tar

- Burt's Bees Outdoor Rosemary Mint Shampoo Bar
- Coastal Classic Creations Shampoos
  www.coastalclassiccreations.com
- Healing-Scents Shampoos
  www.healing-scents.com
  815-874-0924
- Honest Shampoo and Body Wash
  www.honest.com
  888-862-8818
- Morrocco Method International Shampoos
  https://morroccomethod.com
  805-534-1600

- Olivier Soapery Shampoos
  www.oliviersoaps.com
  888-775-5500

Conditioner

Making your hair shine does not require slathering it with a very toxic mix. Choose from the products listed here for beautiful, healthy hair. I have included a number of homemade recipes that were adapted from *Longlocks Hair Care Recipes Cookbook* at www.longlocks.com, which contains recipes that you can make from ingredients in your kitchen.

Hazardous Ingredients and Contaminants: DMDM hydantoin, formaldehyde, coal-tar colors, parabens, propylene glycol, cinnamate, sunscreens, retinyl palmitate, synthetic fragrance, and phthalates

- Coastal Classic Creations Conditioners
  www.coastalclassiccreations.com
- Korres Silk Milk Conditioner
  www.korresusa.com
  877-5KORRES (877-556-7737)
- Morrocco Method International
  https://morroccomethod.com
  805-534-1600
- Non Toxic Skin Care Smooth Ends
  www.thenontoxicshop.com
- Nuture My Body Conditioner
  www.nurturemybody.com
  866-440-8137
- Salon Naturals Conditioning Detanglers
  www.salonnaturalsonline.com
  800-985-3121

Homemade Conditioners

CONDITIONING BREW

1. Pour a cup of warm beer over just-washed hair, then rinse thoroughly with water.
2. For a richer conditioner, add a teaspoon of vegetable oil or jojoba oil to the beer.

VINEGAR SHINE

½ cup cider vinegar
1½ cups cold water

1. Mix the vinegar and water in a bottle.
2. Pour the mixture through freshly washed hair. Be cautious not to get any in your eyes.
3. Rinse thoroughly.

Vinegar will remove buildup on your hair and leave it shiny.

CREAMY CONDITIONER

1. Massage enough mayonnaise into your hair to coat every strand.
2. Cover your hair with a plastic bag for 15 minutes, then rinse with warm water.

- Zosimos Botanicals Conditioners
  www.zosimosbotanicals.com
  877-889-9969

Gel and Mousse

Gel and mousse keep hair in place by coating it with PVP and using solvents to keep the film flexible on the hair. Gel and mousse are safer to use than hairspray.

Hazardous Ingredients and Contaminants: PVP, phthalates, TEA, colors, PEG, 1,4-dioxane, parabens, formaldehyde, and fragrance

- Bumble and Bumble Curls deFRIZZ
  www.bumbleandbumble.com
- Healing Scents Styling Gel
  http://healing-scents.com
  815-874-0924
- Herbaliz Frizz Tamer
  http://herbaliz.com
  334-356-4500
- Salon Naturals Natural Hold Styling Gel
  www.salonnaturalsonline.com
  800-985-3121

Hairspray

Hairsprays rely on polymers and solvents to hold hair. They are usually applied with aerosols or pump sprays. Both produce a fine mist that can be inhaled deeply into the lungs and enter the bloodstream. Pump sprays make larger droplets, which is better. Toxic ingredients in the hairspray are riskier when they are inhaled.

- Beauty without Cruelty Hair Spray, Natural Hold
  www.beautywithoutcruelty.com
  800-824-6396
- Morrocco Method International Volumizer Mist Conditioner and Hair Spray
  https://morroccomethod.com
  805-534-1600
- Shear Miracles by Robyn Organic Body Hair Sprays
  www.shearmiracles.net
  888-223-7986

- Simply Organic Volume Spray
  www.simplyorganicbeauty.com
  866-512-4247

Dye

According to a study by the Harvard School of Public Health, women who have their hair dyed five or more times a year have twice the risk of developing ovarian cancer. Darker dyes pose a greater health risk. The European Union has banned twenty-two ingredients used in hair dyes, but these toxins have not been restricted in the United States.

Hazardous Ingredients and Contaminants: coal-tar dyes and PPD

- Coastal Classic Creations Organic Henna Hair Dye
  www.coastalclassiccreations.com
- Light Mountain Natural Hair Colors
  www.light-mountain-hair-color.com
  262-889-8561
- Morrocco Method International Henna
  https://morroccomethod.com
  805-534-1600
- Rainbow Research Henna Hair Dye
  www.rainbowresearch.com
  800-722-9595

Makeup

Lip Balms and Gloss

Lip balms and glosses are easily ingested, so you should be very careful of what you put on your lips. As many as three chemical sunscreens are often added to lip products. Lead has also been detected in lip gloss and balms. Daily use of lip balms containing conventional sunscreens is taking a risk with chemical exposure.

Hazardous Ingredients and Contaminants: synthetic waxes, mineral oil, petrolatum, lanolin, lead, coal-tar dyes, artificial flavors, BHT, parabens, fragrance, phenol, oxybenzone, cinnamates, retinal palmitate, lead, arsenic, cadmium, and other heavy metals

- Coastal Classic Creations Lip Gloss
  www.coastalclassiccreations.com
- Herbal Choice Mari Lip Gloss
  www.herbalchoicemari.com
  888-417-1375
- Herban Lifestyle Dolce de Limone
  www.herbanlifestyle.com
  905-342-3743
- JayDancin All Natural Lip Balm
  www.jaydancin.com
  519-775-2300
- Loving Naturals 100% Organic Lip Balms
  loving-naturals-skin-care.webstorepowered.com
- Obrien Organics, Inc. Lip Glaze
  www.obrienorganics.com
  941-915-2681
- Smallbones Studio of Home Arts Sustainable Living Lip Balm
  www.smallbones.ca
  905-342-3743
- Welstar Lip Saver Lip Gloss
  www.welstar.net
  800-893-6008

Lipstick

Lead has been detected as an impurity in the colors used in lipstick. Traces of lead, arsenic, cadmium, and other heavy metals have been found in lipstick and glosses. These heavy metals are extremely toxic to the nervous system. Conventional lipsticks contain synthetic oils and petroleum waxes. The safest lipsticks listed next use beeswax or olive oil instead.

Hazardous Ingredients and Contaminants: synthetic oils, petroleum waxes, coal tar dyes, and lead

- Boots No7 Mineral Perfection Lipstick
  www.shopbootsusa.com
  888-476-0035
- Coastal Classic Creations Lipstick
  www.coastalclassiccreations.com
- Green Beauty Cosmetics Lip Tint
  www.greenbeauty.ca
- Real Purity Lipstick
  www.realpurity.com
  800-253-1694
- rms beauty Lip2Cheek Blush/Lipstick
  www.rmsbeauty.com
  877-RMS-1147
- Wine Country Organics Lip Tint Mineral Lipstick
  www.winecountryorganics.com
  877-524-4367

Concealer

The preservatives in concealers can age your skin by reacting to the sun's rays. Retinyl palmitate is a skin-conditioning agent that can damage DNA. You should *not* use a product with retinyl palmitate when you are pregnant.

Hazardous Ingredients and Contaminants: propylene glycol, polyethylene glycol, TEA, 1,4-dioxane,ethylene oxide, alumina, parabens, and retinyl palmitate

- Cargo Wet/Dry Foundation
  www.cargocosmetics.com

- Coastal Classic Creations Refreshing Concealer and Extra Coverage Foundation
  www.coastalclassiccreations.com

Foundation

You wear foundation on your skin for many hours, while your body absorbs the toxic ingredients noted here that are commonly used in foundation products. Some of the safest "clean" alternatives are listed.

Hazardous Ingredients and Contaminants: talc, silica, alumina, aluminum salt, mineral oil, propylene glycol, phenoxyethanal, TEA, parabens, formaldehyde, synthetic fragrances, and coal-tar dyes

- Alima Pure Balancing Primer Powder
  www.alimapure.com
  888-380-5420
- Erth Minerals Foundations
  www.erthminerals.com
  920-819-8228
- Outside/In Cosmetics Mineral Primers
  www.outsideincosmetics.com
- Physician's Formula Organic Wear 100% Natural Origin Matte Finishing Veil
  www.physiciansformula.com
  800-227 -0333
- Real Purity Crème Foundation
  www.realpurity.com
  800-253-1694
- Rejuva Minerals Foundation
  www.rejuvaminerals.com

Blush

Talc is the main ingredient in powder blushes, and it can be contaminated with asbestos fibers. Alumina, a neurotoxin, is used as an anticaking agent. Safer blushes use iron oxides for color and mica instead of talc.

Hazardous Ingredients and Contaminants: talc, asbestos, silica, alumina, coal-tar dyes, parabens, and BHT

- Ada Cosmetics Mineral Blush
  www.adacosmetics.com
- Coastal Classic Creations Blush/Highlighter
  www.coastalclassiccreations.com
- Erth Minerals Bloom Blusher
  www.erthminerals.com
  920-819-8228
- Mineral Concepts Face & Lip Blush
  www.mineralconcepts.com
  951-791-1764
- Premium Minerals Finishing Blush
  www.premiumminerals.com
- Rejuva Minerals Blush
  www.rejuvaminerals.com
- Sappho Cosmetics Solace Mineral Pressed Shader
  www.sapphocosmetics.com
  604-985-8881
- Smashbox O-Glow Intuitive Cheek Color
  www.smashbox.com
  888 763 1361
- Tea Maria Tango Glo
  www.teamaria.com
  406-431-5607

Eye Shadow

The glitter in eye shadows is often created by finely ground particles of aluminum or bronze. You want to avoid those neurotoxins. The same mix of hazardous ingredients found in so many other cosmetics appears in eye shadows, too. Think about what you are exposed to when your face is fully made up.

Hazardous Ingredients and Contaminants: coal-tar dyes, talc, silica, mineral oil, lanolin, particles of aluminum or bronze, lead, cobalt, nickel, chromium, arsenic, BHA, and parabens

- Coastal Classic Creations Eye Shadow/Liner
  www.coastalclassiccreations.com
- Colorescience White Haute, Ice Collection
  www.colorescience.com
  877-754-6222
- Rejuva Minerals Eye Shadow
  www.rejuvaminerals.com

Eyeliner

Eyeliners are made of thickeners like wax and PVPs that form film. The synthetic colors are absorbed into the body through your thin eyelids.

Hazardous Ingredients and Contaminants: PVP, aluminum and bronze powders, coal-tar colors, propylene glycol, parabens, and BHA

- Alima Pure Satin Matte Eyeliner
  www.alimapure.com
  888-380-5420
- Honey Bee Gardens Jojoba Eyeliner Pencil
  www.honeybeegardens.com
- Larenim Odyssey Eyeliner
  www.larenim.com
- Rejuva Minerals Eyeliner Pencils and Crayons
  www.rejuvaminerals.com

Mascara

Mascara is made of waxes that thicken eyelashes as well as color and polymers like PVP that keep the mascara on your eyelashes. Water-resistant mascaras usually contain volatile solvents.

Hazardous Ingredients and Contaminants: petroleum distillates, BHA, phenoxyethanol, propylene glycol, PVP, TEA, and parabens

- Afterglow Cosmetics Pure Soul Mascara
  www.afterglowcosmetics.com
  866-630-4589
- Cleure Mineral Mascara
  www.cleure.com
  888-883-4276
- Coastal Classic Creation Mascara
  www.coastalclassiccreations.com
- Maia's Mineral Galaxy Luxurious Mascara
  www.maiasminerals.com
  877-200-5229
- Rejuva Minerals Lengthening and Thickening Mineral Mascara
  www.rejuvaminerals.com
- Suncoat Products Natural Mascara
  www.suncoatproducts.com
  519-763-9800

Nail Polish

Nail products are among the most toxic products on the market. The Environmental Working Group has named the most harmful ingredients—toluene, formaldehyde, and phthalate—the "toxic trio." Some brands are composed of up to 50 percent toluene. Toluene is a neurotoxin that can raise the risk of birth defects and delayed development. DBP, the particular phthalate used in nail polish, mimics estrogen and can disrupt thyroid function. Animal studies have found that DBP may cause birth deformities like cleft palate.

Hazardous Ingredients and Contaminants: toluene, formaldehyde, phthalate, ethyl acetate, benzophenone-1, triphenyl phosphate, and coal-tar dyes

- Acquarella Nail Polish
  www.acquarellapolish.com
- Avon Nail Experts Nail Enamel Remover Wipes
- Keeki Pure and Simple
  www.keekipureandsimple.com
  866-512-7713
- L'Oreal Pro Nail Polish Top Coat
- Sally Hansen Quick Care Clean-up for Manicures
- Wet 'N Wild Shine Nail Color, No Chip Top Coat

Nail Polish Remover

Hazardous Ingredients and Contaminants: acetone

- Acquarella Remover
  www.acquarellapolish.com
- Cutex Manicure Correction Nail Polish Remover Pen, Non-Acetone

Pets

Shampoo and Flea Collars

Flea collars, flea and tick shampoo, and spot-on pesticides emit a toxic cloud that your dog or cat inhales, and so do you. A recent preliminary study in California discovered a link between pyrenthrin, a pesticide used in pet shampoo and collars, and autism. Mothers of more than five hundred young children participated in the study. They listed products they used from a few months before conception until their baby turned one. Mothers of the 138 children with autism were twice as likely to report using pet shampoos and other household products containing pyrenthrins than other mothers. It is easy enough to avoid using pet products that contain pyrenthrin. Do not risk exposure to this dangerous toxin. There are many natural products available. Check out the following for safer pet products:

- www.onlynaturalpet.com
  888-937-6677
- www.spadiggitydog.com
  866-460-4192
- www.botanicaldog.com
  843-864-9368

Now you truly are a natural beauty. As you get closer to the big day, you will enjoy creating the space where your newborn will live and buying what you need to take care of that new member of your family. Chapter 13, "Planning a Nursery That Is a Healthy Nest," offers guidance on creating that space.

13

Planning a Nursery That Is a Healthy Nest

As your due date approaches, you will be preparing your home to receive your baby. Create a space for your baby that is as toxin-free as possible, whether it is a cradle in your room or a separate nursery. You will be buying or receiving a layette and baby care products. It should come as no surprise that many of those products contain the same toxins found in adult products. Do not rub harmful chemicals into your baby's skin or shampoo his hair with toxins. Since you will be buying and receiving many new things for your baby, you have the opportunity to start fresh. You can also screen hand-me-downs to keep toxins out of the nursery.

Fourteen Hours a Day on a Mattress

One of the most important choices you can make for the health of your child is how you furnish your baby's sleeping environment. My strong recommendation is safe co-sleeping: mom, dad, and baby in the family bed with all the recommended safety precautions, especially no extra pillows or other bedding that could obstruct your baby's breathing. Since many families still buy a crib and a baby mattress, much of the advice in this chapter is for those of you who choose to keep your newborn in a crib in your bedroom. Do *not* put your baby in a separate sleeping room during the first year of life. This is an unsafe sleeping practice.

Your newborn will spend ten to fourteen hours a day sleeping. Every breath your baby takes in his crib is just inches away from dangerous chemicals found in conventional mattresses and bed linens. Polyurethane foam is used to fill baby mattresses, changing pads, nursing pillows, and rockers or gliders. In the past, wool and cotton were used as filler, but polyurethane foam is less expensive. Polyurethane is essentially "foamified" petroleum. Since polyurethane is very flammable, it is treated with fire-retardant chemicals like PBDE. Polyurethane foam disintegrates over time, breaking down into small, easily airborne particles that release volatile organic chemicals (VOCs). The neurotoxin toluene can outgas from mattresses and other products. You do not want your baby sleeping on a toxic mixture like that hour after hour.

Polyurethane foam and PBDEs are just the beginning. Vinyl PVC is used to cover baby mattresses and changing pads to make them waterproof. As you know, vinyl PVC is one of the most toxic plastics in use today. Vinyl contains phthalates and various biocides that are released over time. Awareness of the dangers of phthalates is causing some change, but the chemicals used to replace phthalates remain untested. Lead and cadmium, which are dangerous heavy metals, are used to stabilize some vinyl products.

Vinyl is often used for soft plastic toys like baby books and teething, bath, and stuffed toys. Since babies immediately put toys into their mouths, you should pay attention to what is used to make those playthings.

Cribs and Other Furniture

The most important item of nursery furniture is obviously your baby's crib or the mattress in your bed if you are co-sleeping. She will spend eighteen hours a day there for her first few months, and it will be her headquarters even when she goes off exploring her new world. She will lie in it, sit in it, feel it, taste it, and breathe it in.

The worst choices for cribs are the most common: conventional wood, plywood, particle board, and plastic. They all can be made of chemicals that will increase the toxic load on your baby:

- Commercially produced wooden furniture is often treated with pesticides and coated with toxic finishes like polyurethane or paints with VOCs.
- A padded or upholstered crib will have toxic chemicals in the upholstery, from formaldehyde to flame-retardant PDBEs. If vinyl has been used as an upholstery cover, then lead and phthalates will also be a factor.
- Pressed wood and similar substances—like fiberboard, plywood, and particle board—outgas chemicals, including formaldehyde. Urea-formaldehyde is used as an adhesive to bind the wood together.
- Plastic cribs may contain Bisphenol A, phthalates, or polyvinyl chloride, among other chemicals.

Your best choice is a hardwood crib that is certified organic and nontoxic. Some experts suggest a used hardwood crib, as there will be no chance of outgassing from its original manufacture. (Make sure a used crib meets current safety standards.)

Follow these criteria when selecting the rest of your nursery furniture. If you are furnishing a full nursery, you will want to have a rocker or glider chair, a dresser, and a changing table. Some baby

A Word about Wood

Not all woods—even when untreated—are equally safe choices for your child's crib. Some wood species can cause allergies, sensitivities, and blood poisoning if splinters enter the body. Woods like cherry, fir, and bald cypress are not known to induce allergies or sensitivities. Woods like rosewood, satinwood, and teak have very high incidence rates of allergic reactions, sometimes extreme, and should be avoided. You can find lists of wood species and their risk levels on woodworking websites. Check the following:

www.wood-database.com

dressers come with the changing table on top. The rocker or glider is particularly useful—the gentle motion will soothe your baby to sleep and calm him when he nurses.

Finding hardwood furniture that is guaranteed nontoxic is not always easy, because dealers and websites may not mention all the chemicals—especially stains and finishes—that have gone into making a piece. Many environmentally conscious furniture makers are more concerned about ecologically sound wood sourcing than they are about toxic chemicals. This means that you might have to do a little extra research. Be prepared to settle for furniture that's a good nontoxic choice, not a perfect one.

When you find an eco-friendly furniture dealer, contact the company directly and ask about the kinds of finishes, dyes, and stains they use, and on which pieces. It's important to be specific because a company that uses a nontoxic water-based finish on one piece may use a conventional finish on another. Many pieces may be made primarily of solid woods, but may have some particle-board components. Consider talking to carpenters and cabinetmakers in your area and asking for their assistance—or even commissioning a piece, if you can afford to.

The following list includes furniture companies that are good starting places:

- Baby Eco Trends offers handmade Amish cribs, rockers, rocking horses, and other furniture handmade of solid hardwoods, with an emphasis on nontoxic craftsmanship and extensive environmental information on each piece.
  www.babyecotrends.com
  305-527-8734
- Erik Organic
  www.erikorganic.com
  888-900-5235
- Green Cradle Organic
  www.greencradle.com
  818-728-4305
- Organic Grace—an online retailer of organic and nontoxic furniture and home furnishings
  www.organicgrace.com
  707-923-1296
- Spot On Square—all furniture is free of formaldehyde and VOCs
  www.spotonsquare.com
  800-308-0046

Bedding and Layettes

The Mattress

The crib's mattress is as important as the crib itself. Conventional mattresses are often saturated with toxic chemicals, from polyurethane foam to PDBE flame retardant to PVC vinyl coverings. In fact, as of July 1, 2007, the Consumer Products Safety Commission required that all mattresses be flame-retardant. If you want your child's mattress to be free of fire retardants, you have four choices:

1. Get a doctor's prescription for a chemical-free mattress.

2. Use Naturepedic's organic fire-resistant mattresses, which do *not* require a prescription.
3. Get an organic mattress stuffed with wool, which is a natural fire retardant.

The waterproof layer of these mattresses will be the one area of concern. It will probably not be naturally made, but a nontoxic polyethylene layer is acceptable. Avoid wool, even organic wool, because it is a potential allergen for your child.

Crib Linens and Cushions

Sheets, linens, receiving blankets, and comforters should be made of natural fabrics without chemical dyes, enhancements, or fabric treatments. Do not use crib bumpers, even nontoxic ones, since they present a suffocation hazard.

Cushions for the rocking chair and changing table should be certified organic cotton, grown without fertilizers or pesticides. In addition to being nontoxic, this cotton is also hypoallergenic.

It is especially important that your baby's layette, from onesies to diapers, be made of organic, nontoxic cotton. Not even organic wool is a good choice, because wool can be an allergen. Cover plastic car seats, baby seats, and swings with a towel, a cloth diaper, or a blanket. There should always be a layer between your baby and plastic.

Pajamas are a special concern. In fact, they can be the toxic land mine of your baby's layette. U.S. law requires child garments designated "pajamas" or "sleepwear" to be treated with neurotoxic flame retardants, just like mattresses. There are two loopholes. If the sleepwear has been certified "tight-fitting" by the Consumer Products Safety Commission, it does not have to be treated with fire retardants. The reasoning is that tight-fitting clothes are less likely to catch fire. Sleepwear made to fit children younger than nine months old is not treated with flame retardants. Strangely, the safest sleepwear for your baby is usually labeled "not to be used for sleepwear." I am assuming you are bringing your baby into a nonsmoking household.

You will be receiving many gifts for your newborn. You might even be given a baby shower. Try to make your preferences known and tell family and friends that green gifts would be appreciated. You can register on eco-friendly baby sites. Organic baby clothes and paraphernalia are available just about everywhere these days. Some of my patients put a line on the shower invitation or birth announcement that says, "We are raising a green baby" or "Green goodies appreciated."

If you are concerned about chemical residue from detergents or cleansers used in the production process for your baby's new clothing or bed linens, wash the items several times with a gentle, nontoxic detergent, or soak them overnight in a tub of water with one-half to one cup of vinegar.

Nontoxic baby mattresses, bedding, and layette sets are now relatively easy to find. Here are a few good sources:

- Cotton Monkey—nontoxic baby bedding
  www.cottonmonkey.com
  214-367-0719
- Eco Baby/Pure Rest Organic Crib Mattress—wool-filled cotton mattress made without flame retardants or VOCs
  www.purerest.com
  800-596-7450
- Healthy Home Magazine—online directory of organic children's clothing and furnishings
  http://healthyhomemagazine.com/green-kids-biz-directory
- Kate Quinn Organics—nontoxic baby blankets, sheets, and quilts
  www.katequinnorganics.com
  425-284-1275
- Naturepedic—certified nontoxic, organic mattresses and bedding
  www.naturepedic.com
  800-917-3342

- Organic Grace Cotton/Wool Innerspring Baby Mattress—nontoxic mattress made without flame retardants because of its wool filling
  http://organicgrace.com/node/85
  707-923-1296
- Under the Nile Organic Cotton Bedding
  www.underthenile.com
  800-710-1264

Toxic Playroom

Not long ago, I made a house call to a terrific family who lived on a famous drive in Los Angeles. They were expecting their second child in eight weeks. To prepare for their expanding family, they built a magnificent playroom—about six hundred square feet. They were very proud of it and wanted to show it to me.

They had spared no expense. I looked around the brightly colored room, taking it all in. My heart fell. The floor was covered with wall-to-wall foam-rubber mats. There was a plastic jungle gym and plastic toys on shelving everywhere. Freshly painted murals covered the walls.

It was an uncomfortable moment. They had been so careful to avoid toxins before and during the pregnancy. This was a real blind spot. Their decorator was not aware of the dangers of the materials she had chosen. They had not thought to question the professional. Their newborn baby and young son would be playing in an extremely toxic environment. I said the room was a knockout, but explained how much all the new materials would outgas. I suggested they keep the windows open and start to use exhaust fans immediately. I recommended that the windows stay open when the children played. In time, they could replace the flooring and the toys.

Wall Coverings

The "Grandfather Lead" Problem

Before 1978, indoor paints used lead as both a pigment and an additive. Lead paint has since been banned, but any home built before 1978 may still have it. If your nursery has lead paint, find a contractor who has a license to remove the paint and get it out as far in advance of your pregnancy as possible—months, if you can. Once the contractor has finished, thoroughly clean your home to remove any last trace of lead-bearing dust. If your house's exterior was sanded and repainted, the soil next to the house must be tested for lead contamination.

Painting Your Walls

When painting your nursery, avoid conventional paints. They emit VOCs. Even after that new-paint smell has dissipated, toxins remain. Instead, choose one of the following:

- **Non-VOC paint.** As you remember, volatile organic compounds are toxin.
- **Natural paints.** These are water-based paints, with colors derived from chalk, citrus, clay, and other sources. They're very low in VOCs, do not outgas, and are almost odorless, even when new.
- **Milk-based paints.** These are formed with milk proteins. Like natural paints, they're very low in VOCs and almost odorless. They are sold in powder form.

If you decide to use low-VOC/no-VOC paint, make sure that it conforms to the standards of California's South Coast Air Quality

Management District, which are some of the strictest in the nation. Also, beware of a "low-VOC/no-VOC" paint that uses a standard colorant. In short, if a paint gets its color from a conventional pigment, it's no longer a low-VOC paint.

Whether you choose natural, milk-based, low-VOC, or no-VOC, the paint industry is flourishing, and your options are increasing monthly. Here are some companies to check:

- Anna Sova—natural paints from milk casein, titanium dioxide, and food-grade ingredients
  www.annasova.com
  214-742-7682
- Auro—solvent-free, water-based natural paints and primers, finishes, stains, and adhesives. Ships to the United States and Canada.
  www.aurousa.com
- EcoDesign's BioShield—line of natural paints and finishes
  www.bioshieldpaint.com
  505-438-3440
- Green Planet Paints—high-performance natural paints for interiors based on ingredients from plants and minerals
  www.greenplanetpaints.com
  866-795-4442
- Livos—organic paints, stains, oils and waxes; all natural ingredients. Coatings are based on linseed oil and citrus oil and are nontoxic, low-VOC, and designed primarily for wood.
  www.livos.us
- Masters Blend—natural wood finishes using tungnut oil for wood, furniture, carvings, cutting boards, brick, and concrete
  www.mastersblendfinish.com
  860-651-5531
- The Real Milk Paint Company—nontoxic paints made with milk protein, lime, clay, and earth pigments
  www.realmilkpaint.com
  800-339-9748

- Silacote—paints made from natural mineral compounds for use on masonry, concrete, and wallboard; interior/exterior
  www.silacote.com
  800-766-3157
- Unearthed Paints—nontoxic, vegan, natural paints (including clay paint and lime paint), lime plasters, and wood finishes that are 100 percent zero-VOC. Made in Germany with fully disclosed ingredients.
  www.unearthedpaints.com
- Weather-Bos—line of natural stains, finishes, and paints. Blends of natural oils and resins designed to adhere to wood, forming a monolithic bond.
  www.weatherbos.com
  800-664-3978

Here are some companies to check for more conventional low-VOC/no-VOC paint choices:

- C2 LoVo—high-end, low-VOC paint with a beautiful finish
- The FreshAire Choice from Home Depot—100 percent VOC-free
- Mythic Paint—VOC-free
- Natura by Benjamin Moore—VOC-free

Other Wall Coverings

Natural wall coverings are a much better choice than conventional paper and paste. Conventional wallpapers are often made with vinyl and have inks full of heavy metals. You are much better off with organic alternatives like bamboo, organic cotton, rice paper, flax, cork, and raffia, or at least papers that are guaranteed free of vinyls, VOCs, and heavy metals. You can find them from brands like the following:

- ECO (environmentally conscious options)—cork wall tiles
  http://ecolivingspace.com
  218-626-1118

- Innovations Innvironments—vinyl-free, nontoxic wall coverings
  http://www.innovationsusa.com
  800-227-8053
- Phillip Jeffries—natural-fiber wall coverings
  http://phillipjeffries.com
  973-575-5414

What about the wallpaper paste? Isn't that full of toxins? Yes, if you buy conventional paste. You can use nontoxic paste from brands like Earthborn—but you can also make your own nontoxic wall adhesive from the following recipe.

Nontoxic Wallpaper Adhesive

Makes 1 cup

1 cup flour, wheat, corn, or rice
3 teaspoons alum
10 drops oil of clove oil, a natural preservative

1. Combine the flour and alum in a double boiler. (If you don't have a double boiler, set a smaller pan inside a bigger one that contains enough water that can be brought to a boil without overflowing.)
2. Add enough water to make the consistency of heavy cream.
3. Stir until blended.
4. Heat, stirring constantly, until the mixture has thickened to a gravy texture.
5. Let cool.
6. Stir in the clove oil.
7. Pour into a glass jar with a screw top.
8. Apply with a glue brush.

Shelf life: 2 weeks if refrigerated

Floors

As she gets older, your baby will spend most of her awake time either in your arms or on the nursery floor. She will play on the floor, sleep on it, crawl on it, sit on it, and stand on it. Her skin will be exposed to it for hours at a time. So it is vital that the flooring you choose be safe, clean, and nontoxic.

Many conventional flooring possibilities are very bad choices for a nursery and should be avoided at all costs. Avoid the following:

- **Conventional wall-to-wall carpeting.** Carpeting releases styrene, acetone, ethyl benzene, formaldehyde, and toluene into the air while it is new. When it is old, it can be a breeding ground for mold and fungus.
- **Conventional polyurethane floor finishes.**
- **Vinyl.** Today, most of the floor coverings we call "linoleum" are actually vinyl—polyvinyl chloride (PVC). It is bright, uncrackable, and easy to clean. It is also a source of phthalates and lead. Do not use vinyl flooring in the nursery. Natural linoleum, though, is an acceptable choice.

Fortunately, there is an ever-widening array of safer, more organic floor choices. Most of them involve a hardwood floor covered by smaller rugs that can be washed individually:

- **Hardwood flooring with a nontoxic finish and an FSC certification.** Instead of the standard polyurethane finish, a nontoxic finish uses drying oil, hard wax oil, or water-based polyurethane. The Forest Certification Council (FCC) polices participating lumber organizations to make sure they follow sustainable practices. One of those practices is making sure the wood is free of pesticides.
- **Cork.** These floors are made of recycled wine corks. They do not release toxic chemicals into the air, and they are soft and comfortable. They also muffle sound, making the nursery quieter, and come in a wide variety of colors. It is neces-

sary to make sure that formaldehyde wasn't used as a binder and to use a nontoxic adhesive to secure the tiles. The downside: cork tiles are vulnerable to damage from sunlight, water, and heavy loads.

- **Bamboo** is durable and attractive. You can find bamboo that is free of formaldehyde, but beware of low-quality bamboo that may not meet E1 standards for low formaldehyde emission. Lay down the unfinished bamboo flooring and finish it with a low-VOC/no-VOC, water-based, polyurethane finish.
- **Natural linoleum** is much different from the vinyl flooring covering that is often called "linoleum." True linoleum is made from linseed oil, pine resin, sawdust, and cork dust. It emits very little VOC. There is a strong smell when the linoleum is first laid down, but that dissipates within a few months, however, and is nontoxic.

Area rugs are an important complement to a hard nursery floor. They soften the ground for the baby, provide warmth, and help muffle noise. Choose nontoxic, natural-fiber rugs that are small enough to be easily cleaned, preferably washable, and tack them down to prevent slips.

Carpet is not the best choice for nursery flooring. If carpet is necessary—whether for warmth, price, softness, or other reasons—there are ways to reduce the toxic risk:

- Use carpet made of natural fibers like wool, coir, sisal, jute, or hemp.
- Make sure there are no petroleum-based adhesives in the backing.
- Tack the carpet down, instead of gluing it. If you must glue, use a nontoxic glue.

Even organic carpets and natural-fiber throw rugs collect dirt, germs, mold, fungus, and allergens. Vacuum regularly, every day if possible, to reduce this risk, and shampoo with a safe product frequently. Choose a vacuum with a HEPA filter.

Check US Floors, online at www.usfloorsllc.com or by calling 800-404-2675, to get you started in your search for "green" flooring. This company manufactures bamboo, cork, and other sustainable floorings.

Window Treatments

One of the particular dangers of window treatments is that they are exposed to a great deal of sunlight. Over time, this causes synthetic materials to break down and release toxic chemicals. Avoid synthetic window treatments of all types. Stay away from permanent press window treatments or those that must be dry-cleaned, as these emit formaldehyde.

The best choice for window treatments is flat shades made from untreated fabric like organic cotton, linen, or hemp. Keep them as easy to clean as possible.

Baby Supplies

Buying a crib and painting the nursery aren't enough. Your baby needs supplies as well. To start with, avoid baby cleaners with fragrances or the following chemicals:

- DMDM hydantoin
- Ceteareth
- PEG compounds
- Triclosan
- Triethanolamine
- Oxybenzone
- BHA
- Boric acid
- Bronopol (2-bromo-2-nitropropane-1,3-diol)
- Sodium borate

There are also petroleum-based products like Vaseline and mineral oil that should never be used on a child. There are good organic substitutes for all of these ingredients.

Soap

Use a gentle, mild soap: a plain bar soap without scents or dyes. Antibacterials are usually unnecessary. Many rely on chemicals like triclosan, which has been shown to be a hormone disruptor. Antibacterial soaps can also burn a baby's delicate skin. Instead, consider mild organic soaps like the following:

- Aubrey Organics Natural Baby and Kids Bath Soap
  www.aubreyorganics.com
  800-282-7394
- Dr. Bronner's Mild Aloe Vera Baby Soap
- Weleda Calendula Baby Soap
  http://usa.weleda.com
  800-241-1030

Shampoos, like soaps, often contain unnecessary chemicals. Some better-than-average choices are:

- Burt's Bees Rosemary Mint Shampoo Bar
- California Baby Shampoo & Bodywash Super Sensitive
  www.californiababy.com
  877-576-2825 x207
- Tom's Honeysuckle Baby Shampoo

Baby Wipes

Avoid wipes with fragrance, Bronopol, or DMDM hydantoin. The best wipe at home is simply a cotton washcloth and mild, plain soap. For short trips, put cotton washcloths moistened with water and a gentle, nontoxic liquid soap into a container. Bring a second container for the soiled cloths. If these aren't sufficient, try:

- Honest Wipes
  www.honest.com
  888-862-8816
- Huggies Natural Care Baby Wipes
- Seventh Generation Baby Wipes

Baby Powder

Do not use baby powder. Babies tend to breathe in the powder, which damages their lungs. If necessary to soothe your child's skin, use rice starch, cornstarch, or arrowroot powder instead.

Diapers

Do not use plastic diapers. It may seem like a nuisance, but cloth diapers are a better option, and over time they are less expensive. Plastic diapers contain dyes, dioxins, and VOCs like toluene, xylene, and ethylbenzene. The chlorine-bleached fibers and super-absorbency gels are in contact with your baby's skin twenty-four hours a day. You can find washable, natural-cloth diapers from the following companies.

- Absolutely Diapers
  www.hipbaby.com
  877-836-8020
- www.ecobabyorganics.com
  800-596-7450
- www.mylilmiracle.com
  888-825-4326
- www.royaldiaperer.com
  866-460-8181

If you are traveling, disposables are an option. Readily accessible brands are:

- Honest Diapers
  www.honest.com
  888-862-8818
- Nature Babycare
- Seventh Generation
- Tushies

Lotion and Moisturizer

Avoid strong chemicals and soaps that could dry out your baby's skin. Consider using California Baby Botanical Moisturizing Cream.

Diaper Ointment

Avoid chemicals like boric acid and BHA. Instead, try:

- Baby Bee Diaper Ointment
- Balmex Extra Protective Clear Ointment
- Triple Paste Medicated Ointment for Diaper Rash

Pacifiers/Soothers

These are generally made of rubber or plastic, which shouldn't be in your baby's mouth. If you use a pacifier, use one made of silicone, not latex or any other material. You want to avoid possible latex allergies, latex breakdowns, and carcinogen exposure.

Toys

The first place your baby's toys will go is in her mouth. That makes the question of toxicity much more important. Follow these guidelines:

- Make sure that the toys don't contain materials like toxic paints, glues, dyes, or fabrics.
- Stuffed toys can harbor dust mites, molds, and other allergens. Keep them clean.
- The base materials for your children's toys should be the same as for her nursery furniture: organic cloth and stuffing; smooth, nontoxic, nonsplintering hardwoods; easily washable. No plastics.

Fortunately, there are now quite a few lines of nontoxic toys. Check out these websites:

- www.crocodilecreek.com
  919-598-8152
- www.greentoys.com
  415-839-9971
- www.haba.de
- www.holztiger.de
- www.natureplay.com.au
  61 (0)439515474
- www.parentingbynature.com
  866-864-BABY
- www.playstoretoys.com
  877-876-1111
- www.pkolino.com
  888-403-8992

You can let family and friends know that plastic toys are not welcome in your home. Direct them to these websites—there are hundreds online. People are becoming more and more aware of the toxins found in some toys. Responsible manufacturers are doing something about it. Read the labels and packaging carefully on all toys. Toys bearing the label "Made in China" should be avoided or at least carefully inspected. Even wooden toys can have toxic lead paint.

. . .

While you prepare the nursery, make sure that you are not unnecessarily exposed to any toxins. Wear a mask and make sure the nursery is always well-ventilated when you are painting, hanging wall coverings, or sanding. Always shower thoroughly after working in the nursery. When the room is finally ready, open all the windows to ventilate the room and vacuum and mop to remove all traces of dust and chemicals.

Now you are ready for the big day. Your baby's birth is a watershed point in your life. You have prepared the way.

Now you have a newborn baby to take care of.

PART THREE

Protect Your Newborn

14

Feeding Your Newborn

Toxins have entered every stage of the American food chain, as you learned in chapter 9. The average American carries in his body twenty-three of the twenty-five pesticides monitored by the Centers for Disease Control. Dioxins, benzenes, and the rocket fuel perchlorate have been found in tissue samples across the country. Even Teflon has been found in our bodies. Some of these contaminants are airborne; some infiltrate the body on contact. Most enter our bodies through what we eat and drink.

You cannot trust the conventional food supply to safeguard your baby's health. The simple truth is that no giant food corporation will ever care about your child's safety as much as you do. At this point, everyone knows that the standard is breastfeeding. Your breast milk is the best vaccination your newborn can have. Introducing artificial food to babies is an experiment we have been conducting for only fifty or sixty years.

I take a strong stand about mothers making every effort to breastfeed. I am the first male physician to pass the International Board of Lactation Certification Exam, and I have served on the Professional Advisory Board of La Leche League for twenty-five years. Breast-feeding is the single most important thing you can do for your baby.

If you have difficulty breastfeeding, consult with a lactation coach. Your pediatrician will be able to recommend someone to help you. You can contact La Leche League at www.lalecheleague.org to find local support. Make the best effort you can. I promise you it will be worth it. It has been said that one out of twenty women is unable to breastfeed, but I think the number is far smaller than that. For that 5 percent, I recommend using breast milk from a milk bank. The websites for finding donor breast milk in your area appear on page 230. If all else fails, organic formula is available. A list of guidelines for choosing formula appears on page 231. Discuss the options with your pediatrician.

Toxins in Breast Milk

There has recently been concern that toxins may accumulate in breast milk. Toxins gather in your body, become concentrated in your breast milk, and are transferred to your baby in concentrated form. Pesticides, heavy metals, and pollutants are known to accumulate in breast milk. Breastfeeding infants are exposed to a higher concentration of fat-soluble chemicals like PCBs and DDT while nursing than at any other time in their lives. A six-month-old breastfed baby consumes five times the allowable daily levels of PCBs for a 150-pound adult. After six months of nursing, a baby will receive the maximum recommended lifetime supply of dioxin.

Despite these concerns, there is strong evidence that breastfeeding plays a role in reducing the impact of toxic chemicals on a baby. Even when their mothers have levels of PCBs in their bodies that could be damaging to their babies' health, breastfed babies are more resilient and do not show the effects of PCB exposure that formula-fed babies exposed to PCBs do. This is a tradeoff that is well worth the risk.

Breast vs. Bottle

Breast milk, with its ideal combination of proteins, carbohydrates, and fats, was designed by nature to be your baby's starter food. A mother's breast milk contains antibodies that help her baby fight off infections. Breast milk is also full of long-chain fatty acids like DHA and ARA that are vital to proper brain and visual development.

Always choose breastfeeding over formula, and breastfeed your child as long as possible. The World Health Organization recommends exclusive breastfeeding until at least six months and continued breastfeeding until two years or beyond. I believe that there are benefits to breastfeeding beyond two years.

Studies have found that not breastfeeding at all and early weaning are associated with increased rates of autism. A Japanese study compared 145 autistic children with 224 not-autistic or "control" children. They found that the children in the control group breastfed for a significantly longer time than the autistic children. Another study done in 2006 compared 861 children with ASD with 123 control children. The researchers found that not breastfeeding correlated with a 250 percent increase in the odds of having ASD.

Breastfed children develop more quickly and are more likely to have better visual acuity. A British study found that the percentage of infants who mastered developmental milestones increased with duration and exclusivity of breastfeeding.

Breastfeeding is the best way to enhance your baby's immune system. Breast milk protects the gastrointestinal system and protects against food allergies. Babies who are not breastfed are more likely to develop the following problems:

- Allergies
- Sudden infant death syndrome

- Gastrointestinal problems
- Childhood leukemia
- Type 1 diabetes
- Necrotizing enterocolitis, a condition often seen in premature babies that involves death of intestinal tissue
- Obesity
- Ear, respiratory, and urinary tract infections

There are great benefits for you, too. Breastfeeding helps to strengthen the bond between you and your baby. It helps your body return to its prepregnancy weight. Breastfeeding has been found to reduce levels of certain carcinogenic hormones and cells with damaged DNA. Breastfeeding stimulates the production of oxytocin and endorphins in your brain that promote a positive frame of mind. You have a built-in mechanism that kicks into gear when you breastfeed to combat stress and postpartum depression. Breast milk is ideal for your baby and for you. Nourishing your baby is a natural part of your life cycle. Your body was designed for this. In chapter 9 I discuss what foods to eat and what foods to avoid during your pregnancy. When you are breastfeeding, those rules are even more important for your baby's health.

Breastfeeding increases the nutritional power of what your baby consumes. Even without additives and toxins, the more food is processed—boiled, steamed, flash-frozen, chopped—the lower its nutritional value. If you obtain healthy organic meats and produce, and clean and puree them yourself for your baby when the time comes to introduce solid food, you will have reduced the amount of processing, reduced the toxic exposure, and increased the nutritional power.

Formula, Water, and Animal Milk

Sometimes an urgent situation may arise when you may not have enough breast milk for your child or be with your child to breastfeed when she is hungry. Plan ahead for this by storing your own milk or by finding donor breast milk. You can find a milk bank near you by checking www.milkbanking.net. If you have surplus milk, you can become a donor at that same website or at www.helping handsbank.com. Formula, water, and animal milk are not adequate substitutes for breast milk. None of them, including formula, have all the nutrients your baby needs.

Many baby formulas are loaded with toxic chemicals that enter the formula during the manufacturing process. They can leach into the formula from metal, from the plastic lining of cans, and from plastic containers. BPA is no longer used to line most cans and definitely not formula cans in the United States.

If you feed your baby formula, follow these guidelines:

- Use powdered, not liquid, formula. Liquid formula is likely to have absorbed BPA or other contaminants from the plastic and metal of its container.
- Use an organic formula that does not use brown rice syrup as a sweetener.
- Make sure the formula contains the long-chain fatty acids DHA and ARA.
- Use filtered tap water to reconstitute the formula.
- Make sure the utensils, bottles, and containers you use are nontoxic. That means no polycarbonate plastic, latex, or PVC.

Bottles

For years, BPA was used to make polycarbonate baby bottles. The plastic bottles were hard, lightweight, and translucent. BPA does not belong in baby bottles. Period. BPA is a potent hormone disruptor that interferes with growth and development.

Plastics containing BPA can release the chemical if exposed to heat from a dishwasher, for example, or acids from fruit juices. The older the bottles are, the more BPA is leached into what liquids they hold. You should not use any containers with polycarbonates that might have contact with food. Make sure that your bottles are not scratched or damaged. A scratched plastic bottle is more likely to release chemicals into your stored breast milk or formula—especially if you heat the bottle. Major retailers like Walmart and Toys "R" Us have removed polycarbonate bottles from their shelves. Avoid plastic bottles labeled "polycarbonate" or those that have recycling marks "7" or "PC."

Other plastic bottles may contain PVC, which can be very toxic. PVC plastic can contain the neurotoxin lead. Soft PVC—the vinyl used in bottle liners—may contain phthalates. As you remember, phthalates are hormone disruptors.

If you choose to use plastic bottles, stick with polyethylene or polypropylene plastic, the bottles with a "1," "2," or "5" on the bottom. I strongly recommend that you use stainless-steel or tempered-glass bottles.

Tempered glass and stainless steel are not toxic, but they do present some problems. Glass and steel bottles are heavier, harder, and colder than plastic. Metal bottles can scald a child when

Safe Bottles

Even if you are breastfeeding, you may need bottles for stored milk. Baby bottles made from safer materials are now available:

- Medela, Evenflo, and Born Free make bottles and nursers from non-BPA plastics.
- Born Free, Dr. Brown's, and Evenflo make tempered-glass bottles.
- Klean Kanteen, which makes metal water bottles, now makes stainless steel baby bottles.

A word of warning: The first bottles you try might not be the right ones for you and your baby. Feel free to experiment as long as you remain within the safety guidelines.

heated improperly. If you use metal or glass bottles, make sure they are in good shape. Scratches provide a handy incubating space for bacteria. Glass and metal bottles are also more difficult for your baby to hold. Finally, there is the possibility of breakage with a glass bottle. That risk is minimized by using tempered glass.

Use a clear silicone nipple instead of a latex one on the bottle. Latex contains some carcinogens, and it can also trigger an allergic reaction in your child. If you use plastic bottle liners, use ones that are latex-free, BPA-free, and PVC-free.

Breast Pumps and Stored Breast Milk

For convenience and to help establish a regular supply of breast milk, I suggest that you express milk, store it, and feed it to your baby when breastfeeding is not possible. Storing breast milk is essential for nursing mothers who work or travel. And sometimes your partner will want to participate in feeding your baby. You will especially appreciate it for those feedings in the middle of the night.

When it comes to reducing toxins and germs, follow the same rules with breast pumps as you do with bottles. Find models with plastic parts like suction cups and tubing that are free of BPA, PVC, and latex. Make sure that none of the parts are scratched or damaged, and clean them thoroughly.

The Best Breast Pumps

BPA-free breast pumps are no longer hard to find. The three manual or electric pumps that I recommend are FDA-approved and are easy to find:

- Avent
- Closer to Nature
- Medela

Freezing and refrigerating your breast milk will make your life easier. There are guidelines to doing it safely. Since breast milk is so high in fats and nutrients, it can be a powerful growth source for germs and fungi, meaning that it can go bad. *Never refreeze thawed milk.* Once you thaw a batch, use it all or throw away what is left. Don't refrigerate breast milk for more than twenty-four hours. If your baby has not consumed it during that time, dispose of the breast milk. If you keep milk in the refrigerator, do not store it in the door shelf, because that is a warmer area. Instead, store the milk on a lower shelf in the back of the refrigerator, where it will stay cooler. Treat your breast milk like a dairy product that could spoil.

Bottle Guidelines

- Always wash your hands before you breastfeed or make your baby's bottle.
- Scrub your glass bottles really well by hand and wash them in the top rack of your dishwasher. If you are hand-washing, use hot water with nontoxic dishwashing detergent, and rinse with hot water. I suggest boiling glass or steel bottles in water for five to ten minutes or using a sterilizer.
- If you use plastic bottles, wash them by hand only in hot soapy water. Do not put plastic bottles in the dishwasher, even if they are labeled "dishwasher safe." Plastics can leach chemicals in dishwasher temperatures. Avoid putting any plastic product in a dishwasher, a bottle sterilizer, or a microwave.
- Never heat milk or formula in a microwave.
- Do not leave your baby unattended with a glass bottle. Babies can throw bottles and break them.

Graduating to Solid Foods

At about six months, your baby will be ready to move gradually from breast milk to more solid foods. She should be consuming breast milk for at least the first year if not longer. I prefer six months, but some pediatricians say four to six months.

Your baby will still need your breast milk, but you can now gradually introduce solid food. Consult with your pediatrician about this change in your baby's diet. The key word is *gradual*. A good way to start is with one or two teaspoons of pureed fruit and vegetables mixed with breast milk. I recommend a whole month of gentle organic fruits and vegetables: pureed squash, applesauce, peaches, pears, sweet potatoes. I would avoid citrusy, rashy, allergenic foods like strawberries and tomatoes. Be alert for an allergic reaction in the form of fussiness, rashes, vomiting, or diarrhea. Watch how your baby's digestion adjusts to eating small quantities. Parents always ask me about whether broccoli or cauliflower will make their baby gassy. I tell them, "Babies are always gassy."

After your baby has adjusted to a variety of fruits and vegetables, introduce organic oatmeal or quinoa cereals. I advise keeping the cereal gluten-free. Using breast milk in the cereal is best, but in a pinch you can use almond milk or oat milk. Avoid rice milk. Rice milk has been found to have excessive levels of arsenic. This contamination will be a hot topic for a couple of years. No need to sweeten the cereal, but adding one blueberry also might appeal to your baby. A slice of banana mashed up well might be good for a change.

Between seven and ten months, you can start introducing your baby to soft, organic, nonpureed foods like noncrusty bread, cheese, soft whole-wheat pasta, and diced organic fruits and vegetables cooked soft. I would hold off on the grass-fed organic meat until your baby is a year old. Always watch your baby while he is eating. Do not give your baby small, hard pieces of food like nuts or popcorn that might be choking hazards.

Be a Chef for Your Baby

There are many brands of baby food on supermarket shelves. Some brands are organic. It is important for you to buy your own fruits, vegetables, and meats and to prepare your baby's food yourself. This gives you control of the food you are serving your child. You can be certain that you are serving the freshest, purest food available. You will also reduce the amount of plastic and packaging that commercial baby food can be exposed to during preparation. Making your own baby food will dramatically reduce the potential chemical load of the food.

Becoming your baby's chef enables you to increase his food's nutritional power. Aside from additives and toxins, the more food is processed—boiled, steamed, flash-frozen, and chopped, for example—the lower its nutritional value. If you buy healthy, organic ingredients and clean and puree them yourself, you will reduce the nutrition lost during processing and toxin exposure. Although fresh is best, you can freeze the food you make in ice cube trays and defrost enough for a meal.

In the next section, my wife Meyera has contributed a few recipes for baby food to get you started.

From Meyera's Kitchen

Baby food in jars is expensive. You should have enough vegetables left over from preparing your own meals that you can scoop some off and puree them. There are a variety of small food processors and whips (like a wand or an immersion blender) available at big box stores as well as online. Of course, you do not need a small appliance. You could just mash the vegetables with a fork.

Almost any vegetables and fruits can be softened to suit your baby's tastes. Start out simply, adding organic and naturally sweet products like slices of fruit or cooked yams. Talk to your pediatrician about fruits and vegetables that might not agree with your baby.

None of the recipes included here take more than a few minutes. Once you get the hang of them, you'll find that whatever you are eating or have in the kitchen that can be digested easily will work for your baby.

As far as quantities go, see how much your baby likes. Also, some foods stay fresh in the refrigerator for a few days, like peas and carrots; some discolor, like avocados.

Here are some easy starter purées:

- Purée a sliver of peeled and chopped apple or pear with ½ cup cooked yam in a small processer and puree. The result should be smooth and silky with no lumps or solids.
- Try an avocado with a sliver of peeled and diced pear.
- Cooked peas with cooked carrots are always a hit. Add a sliver of peeled apple for extra sweetness.
- A ¼ cup cauliflower and/or ½ cup spinach with a sliver of peeled and chopped pear is a good combination.
- ½ cup cooked carrots with 2 tablespoons cooked peas and a sliver of peeled and chopped apple works well.
- Purée some banana and peeled apple with a single blueberry.
- Purée peeled pears with a little almond or oat milk, just enough to make it smooth.

There is a wide variety of baby and toddler cookbooks available. I do not agree with everything in these books, but they will give you an idea of how creative you can be in introducing your baby to the wide world of food. Here are a few excellent cookbooks:

- *The Baby and Toddler Cookbook: Fresh, Homemade Foods for a Healthy Start*, by Karen Ansel and Charity Ferreira
- *Top 100 Baby Purées: 100 Quick and Easy Meals for a Healthy and Happy Baby*, by Annabel Karmel
- *The Best Homemade Baby Food on the Planet: Know What Goes into Every Bite with More Than 200 of the Most Deliciously Homemade Baby Food*, by Karin Knight and Tina Ruggiero

- *Cooking for Baby: Wholesome, Homemade, Delicious Foods for 6 to 18 Months*, by Lisa Barnes

An expanded list of terrific cookbooks appears in the Resources.

The Best Ready-made Baby Foods

You may not always be able to prepare your baby's food fresh. The high demand for organic baby food has resulted in a number of very fine products. The brands listed next are a good choice:

- Baby Gourmet was founded by a mother who did not like the taste of grocery store baby food. The recipes come from mothers themselves. The products are all-natural, all-kosher, all-organic, and test-tasted.
  www.babygourmet.com
  780-666-2622
- Ella's Kitchen provides 100 percent organic food with no added sugar, salt, or water. They offer interesting combinations of fruits and vegetables. They have an organic cereal with fruits in one package.
  www.ellaskitchen.com
  800-685-7799
- Happy Baby is known for the variety of foods they make. They offer starting solids, simple combinations, balanced meals, and organic superfoods. Their products are allergy-free and preservative-free.
  www.happybabyfood.com
  212-374-2779
- NurturMe is an all-natural, organic, gluten-free baby food made from quick-dried fruits and vegetables. The quick-drying methods they have developed preserve nutrients and phytochemicals. All you have to do is add breast milk.
  http://nurturme.com
  512-326 4910

- Peter Rabbit Organics offers all-organic fruit and vegetable pouches. 100 percent fruit and vegetables with no added flavor or coloring. They are packaged in BPA-free resealable pouches with a no-choke cap.
  www.peterrabbitorganics.com
  415-867-9545
- Petite Palate offers a line of organic frozen baby food in gourmet flavors. The company packages its products in compostable paper cups.
  www.petitepalate.com
  718-606-8875
- Plum Organics is a great organic baby food company. They have a plum-colored Dispensing Spoon attached to their packaging that makes it easy to feel your baby anytime.
  www.plumorganics.com
  877-914-PLUM

Feeding your baby well from the start will affect his eating habits for life. You will be setting him on a successful course by providing him with all the nutrients he needs to grow and develop—minus the toxins.

Chapter 15, "Your Baby Is Changing Every Day," focuses on the developmental milestones of your baby's first two years of life. Since the early signs of developmental problems involve the absence of a behavior, it is important to know what to expect as your child moves, communicates, and connects to her world.

15

Your Baby Is Changing Every Day

Watching babies grow and relate to the world is a wonderful experience. They seem to learn something new every day. I remain so impressed by how much babies want to do the next thing. They are always trying—to lift their heads, to roll over, to move through space on their hands and knees, to pull themselves up, to take their first steps. The physical effort is remarkable. At the same time, they are also learning to interact with the world and everything in it. Everything is new to them. They form attachments to you and your partner and sometimes to an inanimate object that comforts them. They smile. They taste *everything*. And speech—hearing them babble in imitation of language, react with understanding, and try to express themselves—is amazing. Babies develop in similar ways, but the rate of their development varies from child to child.

If you feel uneasy about your child's development, if something feels "off," trust your instincts. Consult with your pediatrician if you are concerned. No one knows your child as well as you do.

A developmental schedule is a generalization. Few children reach every developmental milestone right on time. Doctors are used to seeing variations. Most development falls in the normal range. That said, your familiarity with your child's growth will be the most important factor in determining whether a particular developmental delay should be addressed.

You are in the best position to catch the earliest warning signs of autism. You know your child better than anyone and can spot behaviors that your pediatrician may not see during a quick office visit. There are many signs and symptoms of autism, and they occur in varying degrees. Problems tend to develop in three main areas:

- Nonverbal and verbal communication
- Relating to others and the surroundings
- Thinking and behaving flexibly

The earliest signs of autism can be tough to spot, because they involve the absence of normal behaviors, not the presence of abnormal ones. Some of the earliest signs of autism can be overlooked or misinterpreted as signs of a "good" baby, one who is quiet and undemanding. You can catch warning signs very early on if you know what to look for. Some autistic infants do not respond to cuddling, do not reach out to be picked up, or do not look at their mothers while being fed.

It is important that you know the cognitive, emotional, and social milestones in order to monitor your baby's development. If ASD is identified in its earliest stages—ideally no later than eighteen months, preferably younger—we have a chance to interrupt the development of ASD and minimize problems. Sometimes overt signs of autism do not appear until twenty months or later. There is no officially recognized psychological test for children under twenty months, but one is being developed and standardized. I believe that well before standard tests begin to measure persistent

Keep a Record

I recommend keeping a careful record of your baby's development. Your pediatrician will make notes at routine check-ups, but you are with your baby every day. Mothers of older children will tell you that as momentous as every milestone is, you stand a good chance of forgetting exactly when that milestone was reached.

The good news is that dozens of infant- and child-themed websites offer ways to monitor your baby's development, from baby journals to online tracking to smartphone apps. The CDC also offers free hardcopy checklists. Take a look at those listed here and choose one that works for you.

- **http://kidmondo.com** This site provides online tracking of your child's growth and development.
- **http://itunes.apple.com/us/app/pregnancy-baby-development/id376210705?mt=8** This site offers a free baby journal app.
- **www.pregnancyguideonline.com** This site offers weekly interactive child-development calendars sponsored by StorkNet.
- **www.babycenter.com** This site offers week-by-week interactive child-development calendars.
- **www.cdc.gov/ncbddd/autism/freematerials.html** You will find a variety of developmental milestone checklists at this website.

Having a complete record of your child's development is a wonderful piece of history. The information is invaluable. I have included a Milestone Tracker in the Appendix that you can copy and take with you to check-ups.

developmental delays, early warning signs can be observed that can lead to earlier evaluation. Parents observing their child and following their own instincts, along with the help of a sympathetic pediatrician, can identify signs of developmental delay as early as six to nine months of age. My job as a pediatrician is to be an expert on the development of a twelve-month-old. You are an expert on *your* twelve-month-old. Observing and evaluating your baby together can help us catch and address early signs of developmental delay.

The younger your baby is, the easier it is to treat developmental delays, because your baby's brain is growing so rapidly during the first two years of life and is still "plastic." Trillions of new neural connections are being made. We are getting better and better at reshaping those connections if there is a problem that is caught early. A child is far from finished developing by the time she is two years old. In fact, brain plasticity continues until about age twenty. The older a child is when ASD is diagnosed, the more difficult it is for some special therapies to work. But age is not everything. I have seen young babies in treatment who remain nonverbal, and as you can see in some of the case histories, I have diagnosed older children who went on to respond very well to ASD therapies. The good news is that the effectiveness of our efforts is improving every day.

The Development Road Map: Milestones and Early Warning Signals, Month by Month

Autism typically first shows up as a detour from the usual developmental path. Certain stage markers, like making eye contact, using complex speech, or communicating emotional empathy, are never reached, or are achieved only to be lost at a later stage.

The developmental calendar that follows lays out the milestones for healthy development and the early warning signals for developmental delays and ASD. Before interpreting possible signs of developmental delays, I usually recommend tests for hearing and vision. Sometimes a lack of responsiveness involves impaired hearing or vision.

Once you understand the calendar, you will be better prepared to know if your baby is on the right developmental path, or if he has taken a wrong turn and needs help. Remember that every child develops at his own rate and that normal development has a broad range. Observe, record, and enjoy your baby's growth. Do not become overly concerned by a slight delay. Your baby is more than likely developing normally. Speak with your pediatrician about what you have noticed so that you can work together to monitor your baby's development.

No one knows your child as well as you do. If you feel that something is wrong, trust your instincts.

Two Months

Your baby's development is just beginning.

- **Social and emotional:** Your baby begins to smile at people. He can briefly calm himself. He tries to look at his parent.
- **Language/communication:** She coos and makes gurgling sounds. She turns her head toward sounds.
- **Cognitive (learning, thinking, problem-solving):** Your baby pays attention to faces. His eyes begin to track, and he recognizes people better at shorter distances. He cries or gets fussy, showing signs of boredom, if there is no new activity.
- **Movement/physical:** She can hold up her head. When lying on her stomach, she will start to push herself up. Her arm and leg movements become smoother.

Four Months

At four months, a healthy baby is starting to interact with people and with his surroundings. He loves to smile. He prefers human beings to objects. He is beginning to babble and to respond to affection.

- **Social and emotional:** Your baby smiles spontaneously, especially at people. She likes to play with people and might cry when play stops. She copies some movements and facial expressions, like smiling or frowning. This is a time when your baby just grabs and holds you with her expression.
- **Language/communication:** He begins to babble with expression and copies sounds he hears. He cries in different ways to show hunger, pain, or tiredness. He communicates happiness and sadness. He responds to affection. He uses one hand to reach for desired objects like a toy.
- **Cognitive (learning, thinking, problem-solving):** She uses her hands and eyes together. For instance, she might see a pretty object and then reach for it. She follows moving things with her eyes from side to side, tracking them. She watches faces closely, and she recognizes familiar people and things at a distance. She shows understanding of what is known as object permanence, knowing that objects exist even when she does not see them. She may look for a dropped toy between four and six months.
- **Movement/physical:** He holds his head steady, unsupported. When his feet are on a hard surface, he pushes down with his legs, which will eventually lead to standing and walking. He may be able to roll over from his belly onto his back. He can hold a toy, shake a toy, and uses one hand to swat at a toy. He brings his hands to his mouth. When lying on his stomach, he can now push up on his elbows.

  The biggest hand-related milestone is not so much grabbing the rattle as wanting to grab the rattle. The umbrella milestone over this whole age period is frustration. Knowing how to reach and grab and sit and crawl, but not being able to. I worry about passive four-month-olds.

Six Months

After half a year, healthy infants have made great strides in social and cognitive development, and some developmental delays are no longer normal. This is when some early warning signals may become obvious.

- **Social and emotional:** Your baby starts to recognize familiar faces and strangers. She likes to play with others, especially her parents. She responds to other people's emotions and often seems happy. She likes to look at herself in a mirror.
- **Language/communication:** Your baby responds to sounds by making sounds. He strings vowels together when babbling, saying "ah," "eh," "oh." He likes taking turns with his parents while making sounds. He makes sounds to show joy and displeasure. He begins to make consonant sounds, jabbering with "m," "b." He recognizes his name and turns more to that word than to others. He begins to recognize a few words spoken along with his name. "Where's Daddy, Bobby?" "Going to take a bath, Bobby."
- **Cognitive (learning, thinking, problem-solving):** Your baby studies things nearby. She brings things to her mouth. She shows curiosity about things and tries to get at things that are out of reach. She begins to move objects from one hand to the other.

Early Warning Signs for Developmental Delays and ASD at Six Months

- Does not smile
- Does not make eye contact
- Does not respond to sounds by making sounds
- Does not "track" objects (follow them with his eyes)
- Does not seem interested in faces

- **Movement/physical:** Your baby can roll over in both directions, front to back and back to front. He begins to sit up without support. When standing, he supports his weight on his legs and might bounce. He rocks back and forth, sometimes crawling backward before moving forward.

Nine Months

A healthy child is now beginning to master fundamentals. She uses the pincer grasp, picking things up or holding them between her thumb and index finger. She is beginning to show her likes and dislikes more clearly. I revel in a nine-month-old who makes strong gestures toward objects.

- **Social and emotional:** Your baby may be afraid of strangers, which is called stranger anxiety, and can cling to Mom when she's around other familiar adults, even Dad! She has favorite toys.
- **Language/communication:** Your baby understands "no," but challenges this idea hundreds of times over, seeming to learn almost nothing when you move her away from the electrical socket or the computer cables. He makes a lot of different sounds, like "mamamama" and "bababababa." He copies the sounds and gestures of others. He uses his fingers or whole hand to point at things, which is known as joint attention.
- **Cognitive (learning, thinking, problem-solving):** Your baby gets better at following the path of an object as it falls. She shows an understanding of what is known as object permanence, knowing that objects exist even when she does not see them. That is what peek-a-boo is all about. She looks for things she sees you hide, and she also plays peek-a-boo. These are both displays of her mastery of object permanence. She puts things in her mouth.
- **Movement/physical:** Your baby can pull himself up to stand and can remain standing while grabbing onto something. He

> **Early Warning Sign for Developmental Delays and ASD at Nine Months**
>
> - Unusual reactions to physical sensations—to the way things sound, smell, feel, taste, and look

can get into a sitting position and sit without support. He picks up things like cereal bits between thumb and index finger—the "pincer grasp." He transfers objects smoothly from one hand to the other. He crawls.

Twelve Months

Your baby is now a toddler, and she should display major social and emotional growth and change. She begins to display joint attention by pointing to objects to show interest. Stranger anxiety may intensify. She may begin to show fear or cry when her parents leave her sight. These developments are all healthy. If she is generally withdrawn and unresponsive, there is a cause for concern. Some children show an attachment to particular objects that are not commonly thought of as transitional ones.

I get more phone calls and questions related to developmental and behavioral behaviors at age one than about any other transition time. Lots of the oppositional and opinionated behavior that parents expect at two actually begins right here.

- **Social and emotional:** He is shy or nervous with strangers. He cries when his mom or dad leaves, and has favorite people and things. He shows fear in some situations. He may hand you a favorite book when he wants you tell him a story. He repeats sounds or actions to get attention. He puts out an arm or leg to help you dress him. He plays object-permanence games like peek-a-boo and patty-cake. He displays joint attention by pointing to objects to show interest.

- **Language/communication:** She responds to simple requests and uses simple gestures—she may shake her head "no" or wave "bye-bye." She makes sounds that have changes in tone, which means they sound more like speech. She says "mama" and "dada" and exclamations like "uh-oh!" She tries to repeat words her parents say.
- **Cognitive (learning, thinking, problem-solving):** He explores objects in different ways, by shaking them, banging them, and throwing them. He finds hidden things easily, showing mastery of object permanence. He connects names with the thing named, looking at the right picture or object when it's named. He copies gestures. He starts to use tools correctly, like drinking from a cup or brushing his hair. He bangs two things together. He puts things in a container and takes them out. He lets go of things without help. He pokes with his index finger. He begins to follow simple directions like "Pick up the toy."
- **Movement/physical:** She sits up without help. She pulls herself up to stand, and cruises, which means walking by holding onto furniture. She may even take a few steps without holding on. She may stand alone.

Early Warning Signs for Developmental Delays and ASD at Twelve Months

- Does not babble or coo
- Does not gesture (point, wave, or grasp)
- Does not respond to his own name
- Does not notice other children or siblings
- Has difficulty with transitions and/or new things
- Displays excessive tantrums or aggressive behaviors
- Displays extreme attachment to particular objects that are not commonly transitional objects

Early Warning Signs for Developmental Delays and ASD at Fourteen Months

- Does not say single words; note that this is a significant sign
- Does not point at objects to show interest, referred to as joint attention

Fourteen to Sixteen Months

At this point, your child should have solidified many of her developmental gains. Single words and joint attention should be part of her repertoire.

Eighteen Months

Your child continues to widen her social, emotional, and cognitive palettes. She will play pretend, throw temper tantrums, play with others, and even walk away from you, often alone.

- **Social and emotional:** Your toddler likes to hand things to others as play. He may have temper tantrums and be afraid of strangers. He should show affection to familiar people. He will play simple pretend games. He may become clingy in new situations. He has mastered pointing. He explores alone but with a parent close by.
- **Language/communication:** She says several single words. She can say "no" and shake her head. She points to show someone what she wants.
- **Cognitive (learning, thinking, problem-solving):** He knows what ordinary objects are for, like telephones, forks, or combs. He shows interest in a doll or a stuffed animal by pretending to feed it. He scribbles on his own. He can follow one-step verbal commands without any gestures. For example, he sits when you say, "Sit down."

Early Warning Signs for Developmental Delays and ASD at Eighteen Months

- Fails to make eye contact as a mode of reading others or responding to another's nonverbal communication
- Displays poor imitative skills
- Displays poor or delayed communication skills
- Does not play pretend games, like feeding a doll

- **Movement/physical:** She walks alone and may run. She can help undress herself. She drinks from a cup and eats with a spoon.

Twenty-four Months

Your child is about to enter the badly misnamed "terrible twos," a time when he begins to assert his independence. I call them the

A Word on Tantrums

Temper tantrums can start at four months and continue into years two and three. Tantrums are an intrinsic part of childhood development, and almost all children have them. Normally, the trigger of a tantrum is obvious—the child does not get what he wants, or maybe he is hungry, scared, tired, or angry. Tantrums will often come as a surprise to children with autism. The outburst may last longer and be more violent. When a child with autism has a tantrum, he may not have the same sense of release or calm attained after he is cried out. I worry at least a little when I see unrelenting tantrums, even though they are often a normal part of a child's development.

"tricky twos," a perfect age to find yourself in exactly the wrong place, a restaurant, for instance, at exactly the wrong time—nap time. Defiance, displays of temper, and outbursts will become more frequent at this age. It is important to separate a two-year-old's sometimes unpleasant, but normal, behavior from the problems that require attention.

- **Social and emotional:** Your toddler copies others, especially adults and older children. He is excited to be with other children. He is more independent. He may display defiant behavior. For example, he may do what he has been told not to. He plays mainly beside other children in parallel play, but is beginning to include other children in his play, in chase games, for example.

Early Warning Signs for Developmental Delays and ASD at Twenty-four Months

- Does not say two-word phrases on his own
- Lacks interest in other children. May not play well with other children but interest is growing.
- Lacks "object permanence," the understanding that objects exist even when they are hidden; peek-a-boo and hide-and-seek are meaningless
- Does not display object-appropriate play
- Has oversensitivity or undersensitivity to sound
- Lacks language comprehension
- Repeats words or phrases over and over, a behavior known as "echolalia"
- Gives unrelated answers to questions
- Has obsessive interests
- Displays hand-flapping, body-rocking, spinning in circles, and other self-stimulatory behaviors called "stimming"

- **Language/communication:** Your toddler points to objects or pictures when they are named. She knows the names of familiar people and body parts. She uses sentences of two to four words. She can follow simple instructions if she chooses to—remember, she is two. She repeats words overheard in conversation. She points to things in a book, displaying an understanding of pictures and words.
- **Cognitive (learning, thinking, problem-solving):** He finds things even when they are hidden under two or three covers. He begins to sort shapes and colors. He completes sentences and rhymes in familiar books. He plays simple make-believe games. He builds towers of four or more blocks. He will usually display right-hand/left-hand preference. He can follow two-step instructions like "Pick up your shorts and put them in the hamper." He names items in a picture book, like "cat," "bird," or "dog."
- **Movement/physical:** She can stand on tiptoe, kick a ball, start to run, climb onto and down from furniture without help, climb and descend stairs, throw a ball overhand, and make or copy circles and straight lines.

Regression, the loss of a skill or developmental milestone—language, coordination, cognitive ability, social skills—is a serious warning signal, a red alert, ay any age.

Communicating with Your Doctor

If you and your pediatrician conclude that your child is experiencing developmental delays and decide to consult with an autism specialist, you should prepare beforehand to make your visit to the specialist productive. You should be ready to provide detailed, organized information about your child. The Milestone Tracker in the Appendix is an easy and convenient way to keep a written record. Just copy the pages and take them with you.

The Autism Triad

We often speak of the "autism triad," three types of symptoms characteristic of autism: impaired communication, impaired social interaction, and repetitive behavior/restricted interests. The first two are deficits, areas in which the child lags. The last are observed behaviors. These signs of autism become significant only when they are recognized in context and at the appropriate stage of a child's development. Grouping classic signs together makes them easier to recognize, and easier to discuss with doctors.

Social Deficits

- Failing to recognize/respond to his name
- Resisting being held or cuddled
- Appearing not to hear you at times
- Lacking the ability to communicate empathy—seems unaware of others' feelings
- Failure to make strong eye contact as a mode of reading or responding to another's nonverbal communication
- Seeming to prefer playing alone—retreating into a private world

Language Deficits

- Losing a prior ability to say words or sentences
- Inability to start or maintain a conversation
- Inability to talk by age twenty-four months
- Repetition of words/phrases without knowing how to use them
- Exhibiting echolalia; may use a sing-song voice or robotlike speech

Behavior

- Engaging in stimming movements like rocking, spinning, or hand-flapping
- Moving constantly
- Becoming disturbed at the slightest change in routines or rituals
- Development of very specific routines or rituals, including the well-known "stacking" behavior
- Becoming fascinated by parts of an object, like spinning wheels on a toy
- Displaying unusual sensitivity to light, sound, or touch
- Seeming oblivious to pain
- Having difficulty sharing experiences with others
- When read to, unlikely to point at pictures in the book (an early-developing skill that is vital to later language and social development)

Even if you alone are worried about your child's development, that is good enough for me. I urge you to get a fuller evaluation and not to be dissuaded by your doctor or anyone else.

Here are some more ways to prepare for your meeting with the autism specialist:

1. Make a baby journal of your child's developmental milestones. Take it with you to the doctor's office.
2. Write down all the changes you see in your child's behavior and abilities.
3. List all the medications and vitamins your child takes, to eliminate possible side effects and drug interactions.
4. Video any unusual behaviors or movements your child displays.

5. Compare your child's developmental milestones to those of his siblings.
6. Record any observations other adults make about your child.

Your baby will most likely breeze through her developmental milestones, but if delays become evident there is plenty of help available. If you have done your best to reduce your family's exposure to toxins, you have already taken the biggest step toward protecting your baby.

I have intentionally left the next chapter for last, because the hysteria about vaccines distracts from the other issues related to autism. I wanted you to have a full understanding of the complexity of ASD before addressing a subject about which you may have preconceived notions.

16

Vaccines
The Middle Ground

One of the agreements I made with myself when I started to think about writing this book was to deemphasize the importance of vaccines in the incidence of autism. That is why I have saved this controversial, contentious, and loaded topic for last. I want the important messages of this book to stand on their own without being overshadowed by the vaccine controversy. I have sat on panels and appeared on talk shows and have listened to different points of view about vaccinations. I am tired of hearing people shout about the issue. I want to talk reasonably about this highly charged subject. I have to say upfront that 99.9 percent of the medical community does not agree with me.

The provaccine and antivaccine camps are entrenched in heated debate. The provaccine people adhere to the need for a rigid, universal protocol. The result is the standard vaccination schedule that requires dozens of vaccines before age six. The vast majority of experts and doctors stand by this protocol. Suggesting changes, flexibility, or reevaluation draws a fast, firm, negative reaction.

The antivaccine activists consider vaccines dangerous. They are responding to the number of children (and adults) who have had adverse reactions to vaccinations.

My thinking falls somewhere between the extremes. I believe that parents should be involved in deciding when and how vaccines are given to their children. I believe in an individualized approach to vaccinations. Changing the protocol might protect a segment of vulnerable children. Unfortunately, we learn about their vulnerability only after problems arise. Since we do not know who these kids are, we must consider giving babies at risk time to develop. In earlier chapters, I identified some risk factors for autism. If there is autism in your family tree, if you are an older father, or if autoimmune disease appears in your family history, it would make sense to proceed with caution. We do not have proof that vaccines can trigger autism, but we have plenty of evidence of adverse reactions.

Evidence of Harm

The doctors and others who adhere to a rigid, unchangeable vaccine schedule claim that there is no proof of harm, and that may be true to a point. But there is enough evidence that vaccines *might* be harmful to warrant more research. Vaccines have been combined to reduce the number of shots given at a time without any testing proving the safety of those combinations. An 11-pound baby gets the same dose of some vaccines as a 180-pound man. The doses of all other medications are adjusted for weight and age. We simply do not know enough to say that vaccines are safe for everyone. Vaccinations are a huge medical intervention that goes right to the heart of a very immature immune system.

Even those experts who favor complete and timely vaccinations readily acknowledge that vaccines work very differently as a child ages. Different cellular responses to illnesses and immunizations have been measured and papers explaining them have been published. Studies have shown that certain groups may be at higher risk to develop reactions to vaccines. Even a U.S. federal court has ruled that some children have been badly harmed by vaccines.

Radical Reaction

This is the story of a rescue. At twelve months, Michael had three vaccines at another pediatrician's office. There may have been a mix-up, and shots may have been switched. We do not know what happened, but we saw the results when his parents brought Michael to our office a few days after he had received the shots. They reported that he had gone blank. He had "disappeared." Immediately after the shot, he flapped his hands and his eyes rolled back in his head. The night of the shots he screamed for forty-five minutes. His parents' instincts told them that this merited fast attention. By the time I saw him, he did not respond even to his name.

I referred him to an MD who is an expert in treating early signs of autism. He recovered within a month and completely returned to himself. He had had a rapid descent, but he came back because of quick and appropriate treatment.

Michael had a radical reaction to a vaccination. If it had not been treated aggressively, he may have developed ASD and never recovered. At age three, he has normal development, social, and cognitive skills.

I studied the charts of some of my patients to prepare cases describing developmental delays for this book. I did not go looking for a connection between vaccines and ASD. In repeated cases, I found notations that parents believed vaccines were temporally related to the onset of autism. In some cases, a child was developing normally, then changed after being inoculated. One eighteen-month-old girl had been meeting all her developmental milestones until she received her delayed MMR vaccination at age two. She then began regressing. She lost language and "went blank," and was diagnosed with autism. Her parents assign the change directly to the MMR shot. One boy was sitting at six months and walking at twelve, an outgoing, expressive child. At thirteen months, he had a severe reaction to an MMR vaccination. He ran a high fever, had to be hospitalized, and was never the same again. He regressed in language skills and withdrew. He received an ASD diagnosis. Years later, he is in special education classes with a shadow companion.

In some cases, mild developmental delays had been recorded. Vaccines precipitated severe responses. One boy was slow to develop age-appropriate sounds and speech efforts and appeared to have social delays. At fifteen months, he was seeing a language specialist and had begun physical therapy. He seemed to be responding well. His parents were doing everything right to support their son's development. His vaccinations a year later set him back, and his progress was reversed. He has not been able to overcome his delays and has been diagnosed with ASD.

You have no doubt heard many of these stories. Parents understandably think vaccines are to blame when they see their children change so drastically shortly after a vaccination. The likelihood is that the susceptibility already existed. The vaccines are a trigger, just as environmental factors are proving to be. We need studies to determine the mechanics of these adverse reactions. I cannot count the number of times other doctors have said to me, "You know the plural of anecdote is not data." But at some point, maybe enough anecdotes and parents' documented stories really do become "data" worth listening to.

Like Mother, Like Daughter

While I took a history from a mother, I learned how her daughter, Brenda, now a teenager, had developed intractable seizures that incapacitated her. After a DPT shot, Brenda began to have major seizures, sometimes as many as twenty-five a day. Many children with autism have a seizure disorder.

While getting papers ready for a consultation with a specialist, Brenda's mother found her own vaccination card from the 1950s. She was surprised to discover that her own vaccines had been stopped after her DPT shot. There was a brief note about a bad reaction to the old DPT vaccine that must have been severe enough to make an exception in her case to stop vaccinating. She regretted not having been familiar with her own history. Had she known about her own physical reaction to a DPT vaccine in her childhood, she surely would have spoken to Brenda's doctor about whether Brenda should receive the same inoculation.

I am not prepared to say that vaccines cause autism spectrum disorders. Vaccines interact with a number of triggers. In the end, ASD has many environmental triggers, and we need to be far more cautious about all of them. That is the fundamental theme of *Preventing Autism.* When I am caring for a newborn child, I consider family history and risk factors and listen to what parents tell me about what they observe in their baby. Then I am able to discuss the right approach to vaccines for that child.

A Schedule Set in Stone?

At the beginning of the twentieth century, children received one vaccine, the smallpox vaccine. By the 1960s, five vaccines—diphtheria, pertussis, tetanus, polio, and smallpox—were part of the protocol. Children received as many as eight shots by the age of two. Today, children can receive more than twenty vaccinations in their first two years of life.

The vaccines work. They do their job. Most parents and doctors today have never seen many of the diseases these vaccines were designed to prevent because vaccine-preventable diseases have almost disappeared in the United States. Smallpox no longer exists. Diphtheria is almost 100 percent eradicated. Polio numbers are down to a few hundred cases among the seven billion of us on this planet. There has been only one very questionable case of polio reported in America in the past thirty-five years. The risk of getting measles, rubella, mumps, or meningitis is just about zero. Tetanus happens very rarely, and statistics show that it mostly affects people in their sixties.

Whooping cough, which the Chinese call the hundred-day cough, is still a nasty, difficult-to-eradicate illness, but most outbreaks are greatly exaggerated by the media. In Indiana in 2012, the Department of Public Health went to great effort to note that when doctors had to do a swab and obtain a positive culture to report pertussis, the number of cases actually documented plummeted to around two hundred instead of the thousands and tens of thousands other states reported. Every four or five years we see an increase in reported whooping cough, because people are not aware that they have it, and it spreads. They cough for two or three months. It occurs often in college students.

There has been talk about dropping some of the vaccines, but we keep adding more. The following chart, adapted from *Pediatrics*, the official journal of the American Academy of Pediatrics, shows the increase of vaccine use in the past century.

Year	Number of Vaccines	Possible Number of Vaccinations by 2 Years of Age	Possible Number of Vaccinations at a Single Visit
1900	1	1	1
1960s	5	8	2
1980s	7	5	2
2000	11	20	5

Note: Many vaccines are combined in one injection, and the rotavirus is given orally.

Currently, federal vaccine guidelines recommend twenty-four immunizations by two years of age and limit the number of immunizations per doctor's visit to up to five shots.

As you can see, since the 1960s, the number of vaccines, injections, and shots given at one visit has more than doubled.

Rather than walk you through all the vaccines given to a child, I have reproduced a chart prepared by the Centers for Disease Control. You can see the conventional protocol at a glance.

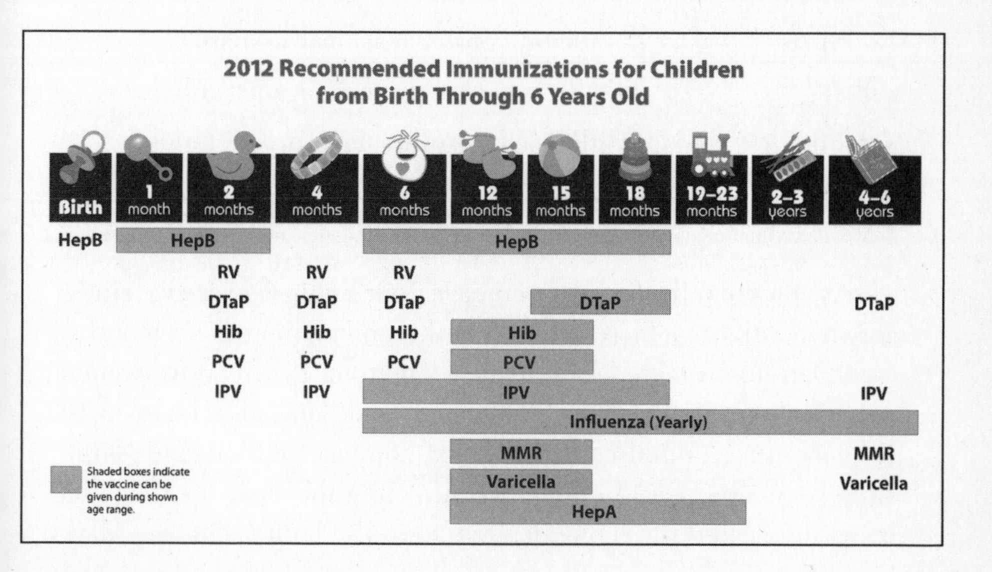

The chart below identifies the vaccines and the combined vaccines.

Vaccine-Preventable Diseases and the Vaccines that Prevent Them

Disease	Vaccine
Chickenpox	Varicella vaccine protects against chickenpox.
Diphtheria	DTaP* vaccine protects against diphtheria.
Hib	Hib vaccine protects against *Haemophilus influenzae* type b.
HepA	HepA vaccine protects against hepatitis A.
HepB	HepB vaccine protects against hepatitis B.
Flu	Flu vaccine protects against influenza.
Measles	MMR** vaccine protects against measles.
Mumps	MMR** vaccine protects against mumps.
Pertussis	DTaP* vaccine protects against pertussis (whooping cough).
Polio	IPV vaccine protects against polio.
Pneumococcal	PCV vaccine protects against pneumococcus.
Rotavirus	RV vaccine protects against rotavirus.
Rubella	MMR** vaccine protects against rubella.
Tetanus	DTaP* vaccine protects against tetanus.

*DTap is a combination vaccine that protects against diphtheria, tetanus, and pertussis.
**MMR is a combination vaccine that protects against measles, mumps, and rubella.

As you see from the chart on page 263, a baby gets six vaccines at two months, five more at four months, and six more at six months (or seven if you include a flu shot). The total is fifteen to twenty vaccines by the time a baby is six months old. At age fifteen to eighteen months, a child can receive as many as four vaccines on a single day. The risk of children contracting the diseases they are being inoculated for is practically zero in the United States today.

I believe that there is no good reason to rush giving so many shots to such young children.

I don't want to change everything about our vaccination policies. I just want doctors to be much more judicious and to look at each child's personal medical issues as well as the family's medical history. I want doctors to look at the way each and every child is developing and be careful not to interrupt the path of normal healthy cognitive and social growth.

We know a baby's brain is developing during the first two years of life. This period is a window of vulnerability. In my opinion, we are giving babies too many vaccines too soon. I believe we should let babies develop more fully before injecting them with viral antigens, bacterial antigens, and live virus vaccines as well as the additives and preservatives found in vaccines. Aluminum levels in particular should be decreased in vaccines.

Why Not Slow It Down?

My position is simple. I want to stop putting kids at risk. I think a safer schedule could be developed for vaccinations. Vaccines might be delayed or spread out depending on family history and risk factors. Since boys are so vulnerable to developmental delays, we should be very careful about how we vaccinate them before they are two years old. Read *The Vaccine Book* by Dr. Robert Sears. He articulately explains about all we know and do not know about vaccines and suggests an alternative schedule that spreads vaccines out over six years.

I care for one child and one family at a time in my practice. I work with the families to develop individualized schedules. I believe we have to do better for our children. We owe it to them to study whether vaccines are a trigger for developmental delays in some children.

Autism rates continue to rise. We have to be open-minded and investigate any possible triggers that are contributing to this epidemic. It is our responsibility to protect all of our children.

Afterword

Better Living without Chemicals

Now you have a plan of action for eliminating harmful chemicals from your everyday life—at least those you can control. Each month, as I worked on this book, new scientific research and publications allowed me to change speculative wording to definitive statements about the origins of the autism epidemic. Proof of environmental impact on genetics gets more and more substantial every day. By the time you read these words, more questions will have been answered, and the cautions and advice offered here will have likely become official medical recommendations. Let's stay ahead of this disorder and act now.

Consider *Preventing Autism* a resource for finding healthy substitutes for toxic food and products. There are so many areas in which targeted change will make a big difference for you and your family. Resist the impulse to be overwhelmed or paralyzed. Don't give up. Every change you make, no matter how small, will be an improvement. Just take one step at a time. When you run out of toothpaste, shampoo, or laundry detergent, replace the product you have been using with a toxin-free alternative. I have given you long lists to choose from, so you don't have to hunt for safe products. Just make a phone call or order them online. You can improve your eating habits by including more delicious, fresh food that has not been contaminated by chemicals. I guarantee that you will not only look and feel better when you clean up your diet, but you will have a real energy boost. Best of all, you will be preparing your body and your home for a healthy new baby and safeguarding the children you already have. Once you start making the shift to healthier living, you will continue to make the right choices without thinking twice. Living clean and green will become a way of life.

As I close this book, I know that what I have written will be considered controversial. Day by day, though, science is proving me right. We have to try to do something to stop autism now. In five, ten, or twenty years a body of "proof" will be discovered. As you can see in the references, many studies are already pointing to a link between environmental factors and developmental delays, and I have included only a few of the thousands of completed studies. In light of the increase in ASD, there is even more funding available for studies, and research is growing exponentially. We have reached a tipping point. I know that the rapid pace of new connections and discoveries will put the pieces of the puzzle together. Check out my website www.drjaygordon.com regularly for updates on the groundbreaking work being done. In the meantime, I cannot remain quiet and wait twenty years for the findings of the National Children's Study on the effects of the environment on children. We cannot continue to put a whole generation of children at risk. I believe that we can begin to combat autism one family at a time. *Preventing Autism* is my attempt to raise your awareness and to recommend a safer path.

Do the best you can.

Appendix
Milestone Tracker

This checklist will help you keep a record of your baby's development. If you write down the date when your child displays a behavior for the first time, you will have a great history to share later. If your baby has not reached certain milestones, you will want to discuss the delays with your pediatrician. Remember that children develop at different paces. Some children develop more quickly verbally, while others might be more physical earlier. Some are more outgoing and social than others. There is a lot of room for variations in their development.

This checklist has been compiled from general guidelines for children's development from the CDC. Copy the pages so you can keep this milestone record handy. Just fill in the blanks with the date that you first noticed the behavior.

Birth to Two Months

__/__/__ Smiles at people

__/__/__ Calming behavior—brings hands to mouth and sucks on one

__/__/__ Tries to look at you and your partner

__/__/__ Makes gurgling sounds and coos

__/__/__ Turns head toward sounds

__/__/__ Pays attention to faces

__/__/__ Begins to follow things with eyes

__/__/__ Recognizes people at a distance

__/__/__ Cries and acts fussy as if bored if activity does not change
__/__/__ When lying on stomach, can hold head up and tries to push up
__/__/__ Movements with arms and legs become smoother

At Four Months

__/__/__ Smiles spontaneously at people
__/__/__ Likes to play with people
__/__/__ Cries when playing stops
__/__/__ Mimics some movements and facial expressions, like frowning or smiling
__/__/__ Babbles with expression
__/__/__ Tries to copy sounds he hears
__/__/__ Different cries for hunger, being tired, pain
__/__/__ Communicates happiness and sadness
__/__/__ Responds to affection
__/__/__ Reaches for a toy with one hand
__/__/__ Uses eyes and hands together—sees a toy and reaches for it
__/__/__ Tracks moving things with eyes from side to side
__/__/__ Watches faces closely
__/__/__ Recognizes familiar people and things at a distance
__/__/__ Holds head steady, unsupported
__/__/__ Pushes down on legs when feet are on a hard surface
__/__/__ Rolls over from stomach to back
__/__/__ Can hold a toy and shake it
__/__/__ Swings at dangling toys
__/__/__ Brings hands to mouth
__/__/__ Pushes up to elbows when lying on stomach

At Six Months

__/__/__ Recognizes familiar faces and knows if someone is a stranger

__/__/__ Likes to play with others, especially parents
__/__/__ Is responsive to the emotions of others
__/__/__ Often seems happy
__/__/__ Likes to look at himself in a mirror
__/__/__ Responds to sounds by making sounds
__/__/__ When babbling, strings vowels together—"ah," "eh," "oh"
__/__/__ Takes turns with parent while making sounds
__/__/__ Responds to her name
__/__/__ Makes sounds to show displeasure and joy
__/__/__ Begins to jabber, making consonant sounds like "m" or "b"
__/__/__ Looks at nearby things
__/__/__ Brings things to mouth
__/__/__ Shows curiosity
__/__/__ Tries to get things that are out of reach
__/__/__ Passes things from one hand to the other
__/__/__ Rolls over from front to back and back to front
__/__/__ Sits without support
__/__/__ Supports weight on legs when standing, and bounces
__/__/__ When on hands and knees, rocks back and forth
__/__/__ Sometimes crawls backward before moving forward

At Nine Months

__/__/__ Shows fear of strangers
__/__/__ Can be clingy with familiar adults
__/__/__ Has favorite toys
__/__/__ Understands "no"
__/__/__ Makes many different sounds like "mamamama," "dadadada," or "babababa"
__/__/__ Imitates sounds and gestures
__/__/__ Points at things
__/__/__ Looks where you point

__/__/__ Watches an object as it falls
__/__/__ Looks for things she sees you hide
__/__/__ Plays peek-a-boo
__/__/__ Puts things in her mouth
__/__/__ Moves things smoothly from one hand to the other
__/__/__ Picks up small things between thumb and index finger
__/__/__ Stands holding onto something
__/__/__ Can get into sitting position
__/__/__ Sits without support
__/__/__ Pulls to stand
__/__/__ Crawls

At Twelve Months

__/__/__ Shy with strangers
__/__/__ Cries when Mom or Dad leaves
__/__/__ Has favorite things and people
__/__/__ Displays fear in some situations
__/__/__ Hands you a book when she wants to hear a story
__/__/__ Repeats sounds or actions to get attention
__/__/__ Puts out arm or leg to help get dressed
__/__/__ Plays games like patty-cake and peek-a-boo
__/__/__ Responds to simple spoken requests
__/__/__ Shakes head for no, waves bye-bye, or makes other simple gestures
__/__/__ Imitates speech with changes in tone
__/__/__ Says "Mama" and "Dada" and exclamations like "Uh-oh!"
__/__/__ Tries to say words you say
__/__/__ Shakes, bangs, throws objects, exploring in different ways
__/__/__ Finds hidden things easily
__/__/__ Looks at the right picture or object when you name it

__/__/__ Copies gestures
__/__/__ Drinks from a cup
__/__/__ Brushes hair and uses things correctly
__/__/__ Bangs two things together
__/__/__ Puts things in a container and takes them out
__/__/__ Pokes with index finger
__/__/__ Follows simple directions like "Pick up the block"
__/__/__ Gets to a sitting position without help
__/__/__ Takes a few steps without holding on
__/__/__ Stands alone

At Eighteen Months

__/__/__ Hands things to others as play
__/__/__ Has temper tantrums
__/__/__ Fears strangers
__/__/__ Shows affection to familiar people
__/__/__ Plays simple pretend, like feeding a doll or driving a car
__/__/__ Clings to caregivers in new situations
__/__/__ Points to show others something interesting
__/__/__ Explores alone, with a parent close by
__/__/__ Says several single words
__/__/__ Shakes head and says "no"
__/__/__ Points to show what he wants
__/__/__ Knows the purpose of ordinary things
__/__/__ Points to get the attention of others
__/__/__ Points to a named body part
__/__/__ Scribbles on her own
__/__/__ Follows one-step verbal commands
__/__/__ Walks alone
__/__/__ Runs
__/__/__ Walks up steps
__/__/__ Can help undress himself

__/__/__ Drinks from a cup
__/__/__ Eats with a spoon

At Two Years

__/__/__ Copies others
__/__/__ Gets excited in the presence of other children
__/__/__ Plays mostly beside other children
__/__/__ Begins to include other children—in chase games, for example
__/__/__ Shows increasing independence
__/__/__ Shows defiant behavior
__/__/__ Points to things or pictures when they are named
__/__/__ Knows the names of familiar people and body parts
__/__/__ Says two- to four-word sentences
__/__/__ Follows simple instructions
__/__/__ Repeats words overheard in conversation
__/__/__ Points to things in a book
__/__/__ Finds things when hidden under two or three covers
__/__/__ Begins to sort shapes and colors
__/__/__ Completes sentences and rhymes in familiar books
__/__/__ Plays simple make-believe games
__/__/__ Builds towers of four or more blocks
__/__/__ Uses one hand more than the other
__/__/__ Follows two-step instructions, like "Pick up the ball and put it in the toy chest"
__/__/__ Identifies pictures in a book
__/__/__ Stands on tiptoe
__/__/__ Kicks a ball
__/__/__ Begins to run
__/__/__ Climbs onto and down from furniture without help
__/__/__ Walks up and down stairs holding on
__/__/__ Throws ball overhand
__/__/__ Makes or copies straight lines or circles

References

This is meant to be a popular book, but I do want to include some key references to support my conclusions and to report the latest findings. I have spent years reading the research on the subject of the environment and children's health. My reading is what prompted me to write *Preventing Autism*.

Introduction and Chapters 1–3

Association for Science in Autism Treatment. "About Autism." http://asatonline.org/about_autism/about_autism.htm.

Autism Society. "About Autism." http://www.autism_society.org.

Autism Speaks. http://www.autismspeaks.org.

Blaxill, Mark F., et al. "The Changing Prevalence of Autism in California." *Journal of Autism Developmental Disorders* 33, no. 2 (April 2003): 227–29.

Centers for Disease Control and Prevention (CDC). "Prevalence of Autism Spectrum Disorders—Autism and Developmental Disabilities Monitoring Network, United States, 2006." *MMWR Surveillance Summaries* 58, no. 10 (2009): 1–20.

Cone, Maria, and Environmental Health News. "Autism Clusters Found in California's Major Cities." *Scientific American*, January 6, 2010. http://www.scientificamerican.com/article.cfm?id=autism-clusters-californiahighly-educated-parents.

Dryden-Edwards, Roxanne, and William C. Shiel Jr. "Autism Spectrum Disorder (in Children and Adults)." http://MedicienNet.com/script/mainart.asp?articlekey+80415.

Dufault, Renee, Walter J. Lukiw, Raquel Crider, Roseanne Schnoll, David Wallinga, and Richard Deth. "A Macroepigenetic Approach to Identify Factors Responsible for the Autism Epidemic in the United States." *Clinical Epigenetics* (April 2012)4:6, (2012): doi:10:1186/1868–7083–4–6.

Environmental Working Group. "New Evidence Suggests Link between Mercury Exposures and Autism." http://www.ewg.org/release/new-evidence-suggests-link-between-mercury-exposures-and-autism.

Esteban-Vasallo, Maria Dolores, Nuria Aragones, Marina Pollan, Gonzalo Lopez-Abente, and Beatriz Perez-Gomez. "Mercury, Cadmium and Lead

Levels in Human Placenta: A Systematic Review." *Environmental Health Perspectives*, May 16, 2012. doi:10.1289/ehp.1204952 Epub 2012 May 16.

Falco, Miriam. "CDC: U.S. Kids with Autism up 78% in Past Decade." *CNN Health*, March 29, 2012. http://www.cnn.com2012/03/29/health/autism/index?hpt=hp_t1.

Goldman, L. R., and S. Koduru. "Chemicals in the Environment and Developmental Toxicity to Children: A Public Health and Policy Perspective." *Environmental Heath Perspectives* 108 (2008): suppl. http://www.ncbi.nlm.nih.gov/pubmed/10852843.

Hertz-Piccioto, Irva, and Lora Delwiche. "The Rise in Autism and the Role of Age at Diagnosis." *Epidemiology* 20, no. 1 (2009): 84–90.

Holtcamp, Wendee. "Obesogens: An Environmental Link to Obesity." *Environmental Health Perspectives* 120 (2012): a62-a68. Published online 2012 Feb 1 hdoi.org/10.1289/ehp.120-a62.

Kalkbrenner, Amy E., Julie L. Daniels, Jiu-Chiuan Chen, Charles Poole, Michael Emch, and Joseph Morrissey. "Prenatal Exposure to Hazardous Air Pollutants and Autism Spectrum Disorders at Age 8." *Epidemiology* 21, no. 5 (2010): 631–41. doi:10.1097/EDE.0b013e3181e65d76.

Kajta, M., and A. Wójtowicz. "Neurodevelopmental Disorders in Response to Hormonally Active Environmental Pollutants." [In Polish.] *Przegląd Lekarski* 67, no. 11 (2010): 1194-9. http://www.ncbi.nlm.nih.gov/pubmed21442975.

Kristof, Nicholas D. "Do Toxins Cause Autism?" *New York Times*, February 24, 2010. http://www.nytimes.com/2010/02/25/opinion/25kristof.html.

Lewandowski, Thomas A. "Evolving Understanding of the Relationship between Mercury Exposure and Autism." *Environmental Heavy Metal Pollution and Effects on Child Mental Development*. NATO Science for Peace and Security Series C: Environmental Security Volume 1 (2011): 65–85. doi:1007/978–94–007–0253_4.

Lord, Catherine. "Searching for the Why behind the Rising Autism Rate." *CNN Opinion*, April 1, 2012. http://www.cnn.com/2012/03/31/opinion/lord-autism-rate/index.html.

Maugh, Thomas H., II. "UC Davis Researchers Find California Autism Clusters, But the Cause Is a Bit of a Surprise." *Los Angeles Times*, January 5, 2010. http://latimesblogs.latimes.com/booster_shots/2010/01/uc-davis-researchers-find-california-autism-clusters-but-the-cause-is-a-bit-of-a-surprise.html.

Mayo Clinic. "Autism." http://www.mayoclinic.com/health/autism/D500348.

Moench, Brian. "Utah's Alarming Autism Rate." *Salt Lake Tribune*, Sunday, April 8, 2012.

National Collaborating Centre for Women's and Children's Health (UK). "Autism: Recognition, Referral and Diagnosis of Children and Young People on the Autism Spectrum." *NICE Clinical Guidelines*, No. 128. London: RCOG Press, 2011.

National Institute of Neurological Disorders and Stroke. "Autism Fact Sheet." http://www.ninds.nih.gov/disorders/autism/detail_autism.htm.

Palmer, Raymond F., Stephen Blanchard, and Robert Wood. "Proximity to

Point Sources of Environmental Mercury Release as a Predictor of Autism Prevalence." *Health & Place* 15, no. 1 (2009): 18–24. doi:10.1016/j.healthplace.2008.02.001.

Van Meter, Karla C., Lasse E. Christiansen, Lora D. Delwich, Rahman Azari, Tim E. Carpenter, and Irva Hertz-Picciotto. "Geographic Distribution of Autism in California: A Retrospective Birth Cohort Analysis." *Autism Research* 3, no. 1 (2010): 19–29. doi:/doi/10.1002/aur.v3:1/issuetoc.

Velasquez-Manoft, Moises. *An Epidemic of Absence: A New Way of Understanding Allergies and Autoimmune Diseases*. New York: Scribner, 2012.

———. "An Immune Disease at the Root of Autism." *New York Times*, August 26, 2012.

Vojdani, A., J. B. Pangborn, E. Vojdani, and E. L. Cooper. "Infections, Toxic Chemicals and Dietary Peptides Binding to Lymphocyte Receptors and Tissue Enzymes Are Major Instigators of Autoimmunity in Autism." *International Journal of Immunopathology and Pharmacology* Sep–Dec;16, (3) (2003): 189–99.

Windham G. C., L. Zhang, R. Gunier, L. A. Croen, and J. K. Grether. "Autism Spectrum Disorders in Relation to Distribution of Hazardous Air Pollutants in the San Francisco Bay Area." *Environmental Health Perspectives* 114, no. 9 (2003): 1438–44. http://www.ncbi.nlm.nih.gov/pubmed/16966102.

Chapter 4

Awylward, E. H., N. J. Minshew, K. Field, B. F. Sparks, and N. Singh. "Effects of Age on Brain Volume and Head Circumference in Autism." *Neurology* 59 (2002): 175–83.

"Autism Brain Secrets Revealed by Scan." BBC News. *Health*. November 3, 2010. http:www.bbc.co.uk/newshealth-11687808.

"Autistic Brains' 'Genes Differ.'" BBC News. *Health*. May 25, 2011. http://www.bbc.co.uk/news/health-13539922.

Belmonte, Matthew K., Greg Allen, Andrea Beckel-Mitchener, Lisa M. Boulanger, Ruth A. Carper, and Sara J. Webb. "Autism and Abnormal Development of Brain Connectivity." *Journal of Neuroscience* 24, no. 42 (2004): 9228–31. doi:10.1523/JNEUROSCI.3340–04.2004.

Cody, H., K. Pepher, and J. Piven. "Structural and Functional Magnetic Resonance Imaging of Autism." *International Journal of Developmental Neuroscience* 20 (2002): 421–31.

Courchesne, E., R. Carper, and N. Akshoomoff. 2003. Evidence of Brain Overgrowth in the First Year of Life in Autism. *Journal of the American Medical Association* 290: 337–44.

Dawson, G., S. Webb, and J. McPartland. "Understanding the Nature of Face Processing Impairment in Autism: Insights from Behaviorial and Electrophysiological Studies." *Developmental Neuropsychology* 27 (2005): 63–74.

Inside Autism. "Lighting Up the Brain." http://whyfiles.org/209autism/4.html.

Minshew, Nancy J., Gerald Goldstein, and Don J. Siegel. "Neuropsychologic Function in Autism: Profile of a Complex Information Processing Disorder." *Journal of the International Neuropsychological Society* 3 (1997): 303–16.

http://www.mendeley.com/research/neuropsychologic-functioning-autism-profile-complex-information-processing-disorder/.

"Protein Found in Brain Cells May Be Key to Autism." BBC News. *Health*. March 20, 2011.

"Researchers Gain Insight into Why Brain Areas Fail to Work Together in Autism." *NIH News*, July 12, 2006. http://www.nichd.nih.gov/news/pr/jul2006/nichd-12.htm.

Scudellari, Megan. "An Autism Brain Signature?" *Scientist*, May 25, 2011.

Sparks, B., et al. "Brain Structural Abnormalities in Young Children with Autism Spectrum Disorder." *Neurology* 59 (2002): 184–92.

Voineagu, Irina, et. al. "Transcriptomic Analysis of Autistic Brain Reveals Convergent Molecular Pathology." *Nature* 474 (2011): 380–4. doi:10.1038/nature10110.

Chapter 5

Carey, Benedict. "Scientists Link Gene Mutation to Autism Risk." *New York Times*, April 4, 2012.

King, Chiara. "A Novel Embryological Theory of Autism Causation Involving Endogenous Biochemicals Capable of Initiating Cellular Gene Transcription: A Possible Link between Twelve Autism Risk Factors and the Autism Epidemic." *Medical Hypothesis* 76, no. 5 (2011): 653–60. http://www.medical-hypotheses.com/article/S0306–9877(11)0026–0.

Kinney, D. K., D. H. Barch, B. Chayka, S. Napoleon, and K. M. Munir. "Environmental Risk Factors for Autism: Do They Help Cause De Novo Genetic Mutations That Contribute to the Disorder?" *Medical Hypothesis* 74, no. 1 (2010): 102–6. http://www.ncbi.nlm.nih.gov/pubmed/19699591.

Kubota, T. "Epigenetics in Congenital Diseases and Pervasive Developmental Disorders." *Environmental Health Preventive Medicine* 13, no. 1 (2008): 3–7.

"Largest-Ever Search for Autism Genes Reveals New Clues." *NIH News*, February 20, 2007. http://www.nichd.nih.gov/news/releases/autism_gene_reveals_clues.cfm.

"Many Tiny Mutations May Contribute to Autism." *Autism Speaks*. April 5, 2012. http://www.autismspeaks.org//print/node/131086.

"New Gene Screen Flags Autism Risk in Infant Siblings." *Autism Speaks*. April 9, 2012. http://www.autismspeaks.org//print/node/131356.

"Newly Discovered Autism Gene Opens New Avenue of Research." *Autism Speaks*. April 5, 2012. http://www.autismspeaks.org//print/node/131091.

Szatmari, Peter. "The Causes of Autism Spectrum Disorders." *British Medical Journal* 326 (2003): 173–74.

Yorbik, O., I. Kurt, A. Hasimi, and O. Ozturk. "Chromium, Cadmium, and Lead Levels in Urine of Children with Autism and Typically Developing Controls." *Biological Trace Element Ressearch* 135, no. 1–3 (2010): 10–15.

Chapter 6

Bello, S. C. "Autism and Environmental Influences: Review and Commentary." *Review of Environmental Health* 22, no. 2 (2007): 139–56.

Deth, R., et al. "How Environmental and Genetic Factors Combine to Cause Autism: A Redos/Methylation Hypothesis." *Neurotoxicology* 29, no. 1 (2008): 190–201.

Dietert, Rodney R., Janice M. Dietert, and Jamie C. Dewitt. "Environmental Risk Factors for Autism." *Emerging Health Threats Journal* 4 (2011): 10. doi:10.3402/ehtj.v4i0.7111.

Grandjean, P., and P. J. Landrigan. "Developmental Neurotoxicity of Industrial Chemicals." *Lancet* 368, no. 9553 (2006): 2167–2178. doi:10.1016/S0140–6736(06)69665–7.

Hallmayer, Joachim, et al. "Genetic Heritability and Shared Environmental Factors among Twin Pairs with Autism." *Archives of General Psychiatry* 689, no. 11 (2011): 1095–1102. doi: 10.1001/archgenpsychiatry.2011.76.

Herbert, M. R. "Contributions of the Environment and Environmentally Vulnerable Physiology to Autism Spectrum Disorders." *Current Opinion in Neurology* 23, no. 2 (2010): 103–10.

Herbert, M. R., J. P. Russon, and S. Yang. "Autism and Environmental Genomics." *Neurotoxicology* 27, no. 5 (2006): 671–84.

Kristoff, Nicholas. "Big Chem, Bog Harm." *New York Times*, August 26, 2012.

Wolstenholme, Jennifer T., Michelle Edwards, Savera R. Shetty, Jessica D. Gatewood, Julia A. Taylor, Emilie F. Rissman, and Jessica J. Connelly. "Gestational Exposure to Bisphenol A Produces Transgeneration Changes in Behaviors and Gene Expression." *Endocrinology*, June 15, 2012. doi:10.1210/en.2012–1195.

Chapter 7

"Autism Sibling Risk: Higher Than Previously Thought." *BBC Health*. August 15, 2011. http://BBC.co.UK/.news/health-14507532.

Berko, Esther. "Genes, Older Dads and Autism." *Autism Speaks*. May 4, 2012. http://www.autismspeaks.org/blog/2012/05/04/genes-older-dads-and-autism.

Burd, Larry, Robin Severud, Jacob Herbeshia, and Marilyn G. Kug. "Prenatal and Perinatal Risk Factors for Autism." *Journal Perinatal Medicine* 27 (1999): 441–50.

Care, Benedict. "Study Finds Risk of Autism Linked to Older Fathers." *New York Times*, August 23, 2012.

Comi, Anne M., Andrew W. Zimmerman, Virginia H. Frye, Paul Law, and Joseph Peeden. "Familiar Clustering of Autoimmune Disorder and Evaluation of Medical Risk Factors in Autism." *Journal of Child Neurology* 14, no. 6 (1999): 388–94. doi:10.1177108830739901400608.

Gardner, Hannah, Donna Spiegelman, and Stephen L. Buka. "Prenatal Risk Factors for Autism: Comprehensive Meta-Analysis." *British Journal of Psychiatry* 195 (2009): 7–14. doi:10.1192/bjp.bp.108.051672.

Hultman, Christine M., Dari Sparen, and Sven Cnattingius. "Perinatal Risk Factors for Infantile Autism." *Epidemiology* 13, no. 4 (2002): 417–23.

Kolevzon, Alexander, Raz Gross, and Abraham Reichenberg. "Prenatal and Perinatal Risk Factors for Autism." *Archives of Pediatric and Adolescent Medicine* 161, no. 4 (2007): 326–33. doi:10.100l/archpedi.161.4.326.

Kong, Augustine, et al.. "Rate of De Novo Mutation and the Importance of Father's Age in Disease Risk." *Nature* 488 (2012): 471–5. doi:10.1038/nature 11396.

Larsson, Heidi Jeanet, et al. "Risk Factors for Autism: Perinatal Factors, Parental Psychiatric History, and Socioeconomic Status." *American Journal of Epidemiology* 161 (2005): 916–25.

"Mom's Age and Autism Risk." *Autism Speaks*. April 23, 2012. http://www.autismspeaks.org/science/science-news/mom's-age-and-autism-risk.

Norton, Amy. "Risk Factors for Autism Remain Elusive: Study." *Reuters Health*. July 11, 2011.

"Prenatal and Perinatal Risk Factors for Autism." JAMA Network. *Archive of Pediatric and Adolescent Medicine*. http://Archpedi.jamanetwork.com/article.aspx?volume=1616issue=4&page=326.

Chapters 10–13

I relied on a number of websites and databases to make product recommendations. They include:

Skin Deep Cosmetics Database of the Environmental Working Group, http://www.ewg.org/skindeep

Guide to Less Toxic Products of the Environmental Health Association of Nova Scotia, http://www.lesstoxicguide.ca

Organic Consumers Association, http://organicconsumers.org

In Chapter 10 the material from Mary Cordaro is adapted from "Seeking a Cure for the Sick Home" from her website, http://marycordaro.com.

Some of the recipes for homemade household cleaning supplies were based on recipes in *Clean and Green* by Annie Berthold-Bond (Woodstock, NY: Ceres Press, 1994).

In chapter 11 the reporting on Greenpeace's toxin tests, "Dirty Laundry 2: Hung Out to Dry," on brand-name clothing dates from September 27, 2011. By that date, Nike, Adidas, Puma, and H & M were taking steps to eliminate the use of hazardous chemicals in their products. Most of the international brands said they were "cut-and-sew" customers, and they did not use the dye services at the two factories that were responsible for the hormone disrupting discharges.

The recipes for hair care products in chapter 12 are from The LongLocks Natural & Organic Hair Product Recipes Cookbook, http://www.longlocks.com/hair-care-recipes-cookbook.htm.

Sole-Smith, Virginia. "The High Price of Beauty." *Nation*, October 9, 2007.

Chapter 14

American Academy of Pediatrics, Work Group on Breastfeeding. "Breastfeeding and the Use of Human Milk." *Pediatrics* 100, no. 6 (1997): 1035–9.

Blumberg, J. "Organic Food Sweetener May Be a Hidden Source of Dietary Arsenic." *Dartmouth Now*, February 16, 2012.

Centers for Disease Control. "Fourth National Report on Human Exposure to

Environmental Chemicals." 2009. http://www.cdc.gov/exposurereport/pdf/FourthReport.pdf.

Sacker, A., M. A. Quigley, and Y. J. Kelly. "Breastfeeding and Developmental Delay: Findings from the Millennium Cohort Study." Department of Epidemiology and Public Health, University College London, London, United Kingdom. *Pediatrics*. 2006 Sep 1; 118 (3)e 682-689.

Schafer, Kristin S., and Margaret Reeves. "Chemical Trespass: Pesticides in Our Bodies and Corporate Accountability." Pesticide Action Network. 2004. This booklet can be found at http://pesticideresearch.com/site/docs/ChemTrespass.pdf.

Shultz, Stepehn T., Klonoff-Cohen, Hillary S., Wingard, Deborah, Askshoomoff, Natacha A., Macera, Caroline A., Ji, Ming, and Backer, Christopher. "Breastfeeding Infant Formula Supplementation and Autistic Disorder: The Results of a Parent Survey." *Int Breastfeed* J. 2006; 1: 16. Published online 2006 September 15. doi: 10.1186/1746–4358–1–16.

Tanoue Y., and S. Oda. "Weaning Time of Children with Infantile Autism." *Journal of Autism and Developmental Disorders* 19, no. 3 (1989): 425–34.

Chapter 15

Ennis, Diana and Manns, Cath. "Breaking down Barrierers to Learning." The National Autism Society U.K. June 2004. http://www.autism.org.uk/working-with/education/educational-professionals-in-schools/breaking-down-barriers-to-learning/asperger-syndrome-the-triad-of-impairments.aspx.

Eikeseth, S. "Outcome of Comprehensive Psycho-educational Interventions for Young Children with Autism." *Research in Developmental Disabilities* 30, no. 1 (2009): 158–78.

Lam, Kristen S. L., and Michael G. Aman. "The Repetitive Behavior Scale-Revised: Independent Validation in Individuals with Autism Spectrum Disorders." *Journal of Autism and Developmental Disorders* 37, no. 5 (2007): 855–6. doi:10.1007/S1083–006–0123-z.

Shattuck, P.T., et al. "Timing of Identification among Children with an Autism Spectrum Disorder: Findings from a Population-based Surveillance Study." *Journal of the American Academy of Child and Adolescent Psychiatry* 48, no. 5 (2009): 474–83.

Chapter 16

Centers for Disease Control and Prevention. "2012 Recommended Immunizations for Children from Birth through 6 Years Old." http://www.cdc.gov/vaccines.

National Vaccine Information Center. "49 Doses of 14 Vaccines Before Age 6?" http://www.nivc.org/downloads/49-doses-posterv.aspx.

Resources

Autism Societies

Autism Society of America

The Autism Society exists to improve the lives of those affected by autism by increasing public awareness about the day-to-day issues faced by people on the spectrum, advocating for appropriate services for individuals across their lifespan, and providing the latest information regarding treatment, education, research, and advocacy.

www.autism-society.org

800-328-8476

US Autism and Asperger Association

The USAAA's mission is to provide the opportunity for everyone with autism spectrum disorders to achieve their fullest potential by enriching the autism community with education, training, accessible resources, and partnerships with local and national projects. The website has information on research, therapies, intervention, and legal issues.

www.usautism.org

801-816-1234

Autism Speaks

Autism Speaks funds research into the causes, prevention, treatments, and cure for autism; increases awareness of autism spectrum disorders; and advocates for the needs of individuals with autism and their families.

www.autismspeaks.org

888-288-4762

National Autism Association

NAA creates and implements direct-assistance programs for the growing number of families affected by autism. Along with these services, NAA provides autism research funding, ongoing advocacy, support, and education.

http://nationalautismassociation.org

877-622-2884

Association for Science in Autism Treatment

ASAT educates parents, professionals, and consumers by disseminating accurate, scientifically sound information about autism and its treatment and by combating inaccurate or unsubstantiated information.
www.asatonline.org

The Autism Research Institute

ARI conducts and fosters scientific research designed to improve the methods of diagnosing, treating, and preventing autism. The ARI data bank contains more than forty thousand detailed case histories of autistic children from more than sixty countries.
www.autism.com
866-366-3361

Generation Rescue

Generation Rescue brings together scientists, physicians, and community members who believe in recovery; they are powerful advocates for families living with autism.
http://generationrescue.org
1-877-98AUTISM

AutismOne

AutismOne educates parents, professionals, and the public about the care, treatment, and prevention of, and recovery from, autism and related disorders by making critical information available through new and traditional channels.
www.autismone.org

Autism Support Network

The Autism Support Network connects families and individuals touched by autism, provides support and insight, and acts as a resource guide for education, treatments, strategies, and therapies for autism.
www.autismsupportnetwork.com
203-404-4929

Talk About Curing Autism

TACA educates, empowers, supports, and connects families with the resources they need to secure the best possible future for their children.
www.tacanow.org
949-640-4401

Books on Living Toxin-free

Healthy Child Healthy World: Creating a Cleaner, Greener, Safer Home by Christopher Gavigan. For additional information check out the Healthy Child Healthy World organization: http://healthychild.org.

The Economical Baby Guide: Down-to-Earth Ways for Parents to Save Money and the Planet by Joy Hatch and Rebecca Kelley. They also have a blog: http://greenbabyguide.com.

Raising Baby Green: The Earth-Friendly Guide to Pregnancy, Childbirth, and Baby Care by Dr. Alan Green

Green Babies, Sage Moms: The Ultimate Guide to Raising Your Organic Baby by Lynda Fassa

The Everything Green Baby Book: From Pregnancy to Baby's First Year—An Easy and Affordable Guide to Help You Care for Your Baby—and for the Earth! by Jenn Savedge

Growing Up Green: Baby and Child Care by Deirdre Imus

Organic Baby: Simple Steps for Healthy Living by Kimberly Rider

Smart Mama's Green Guide: Simple Steps to Reduce Your Child's Toxic Chemical Exposure by Jennifer Taggart

Raising Healthy Children in a Toxic World: 101 Smart Solutions for Every Family by Phillip Landrigan, Herbert L. Needleman, and Mary Landrigan

Spit That Out!: The Overly Informed Parent's Guide to Raising Children in the Age of Environmental Guilt by Paige Wolf

Clean & Green: The Complete Guide to Nontoxic and Environmentally Safe Housekeeping by Annie Berthold-Bond

Slow Death by Rubber Duck: The Secret Danger of Everyday Things by Rick Smith and Bruce Lourie

Fit Pregnancy Magazine
www.fitpregnancy.com

Farmers' Markets and Local Food Sources

Farmers' markets are the best sources of organic produce, free-range eggs, artisanal cheeses, and grass-fed meats. This website will help you to locate markets nearby:

http://search.ams.usda.gov/farmersmarkets

Local Harvest
Local Harvest has a wonderful website that will give you information about markets in your area, family farms, food coops, CSAs, and where to buy local products like grass-fed meats and many other treats in your area. There is also a mail-order section.
www.localharvest.org

Breastfeeding

La Leche League
www.llli.org

International Lactation Consultant Association
www.ilca.org

Great Cookbooks for Baby and Toddler Food

Cooking for Gracie: The Making of a Parent from Scratch by Keith Dixon

201 Organic Baby Purees: The Freshest, Most Wholesome Food Your Baby Can Eat! by Tamika L. Gardner

The Everything Organic Cooking for Baby and Toddler Book: 300 Naturally Delicious Recipes to Get Your Child Off to a Healthy Start by Kim Lutz and Megan Hart

Organic Baby and Toddler Cookbook by Lizzie Vann and Daphne Razazan

Cooking for Baby: Wholesome, Homemade, Delicious Foods for 6 to 18 Months by Lisa Barnes

Organically Raised: Conscious Cooking for Babies and Toddlers by Anni Daulter and Shante Lanay

The Petit Appetit Cookbook: Easy, Organic Recipes to Nurture Your Baby and Toddler by Lisa Barnes

Great Cookbooks for the Entire Family

I am a vegetarian. At the very least, your family should be eating more fresh fruits and vegetables than they are now. The following cookbooks are filled with recipes you can serve even to carnivores.

Simple Pleasures: Healthy Seasonal Cooking and Easy Entertaining by Cornelia Guest

Forks Over Knives—The Cookbook: Over 300 Recipes for Plant-Based Eating All through the Year by Del Sroufe, Isa Chandra Moskowitz, Julianna Hever, and Judy Micklewright

How to Cook Everything Vegetarian: Simple Meatless Recipes for Great Food by Mark Bittman

Veganomicon: The Ultimate Vegan Cookbook by Isa Chandra Moskowitz and Terry Hope Romero

Quick Fix Vegetarian: Healthy, Home-Cooked Meals in 30 Minutes or Less by Robin Robertson

Skinny Bitch: Ultimate Everyday Cookbook: Crazy Delicious Recipes That Are Good to the Earth and Great for Your Body by Kim Barnouin

Vegetarian Cooking for Everyone by Deborah Madison

1,000 Vegan Recipes by Robin Robertson

Index